MILLIONAIRES AND GRUB STREET

Comrades and Contacts in the Last Half Century

by

JAMES HOWARD BRIDGE

Foreword by DON C. SEITZ

THE BEACON-LIGHTS OF LIFE ARE ITS FRIENDSHIPS.
William Tecumseh Sherman

New York
BRENTANO'S · PUBLISHERS
Mcmxxxi

HERBERT SPENCER [1820-1903]
From the Portrait in the National Gallery by J. B. Burgess.

MILLIONAIRES
AND GRUB STREET

FOREWORD

Too modest to say anything in preliminary about himself and the fortunate associations he has enjoyed, Mr. James Howard Bridge, author of this diverting volume has asked me to perform the task. He could do it much better himself, he balks at the task. Not only has he kept good company but much of it has been great. He has seen a world-revolution in science and industry, together with such accumulation of wealth by individuals as to make Midas but a puny adventurer. Knights of science and barons of industry have been his friends, while above all he has made for himself a beloved place in a wide literary circle.

It would appear to have been enough glory for one career to enjoy the confidence of Herbert Spencer, of whom he gives us such an attractive picture; yet he makes the shift from Science to Big Business and is just as entertaining in the second role. Next he sits in the sanctum of the famous *Overland Monthly* with its memory of Bret Harte and the exotic men of letters who flamed out on the Pacific coast, following the gold-diggers.

Back from his adventures on the Western coast, Mr. Bridge became a true New Yorker and an active member of that distinguished body of American authors who make the city their headquarters. Indeed the Authors Club owes its good fortune largely to him. His friend Andrew Carnegie endowed it with a sufficient fund for the relief of men who might not find the pen always sufficient for their support, and whose estate contributed the handsome donation that gave the club its home. His book is panoramic of a period so near that we know very little about it, dealing as it does with familiars, with whom the public had only a hearsay acquaintance. They are here met in the atmosphere of intimacy and prove to be very human and genial. Spencer, Youmans and Carnegie were true builders, who left much behind. From Mr. Bridge we learn what manner of men they were. The lesser figures pass in pleasant review: Mr. Bridge turns them into intimates.

Crisp and entertaining is this charming exhibition of a cross-section of life in Europe and America. Surely no one has ever introduced his readers to a more entertaining companionship.

DON C. SEITZ

CONTENTS

LIST OF ILLUSTRATIONS

xi

List of Illustrations

MILLIONAIRES
AND GRUB STREET

HERBERT SPENCER

AT WORK AND AT PLAY

A GROUP of men and boys stood at the back-door of a Derbyshire spinning mill on the banks of the Derwent, whiling away the remnant of their dinner hour, and waiting for the bell to call them back to work. Across the stream, a small boy—a child of nine or ten —sat on the green bank, dangling a tiny fishing rod over the water. He was a bright little fellow, with a pale thin face, and quick nervous manner. Just as the factory bell sounded, and the mill hands turned with noisy bustle into the works, the young fisherman observed his float in violent motion. He sprang to his feet, and a few of the men waited to see him land his prize. But the bank was slippery; and before they could utter more than a cry of alarm, the men saw the child disappear under the dark surface of the water. None of them seemed to know what to do. They ran up and down the bank shouting conflicting advice. The boy's cap and rod floated placidly down the stream, and with a few rising bubbles marked the spot where he had sunk from sight. The bell clanged unheeded by the excited workmen; but none ventured to cross to the drowning child. For a moment a dark head appeared near the surface and sank again. The men ran hither and thither in purposeless agony. Again a little round patch of hair showed itself near the surface; and began to sink from

THE DERWENT AT DERBY.
Here Spencer, aged ten, was nearly drowned while fishing.

sight. But the incoherent shouts of the crowd had been heard by one who had both wits and courage. A stout youth of fourteen sprang through the open door, flinging off his clothes as he ran. In a moment he had plunged into the stream; in another moment he had dragged a still white face to the edge, and was helped by fifty eager hands on to the bank. The limp figure was that of Herbert Spencer. The gallant youth who had rescued him was a mill hand named George Holme; and the quick thought and ready action which saved to his age its brightest intellect, afterwards won for himself both riches and honor: he became the owner of a mill himself and the mayor of his native town of Derby. In my sitting-room, fifty years afterwards, he described the incident to me with a pride

2

that betokened his realization of the service he had rendered mankind in saving this valuable life.

That sitting-room, after another fifty years, is still full of memories for me, though ghostless to its present tenant. Here is one—a mental picture of Herbert Spencer sitting in a cushioned steamer-chair in front of a coal fire, feet stretched well out toward the fender, hands clasped over the top of his head, and dictating, without reference to a single note, a long list of researches to be made at the British Museum, while he was absent from London for a fortnight. The room was one that he had rented as a workroom, near the boarding-house where he lived. It was on the second floor of No. 2, Leinster Place, Bayswater, above a dairy, and, with a bed-room at the back, it served as my own living quarters. It was a large room, with two windows overlooking Porchester Terrace, and was furnished with a felt carpet, much the worse for wear; an old-fashioned roll-top desk, kept locked when not in use; two hair-seated arm-chairs of uncertain date; an iron tripod-table, once gilt lacquered; and two drop-leaf side-tables. Under one of the tables a sheet-iron trunk full of papers was kept locked. Book-shelves, reaching to the ceiling, covered one wall; and in a corner closet other books disputed the space with my simple housekeeping paraphernalia. The steamer-chair was the one Mr. Spencer had bought and used when he visited America; and I had had cushions made for it at Whitely's "emporium" in Westbourne Grove, nearby.

It was Spencer's belief that profound thought called for increased blood-pressure in the brain, and that this was facilitated in a partly bald head by clasping the

3

NUMBER 2, LEINSTER PLACE, BAYSWATER

The second floor above the dairy was used by Mr. Spencer as
workroom for more than ten years. In this room were written
parts of the *Principles of Biology,* the whole of the *Principles
of Sociology,* the *Data of Ethics* and many of the later essays.

hands over it. This attitude was usual with him when
he was dictating.

The memoranda in which he thus embodied a fortnight's task for me are now before me. They are worth
quoting at length :—

Read the oldest medical works, and observe (1) : How there
is associated with the natural effects of medicine the notion of

4

supernatural agency to be dealt with, in the shape of demoniacal cause, etc., and also (2) : How, in the early prescription, there is an habitual choice of ingredients akin to those used in sorcery; and (3) : How, further, there is a predominant notion that the repulsiveness of medicine is an element in its curative effect; this repulsiveness having originally been a trait of something given to drive out the demon. (4) : Is not the practice of bleeding traceable back to a propitiatory rite? (In Yucatan, the medicine men and sorcerers wrought their cures by bleedings; and in this region bleeding was a propitiatory act.)

Read the newest books on Burmah, and extract passages relating to education by the priesthood.

Observe, throughout reading, cases of jealousy of the different priesthoods of one another, and the tendency to struggle for supremacy.

Observe similar feelings in the votaries of saints.

Mark the tendency from polytheism to monotheism, as resulting from supremacy of one god.

Copy out of Dalton the industrial arrangements of the Padám [i.e. a primitive hill-tribe of Bengal].

Find where the Hebrews, having taken God's advice in fighting, are beaten.

Look up the passages in Plato in which there is reprobation of the more brutal and sensual attributes ascribed to gods, and the growth of the higher notion of gods, and a tendency toward monotheism.

Collect general facts bearing on the history of morals. For this read Homes' (afterward Lord Kames) Sketches of the History of Man, and Sismondi's Literature of Southern Europe.

Does Luktas form a part of Mount Ida or Ada in Crete?

Extract facts (from recent books of travel) bearing on the general developments of labor.

Grote somewhere gives an account of Hannibal sacrificing 3000 Greeks. Get the extract.

Read histories of non-conformity and ascertain (1) : Social condition under which sects have arisen (amount of general free-

5

dom, etc.) (2): Prompting motives—whether rebellion against a tyrannical creed, or whether in re-assertion of neglected moral principles.

Look in Blunt for mention of oaths administered in sacred places.

Inquire as to the Roman Catholic theory of nuns married to Christ.

To see how religion and immorality may be conjoined, read History of the Maharajahs in Western India, published, I think, by Trübner.

Truly, a pleasant little holiday task! But it was not to illustrate this that I have made the long quotation. It shows in a marked way the wonderful activity of Spencer's mind. The list was dictated as rapidly as it could have been read aloud. These widely-divergent interests were simultaneously occupying his thoughts. In the chapter "Religious Retrospect and Prospect," Spencer speaks of every point in space thrilling with an infinity of vibrations passing through it in all directions. Could he have given a better description of his own mind? His encyclopedic range of knowledge was amazing when we remember that he never read a book. Though, perhaps, that is the reason. He glanced at books—barely touched them, as it seemed; and assimilated all that was nutritious in them, much as certain of the amebæ absorb, by contact, every smaller organism they touch. His wonderful power of induction did the rest.

Then his memory was phenomenal. He once directed me back seven years to an article in the *Révue des Deux Mondes,* by Taine, on "Linguistic Development in Childhood," to copy and translate a passage in which Taine tells how his infant personalized the moon. And

6

once he referred me back fifteen years to an incident related of M. Thiers by Mr. Vignoles, the president of the Institution of Civil Engineers, in his inaugural address. He had pigeon-holes in his mind where he stored scraps of knowledge until he should need them; just as, in his boarding-house, he had a cupboard divided into little racks and compartments labelled with dates, for the saving of biographical data.

This list also serves to illustrate Spencer's methods of work. The material to be thus collected was for use in certain parts of the *Principles of Sociology*. "Political Institutions" was being written; and, as the work progressed, verification of statements was daily called for, together with additional illustrative data, necessitating frequent visits on my part to the London Library or the British Museum. Simultaneously material had to be collected for use in "Industrial Institutions," which was the next division to be taken up; and this material was sorted from time to time and distributed into envelopes marked with the title of the chapter for which it was intended. Moreover, some additions to the "Data of Ethics" were contemplated; and material for these, as well as for the later divisions of the *Principles of Ethics*, had to be sought, copied and classified. In this way provision was made that my own holiday might not be entirely profitless.

The act of classifying the extracts and notes, when thus collected, would have looked like a strange ritual to any casual observer. He would have seen the tall figure of Spencer stooping over a ring of brown-paper envelopes spread upon the floor, with a handful of notes which, one by one, he read aloud and then dropped on the floor near to their appropriate envelopes. Hovering outside the magic circle, like an acolyte, was myself, suggesting from time to time a different receptacle for some note that I had made with another end in view. This giving rise to a polite exchange of ideas, the chief functionary, in his long Prince Albert coat, would then stand erect and deliver himself of a miniature essay, couched in the choicest language and enunciated in the most musical of voices, on, say, the use of cavalry in mediæval battles; the altruistic attributes of Arafura chieftains; the other characteristics of the Aloe which are related to the long delay in flowering and which make the delay profitable to the species; or some other more or less recondite subject that would have strangely puzzled the casual listener. The matter having been thus settled, the tall figure would stoop again; and the sorting would go on until interrupted afresh by a new difference of opinion, and a new disquisition, perhaps on planetoids, or priesthoods, or the marital customs of Central Africans.

This marshalling of facts to support an *a priori* induction had the merit of simplicity; but it occasionally failed, with results that recall a bright saying of Professor Huxley's which Spencer used to relate at his own expense. It was at a dinner of the X Club. Among those present were Tyndall, Huxley, Hooker, Lewes and others of the scientific stars that formed such a brilliant *Corona Borealis* over England at that time. The talk had turned on the drama, and tragedies being mentioned, "Oh," says Huxley, "Spencer's idea of a tragedy is an induction killed by a fact!"

A minor tragedy of this order occurred during one of the rituals of sorting and classification just described. Some reference was made by Spencer to the great industrial development in England during the reign of Queen Elizabeth—a perfectly justifiable inference in view of other notable activities of the period. I ventured the opinion that there had been no such development, but that the contrary had been the case. Now the statement of an error of fact was to Spencer as irritating as the pronouncement of a false opinion or an unscientific heresy; and looking at me with a severe expression, he began to censure my ignorance, or, rather, my erroneous interpretation of history. With the assurance of youth, however, I held to my opinion; and, in response to his demand for justification of it, I cited the well-known destructive effects of monopolies as farmed out wholesale by Elizabeth among her favorites. As he remained unconvinced, and as the matter concerned a part of the chapter we were working on, I hied me to the British Museum, and next morning gave him chapter and verse from Hume in proof of my position. He then conceded his defeat, and made me a pretty compliment. From him, this meant much; for he used to say: "I always spell compliment with an 'e,' meaning 'that which is due.' "

Francis Galton in *Memories of My Life* describes another "tragedy" in which a Spencerian induction was killed by a fact. Writing on finger-prints, he says:

Much has been written, but the last word has not been said, on the rationale of these curious papillary ridges; why in one man and in one finger they form whorls and in another loops. I may mention a characteristic anecdote of Herbert Spencer in connection with this. He asked me to show him my laboratory and to take his prints, which I did. Then I spoke of the failure to discover the origin of these patterns, and how the fingers of unborn children had been dissected to ascertain their earliest

9

8 Sep 81

Dear Mr Bridge

Please inquire of Mr
Harrison or Mr Jones what
books he has about
military organization — histories
of its successive stages; and
then begin to read up so
as to collect the facts
showing the differentiation &
integration that has gone
on since savage times.

I shall be back in
about ten days.

Faithfully yours
Herbert Spencer

stages, and so forth. Spencer remarked that this was beginning in the wrong way; that I ought to consider the purpose the ridges had to fulfil, and to work backwards. Here, he said, it was obvious that the delicate mouths of the sudorific glands required the protection given to them by the ridges on either side of them, and therefrom he elaborated a consistent and ingenious hypothesis at great length.

I replied that his arguments were beautiful and deserved to be true, but it happened that the mouths of the ducts did not run in the valleys between the crests, but along the crests of the ridges themselves. He burst into a good-humored and uproarious laugh, and told me the famous story—the Huxley one already quoted—which I have heard from each of the other two who were present on the occurrence. Huxley was one of them. Spencer, during a pause in conversation at dinner at the Athenæum, said, "You would little think it, but I once wrote a tragedy." Huxley answered promptly, "I know the catastrophe." Spencer declared it was impossible, for he had never spoken about it before then. Huxley insisted. Spencer asked what it was. Huxley replied, "A beautiful theory, killed by a nasty, ugly little fact."

Huxley said another clever thing at one of the dinners of the X Club, which I have heard Spencer quote. The conversation had turned upon habits of composition; some confessing frankly that they had difficulty in starting a subject, others that they required to have a pen in hand before the thoughts would come, and some that they were always ready. This was the case with George H. Lewes, who, saying that he quickly got up steam, added "I boil at a low temperature!" "But," queried Huxley, "does not that imply a vacuum in the upper regions?"

This recalls an incident which Spencer related to me on one of our walks concerning George H. Lewes, which puts that somewhat volatile personage in a bad

light. It appears that in the early days of their acquaintance Spencer and Lewes were in the habit of taking
long Sunday walks into the country; and, on one of
these occasions, Spencer, in the course of conversation,
outlined a theory of population which he had developed
during the previous week, and which was afterward
elaborated in one of his essays. A few weeks later, to
Spencer's surprise and annoyance, he found that Lewes
had coolly appropriated the idea, and embodied it in
an article for one of the periodicals to which he was a
regular contributor. Lewes gave no credit to Spencer
for it; and the dishonesty was never forgotten nor
wholly forgiven.

One day Spencer came into our workroom with Frederick Harrison, the great Positivist; and, after intro-
ductions, we all mounted to my bed-room on the floor
above, and carried down a heavy and clumsy-looking
bundle in canvas, which had always stood against the
wall at the head of my bed. On being opened, this
turned out to be an invalid's couch, made of iron, with
a tripod support instead of legs, and some sort of ball-
and-socket joint, so that it could be tipped at any angle.
It had been invented by Spencer, but as he had refused,
for altruistic reasons, to patent it, he could find no
manufacturer to put it on the market. Harrison's father
was bedridden; and the suggestion had been made to
let him have the use of it. To show how it worked I
was required to lie upon it, while Spencer manipulated
the levers. The resultant attitudes into which I was put
would have done no discredit to a professional gym-
nast. My feet were elevated far above my head; I was
thrown first on one shoulder and then on the other;
then tipped forward till I almost slid to the floor. At

one time I was suddenly jerked into a sitting posture; then tilted back until I almost stood on my head. Stretched out at full length, I was made to rotate like the needle of a compass; and suddenly stopped to find myself sliding over the edge of the bed. All the time Spencer was talking in his book-language about the impossibility of bed-sores developing where the patient's weight could be shifted to any part of his body; but he insisted that during these manipulations the nurse should never release the lever controlling the ball-and-socket joint, lest the whole thing collapse and the patient be shot to the floor—or through the open window, as seemed likely to happen to me. The contraption was duly tried on Harrison senior, probably with disastrous results; for it was returned two days later with no explanation and no provision for re-packing. This omission displeased Spencer, and he gave free expression to his annoyance. Many years afterward I reminded Mr. Harrison of the incident, but he made no rejoinder. The subject was evidently not pleasant.

Those who have read Spencer's story of his own life will recall that, during his early manhood, he was engaged in a subordinate capacity in building railways in England. In the Spring of 1882, I stood with him on a bridge crossing the London and Northwestern Railway at Harrow Road, near Willesden Junction; and he pointed to the sloping embankment edging the railway as one that he had constructed forty-four years earlier. A short distance across the fields we could see a farm-house at which he had lodged when so engaged; and it was while returning to this lodging that he had had an exciting adventure with a runaway truck. This

PORTER'S LODGE, KENSINGTON PALACE GARDENS

In this little room, behind the lampost, was written part of
Man versus The State, in the intervals had between games of
quoits in the adjoining gardens.

he narrated as we leaned on the parapet of the bridge. The story is told in the *Autobiography*; but there it lacks the vivid, colorful quality it had when I first heard it.

The occasion was one of those delightful walks in which Spencer was wont to indulge when his work was possible without frequent reference to notes. Taking a cab or train to the outskirts of London, we would start briskly across the country by paths known to him from long familiarity; and finding a shady knoll or grasssy nook he would recline with hands clasped behind his head, and dictate for ten or fifteen minutes. Then up again for a brisk spurt of a mile or two, until another quiet spot tempted to physical relaxation and the expression of thoughts that had crystalized during the walk. This was how parts of *Ecclesiastical Institutions* were written, especially the last chapter, entitled "Religious Retrospect and Prospect."

The four essays comprising the volume entitled *Man versus the State,* were dictated in the intervals between games of quoits, which we use to play in a garden behind the old tavern "William the Fourth," nearly opposite the gates of Kensal Green cemetery. Here Spencer paid a few shillings a week for the privilege of using a beery-smelling room with sanded room, just off the tap room to work in, and a piece of the garden behind in which to play. This old tavern—since rebuilt—was a hundred yards or so beyond the post marking the four-mile circle from Charing Cross; and the first time we drove there the cabman naturally charged the excess fare which the law allowed for passing beyond the four-mile limit. Spencer disputed the charge, saying that the cabman ought to have notified us before passing the mile post; and Jehu, recognizing that an altercation presaged no tip, promptly took up the challenge. The wordy warfare that ensued would have required the pen of Dickens to report it faithfully. Even when angry, Spencer talked "like a book" in polysyllabics of Latin derivation; while Cabby had at command the rough Saxon eloquence of his kind. The quoits, which were new, fell from their paper wrapping under Spencer's arm as the dispute waxed in vehemence, and I rescued them from the gutter. Thereafter it was his habit to stop the cab a few feet before the fateful boundary was reached, greatly to the disgust of the cabman, and we walked the rest of the way, rejoicing that one of the extortionate fraternity had been disappointed in his expectations. After a time permission was obtained to play in Kensington Palace Gardens, a tiny room in the gatekeeper's lodge having been secured for a small weekly sum to work in during the intervals between games.

At other times we have alternately worked and rowed in boats on a Scotch loch or along the Sussex shore. In Scotland we once played at fishing from a boat; but Spencer quickly tired of catching perch, which bit too freely and came in too tamely to afford sport for one accustomed to salmon. I remember that here he took out his pocket knife to give the wriggling fish its *coup de grace,* and he looked disgusted while doing it. The gaff promptly ended the struggles of the salmon I saw him catch; and doubtless his sportsmen's instinct was thus gratified without painfully violating his humanitarian impulses.

One evening while sitting over the fire which the Scotch evening chill made comfortable, and sipping

glasses of hot toddy—the wee doch and doris that
Harry Lauder has popularized—Spencer devised a new
kind of knot to fasten the hook to his line—one that a
single pull would untie whenever he wanted to change
the fly. He handed it to me to duplicate if possible;
and I surprised him by doing this at once. Answering
his puzzled inquiries, I told him that I had learned the
trick, and many others with string from my father, who
had been a weaver. "Ah! an illustration of the specialization of functions!" was his gratified comment.

He was ever thus alert to recognize such *a posteriori*
proofs of his doctrines. At Brighton, one day, as we
walked along the Esplanade, he suggested that we
should take a run into the country, he on a tricycle and
I on one of those old-fashioned aerial bicycles with a
high wheel in front, on which in those days I was somewhat expert. As he proposed to hire these machines
forthwith, I smilingly objected that we should look
unpleasantly conspicuous riding such machines in high
silk hats and frock coats, such as we both were wearing
in response to the absurd conventions of the day. Again
there were comments on "specialization," extending to
the minor details of dress; and but for my own reluc-
tance to attract the amused attention of passers-by, I
believe Spencer would gladly have seized the opportunity of displaying his independent spirit by riding a
tricycle along the Brighton Front in a tall silk hat and
frock coat!

At frequent intervals, as the *Autobiography* shows,
Spencer absented himself from London, to visit friends
in the country or to make short trips with some genial
companion. On these occasions my own work consisted
in gathering material to illustrate the arguments in

17

forthcoming divisions of the *Synthetic Philosophy;* and as a guide to research at the British Museum, where most of my reading was done, I had a series of memoranda, which varied from time to time according to the character of the subjects to be investigated. For the essays comprising *Man versus the State,* old legal enactments which had turned out disastrously had to be hunted through scores of volumes of histories and parliamentary documents, and proved an alternative kind of sport and one equally fascinating as the other games we played. In collecting data for the *Principles of Morality,* I had a little book, now before me, in which a page is given to each of sundry moral or immoral attributes accompanying advancing civilization. Here are examples of these pages, which vividly present methods of research by proxy, as well as the mechanics of book-making of a certain kind.

Excess and Abstinence in Food or Drink.

Primitive gluttony—its adaptation to conditions of irregular supplies of food.

Rise of reprobation of over-eating, when and where and under what conditions.

Over-drinking—considered as subject to no moral criticism; considered as applauded in certain times; considered as reprobated; in relation to societies, habitats, classes, temporary states.

Kindred data in respect of nervous stimulants of various kinds —the approval and disapproval of their use.

Regard for Others' Property.

Plundering of enemies held praiseworthy during high militancy; plundering within the society honorable as marking supremacy; theft praiseworthy if not discovered; respect for property rights increasing as the relation of contract grows; property rights of individuals as coming to be held sacred one against another; ditto as getting more and more sacred in relation to the aggregate of individuals represented by the State; reprobation of injury to property.

Obedience and Independence.

The idea and the sentiment of loyalty as growing with militancy; the accompanying duty of submission and viciousness of resistance.

The idea and sentiment of independence as accompanying the growth of industrialism; the duty of asserting personal claims, with the contemptibleness of servility and the surrender of rights.

There are numerous other pages under the headings of Labour and Rest; Revenge and Forgiveness; Courage and Cowardice; Endurance and Impatience of Pain, Cold, Hunger, &c; Sexual desires Restricted or Unrestricted; Regard for Others' Lives; Regard for Others' Liberty; Marital Duties; Parental Duties; Humanity; Generosity; Desire to Please; Etc.

Then came the following general directions to be observed.

Note the end which injunctions have in view—divine approval,—approval of a living superior, welfare of the community, personal welfare, or a moral ideal.

The facts to be gathered together under the foregoing heads should at the same time be noted in their relations primarily to types militant and industrial.

They should also be considered in their relations to the characters ascribed to the god or gods, and the tacit implication as to what are considered virtues as possessed by him.

Further, the ethical sentiments and ideas are to be considered as being simply identical with the ideas of what the god or gods will, and contrariwise as being separate from, and in the course of time independent of, the ideas of what is willed by the gods.

And in the same way they are to be considered as identical

with the requirements of established law or custom, and again later as being independent of, and from time to time opposed to, human law and culture, with the effect of showing under both these heads the rise and development of the ethical ideas and sentiments as independent of the religious and political.

It may be also noted so far as can be, that this rise of the ethical ideas and sentiments into independence of authority, theological and political, is a comcomitant of industrial progress.

Attention may also be paid to the relationship which exists between the rise of ethical ideas into precision and the growth of intelligence, and especially scientific intelligence.

Then follow suggestions as to the sources from which these facts are to be gathered: the *Zendavesta;* the Veddas; the Egyptian Book of the Dead; histories of the Mahabarata; the Sacred Books of the Chinese; collections of proverbs belonging to different races; *An Ethical Anthology* by Moncure D. Conway; Grote's *Greece;* Gibbon's *Rome;* Lecky's *European Morals,* etc., etc.

"These" concludes Spencer, "sufficiently indicate the scope of the inquiry, and you will be able to fill in the details of it more fully than I can."

Spencer's habit of spelling "compliment" with an "e"—meaning "that which is due," again gives a double value to the compliment implied in the closing sentence of this long quotation.

Much has been said and written concerning the value of the Spencerian doctrine as a basis of religion; and the question was well debated at the time of the famous controversy between Frederick Harrison and Herbert Spencer in 1884. At that time Spencer was in unusually poor health, and perhaps did not make so notable a fight as he might otherwise have done. Yet the noise of it was heard around the world. His first contributions to the controversy were made from Brighton, where we used to take long walks over the downs, occasionally resting on some grassy bank to write a few paragraphs. The later ones were written in intervals between our games of quoits in Kensington Palace Gardens.

The immediate cause of the controversy—which, besides Frederick Harrison, the high priest of Positivism involved Sir James Stephen, one of England's most noted jurists, Mr. Wilfred Ward, an ardent Catholic, Count Goblet d'Alviella in France, and started an infinity of minor polemics throughout England and America, extending also to Germany and Italy—was the chapter previously referred to, entitled "Religion: a Retrospect and Prospect," now included in the division *Ecclesiastical Institutions* in the *Principles of Sociology*. This short essay of a dozen pages, dictated to me during our strolls over the downs above Brighton, was written within a week, and formed the capstone of the elaborate edifice which had taken more than thirty years to build. It is the most important part of the *Synthetic Philosophy*, containing as it does the first presentation of the evolutionist creed by one authorized to make it. It was simultaneously published in London, New York, Paris, Berlin, Milan, St. Petersburg, Budapest, Calcutta, and, a week or two later, in Australia, New Zealand and Japan—in Japanese. The special effort taken to obtain simultaneous publication throughout the world is an indication of the high importance Spencer attached to this brief statement of evolutionary belief. Tyndall and Huxley both read it in proof, and subscribed to its doctrine.

Count Goblet d'Alviella thus speaks of this important part of Spencer's work in its relation to current religious beliefs:

The last word of Evolution agrees with the definitions of the most refined theologists, which, transcending vulgar symbolism, have constantly recognized God in the double character of reality and incomprehensibility. We may add that, before becoming the scientific faith of Spencer, Huxley, and even of Haeckel, this religious conception has sufficed for men of the highest mind and the most pious imagination, such as Giordano Bruno, Spinoza, Kant, Goethe, Shelley, Wordsworth, Carlyle, Emerson, and even M. Renan. It can lead not to religion only but to mysticism. And then Count d'Alviella cites a passage from a Hindoo mystic:

For the true Yogi, forms become informal, the informal takes form. Mind discovers itself in matter, matter forms itself in mind. In the glorious sun is revealed the glory of glories. In the serene moon mind imbibes of all serenities. In the reverberation of the thunder is the voice of the Lord which makes itself heard afar. All things are full of Him. Open your eyes, behold, He is without; shut them, He is found within.

This reads like a paraphrase of one of the Psalms of David. "Yet," contends Count d'Alviella, "there is not a word in these exalted conceptions in contradiction with the religious conceptions of Mr. Spencer."*

In this aspect the *Synthetic Philosophy* becomes a

*William Herbert Carruth, unknown to Spencer, in eight short pregnant lines has summarized, with a touch of genius, the entire *Synthetic Philosophy*.

> A fire mist and a planet,
> A crystal and a cell,
> A jellyfish and a saurian,
> And caves where the cavemen dwell—
> Then a sense of Law and Beauty,
> And a face turned from the clod;
> Some call it EVOLUTION,
> And others call it—GOD.

glorified Pantheism. But it is not only a transfiguration
of nature; it is also an exaltation of theology; for it
teaches the universal fatherhood of God, and the universal brotherhood of man—aye, and of all sentient
creation. It is as far removed from materialism as is
the Song of Solomon, or the teachings of St. Paul. The
Power that holds the planets in their courses and gives
the lily its fragrance; that guides the mighty rush of
a comet and directs the movement that in ten thousand
years produces a microscopic crystal; that has sprinkled the universe with star-dust, and put three thousand
lenses within the minute dimensions of an insect's eye;
that has given the glow-worm its lamp and the sun its
fire; is the same Power—call it God, the All-Father,
the Ultimate Reality, the Great Unkown, the Absolute
—which wells up in consciousness, inspires our Shake-
speres and our Miltons, which breathes indeed through
every living soul, and is behind every impulse for good
within us. Not in the material world alone is its presence everywhere seen and felt; it is manifest in the
growth of intellect no less than in the rising sap of
every grass-blade; in the voice of conscience as in the
song of birds; in the beauty of charity and all kindly
sentiment, as in the verdure of awakening Spring; in
the glow of the poet's fancy as well as in the pink and
gold of the sunset sky. To give a scientific basis to this
sort of belief is what Spencer has done; and it is this
which, above all the brilliant details of his great Cos-
mogony, entitles him to the everlasting gratitude and
veneration of mankind.

I have another mental picture which I love to recall.
In a highland glen; Scotch mists drifting along the

mountain sides and occasionally dissolving into rain. On the margin of the stream Spencer, in goloshes, Inverness cape and deer-stalker cap, thrashing the water with rod and line for salmon. In the imperfect shelter of a stunted tree, the gillie and I talking in low tones lest the fish should hear and be frightened away!

"They tell me," says the gillie, with the richest of Scotch burrs, "that Meester Spencer-r mak's books, and that 'tis ye that wr-rite them doon f'r him?"

I assented.

"Ah suppose ye've mony lang wur-rds to wr-rite?"

Again I assented; and frank admiration shone in the freckled face. After a thoughtful silence:

"An' is Meester-r Spencer-r a gude speller too?"

A few minutes later this gillie, through his clumsy failure to gaff the fish that had been hooked, received a personal introduction to some of those "lang wur-rds" that flowed so easily from the Spencerian tongue; but he recovered favor when I related the story of the "gude speller." The implied compliment was irresistible!

Herbert Spencer was the son of a schoolmaster, and studied under his uncle Thomas, who also kept a school. The critical and didactic attitude, which was his most marked characteristic, was thus honestly inherited. He deemed it his duty to combat on the instant every erroneous statement, false reasoning or foolish opinion; and this led to frequent homilies. At his boarding-house, where I sometimes lunched with him, corrective or expostulatory explosions came from him as regularly as the dessert followed the roast. The inconsequent chatter around the table seemed marked with more than

24

the usual inaccuracies of fact and fancy; so that, to preserve his temper—which was of the hair-trigger type—Spencer finally hit upon the expedient of closing his ears to it. This he did literally, by applying ear-pads similar to those protective coverings used by policemen in zero weather. These he carried in his coat-tail pocket; and, when the talk became unbearably frivolous, he ended it for himself by taking out the ear-pads and slipping them on. This always proved a death-blow to conversation of every sort; but as he believed that talking fatigued him and diminished his power for work, and as he regarded his work as the greatest thing in life, he was never deterred by consideration for others from abruptly ending a conversation. Mr. William M. Evarts, presiding at the complimentary banquet to Spencer in New York, was visibly annoyed when asked by the guest of honor to refrain from trying to entertain him with playful remarks, because of the customary after-dinner speech which Spencer dreaded as likely to result in a nervous breakdown.

This fear of a breakdown was ever present, and controlled every thought and act of Spencer's during the greater part of his life. He frequently interrupted his work to feel his pulse or to note whether the temperature of his head was falling. His anxiety to sleep kept him awake. Believing that somnolence is due to a mild form of cerebral congestion, he frequently took the pillow from under his head and placed it beneath his feet, so as to help gravitation in producing this condition. This was done in all seriousness, and mentioned by himself without a smile.

I never heard Spencer make a joke, nor even indulge in playful badinage. On the contrary, we have sometimes walked miles across the downs of Sussex without exchanging a word. Sometimes, however, he would momentarily forget himself; and then it was a delight to listen to him. On these occasions it seemed as if nothing in Nature escaped his notice. The first skylark in Spring —February 18th is a date I recall; the track of earthworms on the wet country road; the reflex waves that run back from the shore; the golden beauty of the budding gorse-bush—these and many others I recall as furnishing the subject of charming little essays, had I been able to take them down as uttered. At the same time, it was the scientific rather than the æsthetic aspects of Nature which appealed to him; and the fragrance and coloring of the rose seemed chiefly to interest him in their relation to fertilization by insects. The early song of the skylark simply meant an open winter, with an abundance of bird food, and was not the love-note that Darwin had found it.

In his rare expansive moments we have discussed poetry, music and sculpture; and here again his concepts had a scientific and non-emotional basis. Tennyson he admired for his poetry, but was impatient of his dogmatism. He told me that when, with a party of his friends, he once called on the poet at his residence in the Isle of Wight he soon left the group and wandered about the garden alone, having found Tennyson's talk irritating. Berlioz he ranked among the greatest musicians; and esteemed his "Damnation of Faust" above every similar work. His appreciation of sculpture was proportioned to its anatomical accuracy; and his criticism of paintings had a similar bias in favor of the laws of optics. Although he wrote much on æsthetics, he was so critical, and so bound by scientific formulæ,

26

that the beautiful in art and nature gave rise to none but intellectual reactions: received from him little if any emotional recognition. John Fiske noticed this, and commented on it in a letter to his family, which was published while the foregoing passages were undergoing revision. "Yesterday," wrote Fiske in 1873, "I lunched with Spencer and walked through Kensington Gardens and Hyde Park with him. It was a beautiful day—warm as summer and such a delicious blue-gray sky as I never saw before. I was wild with delight. But Spencer never seems to warm up to anything but ideas. He has got so infernally critical that even the finset work of God—a perfect day—is not quite fine enough for him." I used to think of Spencer as living on a mountain top—a snow capped mountain where he dwelt in glacial isolation. At times he seemed to be the mountain itself, dominating all the surrounding terrain to horizon limits, but frigid, remote, unapproachable.

I have said that I never heard Spencer make a joke. The nearest approach to a whimsicality of his that I recall was his statement before the Royal Commission on copyright. "Now," said he, "take one of my books, say the *Principles of Psychology*. Instead of calling it '*caviare* to the general,' let us call it 'cod-liver oil to the general.' I think it probable that if you were to ask ninety-nine people out of one hundred whether they would take a spoonful of cod-liver oil or read a chapter of that book, they would prefer the cod-liver oil." A joke truly, with a melancholy tinge, and an implied criticism of the intelligence of the ninety-nine!

Stay! There was a joke, purely Spencerian! It is as follows, transcribed from letters to E. L. Youmans, in

27

Duncan's *Life and Letters of Herbert Spencer*, pp. 238-9:

12 *January* (1883). The programme of the forthcoming number of the *Edinburgh Review* I see contains an article on "The Spencerian Philosophy." I expect it will be civilly dissident.

28 *January.*—I went yesterday to look at the article to find a sentence which would serve my purpose, and found one on the last page admirably fitted, which I inclose. I am going this week to issue advertisements of *First Principles* in all the leading papers, to which I shall affix this adverse opinion of the *Edinburgh* by way of showing my contempt for it.

The advertisement accordingly appeared with the selected sentence: "This is nothing but a Philosophy of epithets and phrases, introduced and carried on with an unrivalled solemnity and affectation of precision of style, concealing the loosest reasoning and the haziest indefiniteness." A copy was sent "to the editor and another to the contributer, who, I find, is Sir Edward Beckett."

Spencer copied the sentence himself at the Athenæum Club, and gave it to me next morning when I was writing out the advertisements mentioned. I kept the original as a curiosity, and reproduce it here.

"This is nothing but a philosophy of epithets and phrases introduced and carried on with an unrivalled solemnity and affectation of precision of style, concealing the loosest reasoning and the haziest indefiniteness"
Edinburgh Review

At times he found his physical condition inadequate to the demands of his regular work on the *Synthetic Philosophy;* and then he would engage in some light work that filled in the time and enabled him to give definition to ideas which had been shaping in his mind. During an attack of lumbago, for instance, he dictated while in bed an essay on the "Physiology of Character" —a fascinating analysis of the co-relation of bodily conditions and mental states, which is published as an appendix in the *Autobiography*.

The essays, "The New Toryism," "The Coming Slavery," "The Sins of Legislators," and "The Great Political Superstition," constituting, with a postscript, the volume *The Man versus The State,* were easy for Spencer; but, as the subjects were new and no material had been collected for them, they entailed a good deal of extra work on me. Every afternoon and late evening found me at the British Museum, getting together the references required for the next day's work; and, while I thought little of this at the time, I have since come to feel that I was inadequately compensated for the work I did, not only then but always. For, by our agreement, my time was my own after two o'clock; and, looking back over the years, it seems to me that thirty shillings a week was scant pay for the services I rendered. I had to make researches in French, German, Italian, and Spanish—usually in my own time; take dictation in shorthand while transcribing it into longhand; and carry a dozen books twice or thrice a week from Bayswater to the London Library in St. James's Square and back again, a distance of nearly six miles. The propriety of his supplying bus-fare for the transportation of these heavy loads was as completely overlooked as was the fact that this and other necessary work could not be done within the stipulated hours of my employment. That he was unconscious of any unfairness to me in all this is amusingly shown in that on my notifying

WILMOT STREET, DERBY
Where Spencer spent his childhood. He was born in Exeter
Street, nearby.

him, by letter to Scotland, of my intention to leave him, he telegraphed back saying, "If you stay I will give twenty pounds more for equivalent extra time!" He had not even noticed that all along I had been giving him practically all my time!

Generally speaking, however, his sense of justice was as delicately poised as a chemist's balance. Also it was just as automatically mechanical, just as mathematically precise, and just as insensible to emotional appeal. It was like a law of Nature. If you fell, you hurt yourself. If you made a mistake you suffered the natural consequences; and if these consequences reached others, the mistake became an injury. His father's loss of money in a lace business, for which he had had no experience, was more than an error of judgment; it was a wrong done to his mother and himself. His own conduct was regulated by the same severe and scientifically conceived rules. If he came to my room on Sundays, he knocked at the door and waited on the mat until I called "Come in!" If on week days he came at irregular hours, he made a noise outside the door and came in without knocking. Between ten and one o'clock he walked right in. Such graduated punctiliousness suggests nothing so much as a chemist's balance.

Contrariwise—to use an expression greatly in favor with himself—he was habitually so self-absorbed, so completely possessed—I almost wrote "obsessed"—by the work to which he had devoted his life, that he was not even conscious of many things that called for recognition and in fairness were entitled to it. Beyond an occasional warning—which he took no pains to make effective—he gave himself no concern for the health and comfort of his assistants. Collier, my immediate predecessor, who lived the same lonely life that I did, suffered a breakdown from which he never recovered. Dr. Sheppig was years convalescing from a collapse suffered while working for Spencer. We were simply mechanical accessories to the *Synthetic Philosophy!* Except for the gift of a complimentary ticket to the Royal Academy, which he was unable to use himself, Spencer never gave me a diversion that was independent of our work during the years I was with him. In a strange city, with no friend and hardly an acquaintance, my life, in that lonely workroom, inevitably became that of a studious recluse. I recall whole days, and almost weeks, when I did not speak to a soul except Spencer and the waiter who served my dinner in a restaurant. In his early life he had been warned by his physician against living alone; and so he took up his abode in a boarding-house, where he had some sort of human contact. His oversight of the danger to his assistants from loneliness was, therefore, all the more incomprehensible, except on some ego-centric theory like that suggested.

Despite all this, the experience, which in my own case lasted nearly five years, was invaluable; and I would not part with the memory of it for any material gain. One day, years after my connection with Spencer, Andrew Carnegie and I were looking into Fifth Avenue from a window of the Windsor Hotel. "There goes the richest man in the world," said Mr. Carnegie, indicating William K. Vanderbilt, who was passing on the opposite side of the street. "And I would not exchange my knowledge of Shakespere, or my knowledge of Herbert Spencer for all his wealth. So," he added, turning to me, "you may figure up what you are worth!" And, making due allowance for Mr. Carnegie's well-known prejudice in favor of poverty, I am inclined to think that his estimate of comparative values was true.

Parts of this chapter appeared in *Liber Scriptorium,* the Second Book of the Authors Club and in the *Unpartizan Review,* published by Henry Holt & Co. who have kindly authorized their republication here.

Dr. Will Durant, speaking of Spencer as "the greatest English philosopher of his century," says "he gave to philosophy a new contact with things, and brought to it a realism which made German philosophy seem, beside it, weakly pale and timidly abstract. He summed up his age as no man had ever summed up any age since Dante; and he achieved so masterly a co-ordination of so vast an area of knowledge that criticism is almost shamed into silence by his achievement. We are standing now on heights which his struggles and his labors won for us; we seem to be above him because he has raised us on his shoulders. Some day, when the sting of his opposition is forgotten, we shall do him better justice."

To my friends D H Bridge
with best wishes
Andrew Carnegie
May 19 1913

ANDREW CARNEGIE

THE STAR-SPANGLED OPTIMIST

IF Herbert Spencer's glacial isolation suggested a snow-capped mountain, Andrew Carnegie's smiling geniality recalled an Alpine meadow, lush with a tender herbage and dappled with wild flowers. In contrast with Spencer's icy aloofness, Carnegie's sunny personality radiated warmth and light: he loved to find his own joy of living reflected by those about him. He was the most consistently happy man I ever knew. He enjoyed the perpetual miracle of life.

Early in our acquaintance he unwittingly gave a clue to the sympathetic side of his nature. It was early summer. We had that day moved from the Windsor Hotel in New York to his mother's little frame cottage at Cresson Springs in the Allegenies. No provision had been made for our coming and there was a good deal of confusion, which was cheerfully endured. At night the restricted space in the cottage forced him and me into adjoining beds in the same room. From a near-by room the noisy gossip and laughter of the Irish cook and waitress came through the thin partition in disturbing volume. After a while my own reaction to it became one of impatience, for I wanted to sleep. Presently, in response to a loud peal of laughter from the next room, I heard a chuckle from the adjoining bed followed by a sympathetic laugh. "My, how those girls

35

are enjoying themselves!" Such was Andrew Carnegie's only comment on what most people in his position would have met with a harsh demand for "less noise in there!" For him the phrase "our common humanity" had a real meaning.

Of lowly origin himself, Carnegie's sympathetic understanding of the trials and hardships of the wage-earner never faltered. The best-known and most frequently garbled saying of his was the one supposedly addressed to his own workmen: "Thou shalt not take thy neighbor's job." I was with him when he wrote this sentence. Separated from its context it became the strikers' slogan, such as was never intended. Here is the full passage, which far from inciting to violence, as often asserted, is simply a well-phrased analysis of the emotional reactions of the laborer under severe stress:

While public sentiment has rightly and unmistakably condemned violence even in the form for which there is most excuse, I would have the public give due consideration to the terrible temptation to which the workingman on a strike is sometimes subjected. To expect that one dependent upon his daily wage for the necessities of life will stand by peaceably and see a new man employed in his stead is to expect much. This poor man may have a wife and children dependent upon his labor. Whether medicine for a sick child, or even nourishing food for a delicate wife, is procurable, depends upon his steady employment. In all but a very few departments of labor it is unnecessary and I think improper to subject men to such an ordeal. In the case of railways and a few other employments it is, of course, essential for the public wants that no interruption occur, and in such cases substitutes must be employed; but the employer of labor will find it much more to his interest, wherever possible, to allow his works to remain idle and await the result of a dispute than to employ a class of men that can be induced to take the place of

36

other men who have stopped work. Neither the best men as men, nor the best men as workers, are thus to be obtained. There is an unwritten law among the best workmen: "Thou shalt not take thy neighbor's job."

I recall that he wrote this passage with a pad on his lap while seated with one leg tucked under him—a favorite position of his, and as he finished it he read it aloud with sparkling eyes and declamatory voice.

"There, what do you think of that?" he asked.

"I think it's great, and shows an understanding of the workman's mind that few employers ever attain. But it may be misunderstood by the workman himself —misunderstood because it comes from a great employer of men."

"You are wrong! It is because it comes from an employer that it will have its greatest effect."

We were both right—as the Homestead strike demonstrated.

Carnegie gave a flat contradiction to the silly saying that Scotchmen are devoid of humor. With him life itself was a jest and a jewel, and every one of its many facets sparkled into ripples of light and laughter. Once while absorbed in the study of Scribners' chart of the industrial progress of the United States, for illustrations in Carnegie's forthcoming *Triumphant Democracy,* I was startled as a book came hurtling through the air, striking the wall above my head.

"Let's leave these statistics—these dry bones, and get out into the sunshine!"

A moment later Carnegie had joyously herded everybody—'Liza, Fanny, Mary, Victor and myself—on to the porch and away into the woods. There Victor—a leading lawyer and afterwards head of a great trans-

37

THE LITTLE COTTAGE AT CRESSON SPRINGS
Photographed during Carnegie's sickness.

continental railway system—in the contagion of the
Carnegie spirit of fun, essayed to climb a tree. Chagrined by his failure and our shouts of laughter, he
challenged me to attempt the feat, offering to buy me a
new suit of clothes if I spoiled those I was wearing. But
Carnegie vetoed the contest, declaring he could not
risk the neck of his literary assistant until *Triumphant
Democracy* was finished and in the printers' hands!

About this time he bought all of this land, covering
the entire mountain top; and we had many tramps
through the woods seeking the best site for the big

38

house he intended to build there. Then it was that he let me climb a tree—with an anæroid to determine the highest point of land on which to put the building. It was a beautiful spot, overlooking all but the highest ridges in that part of the Allegenies. Later Frederick Law Olmstead was engaged to make the final selection of the building site; and, as he was lame, we saddled a couple of horses and rode all over the terrain. Mr. Carnegie was not feeling well and did not come. When I joyfully reported that Mr. Olmstead had confirmed our selection, Mr. Carnegie showed an unusual irritation, saying that I must have led Mr. Olmstead to the spot, whereas what he had wanted was an independent judgment, for which he was paying a good fee. All of which was true and I had no excuse to offer for my thoughtlessness.

That which had seemed a slight indisposition, in one who had always been robust and in good spirits, took a serious turn, for it developed into typhoid fever. Dr. Fred S. Dennis was sent for, and he practically gave up his New York practice to attend to his distinguished patient. Dr. Jasper Garmany was Dr. Dennis's chief assistant, and he and the nurse whom he afterwards married took up their abode in our restricted quarters.

It was during these tragic days that Tom Carnegie died, and a few days later the idolized mother followed him. The partners came up from Pittsburgh, and none of them was willing to break to Andrew the news of his brother's death. As I was in the way of going freely into the sick room to give the patient news of outside happenings, or occasionally to read to him, the painful duty fell to me.

"George Lauder has come up from Pittsburgh," I said, "and Tom is very sick."

"What's the matter with him?" asked Andrew.

"He has pneumonia."

"Then he'll never get over it! That's the end of Tom! Oh this life, this life!" And with that he threw up his hands and turned his face to the wall. Nothing more was said, and I tip-toed out of the room to report to Lauder, Phipps and John Walker.

Tom was his mother's favorite, her younger son, and Andrew knew that in her weak state and advanced years the effect of his death would be fatal. So he called Dr. Dennis in, and quietly said,

"When Mother goes, you attend to everything."

And so it was—quietly and with muffled feet, we gently carried her out, across the snow, down the hill to the station, and so to Pittsburgh, to rest beside her beloved Tom.

A mile or so back of the little wooden cottage where Mrs. Carnegie died was the Old Portage Road, now overgrown with mountain laurel, and the solid stone ties on which the old rails had rested half covered with grass and wild flowers. This was the road over which the Carnegies had travelled to Pittsburgh nearly forty years earlier, when they came from Dunfermline in 1848—by canal boat to the eastern foot of the mountains, then hauled up and across them by cable, and so down the western slope and on to Pittsburgh. These boats were built in sections, to facilitate the hauling of them over the mountains.

Winter set in early that year, but Mr. Carnegie's condition was such that he could not be removed from his arctic surroundings. The cottage had no heating

CROSSING THE ALLEGHANIES IN 1840
How Andrew Carnegie, aged twelve, crossed the mountains to
Pittsburgh in 1848. The Canal boats were constructed in Sections and were pulled over the mountains by stationary Engines
on eleven inclined planes.

facilities except open log fires; and those of us who
remained hung rugs against the windows and crouched
in front of the open fire, puffing our tobacco smoke up
the chimney so that it would not get into the sick room.
Mr. Carnegie never smoked himself and abhorred the
smell of tobacco. I have known him open a window
at the Windsor Hotel, to drive out the smell of tobacco
left by some bell-boy who had just brought in a letter
or telegram.

When convalescence set in and it was safe to remove
the patient to New York, Robert Pitcairn, one of Andrew's boyhood chums who had become an important
official of the Pennsylvania Railroad, lent his private
car. And I am reminded of a characteristic incident that
happened on our way to New York. The car at Cresson

41

Springs had been put at the end of the train, which had come through from Chicago or St. Louis. As we approached Elizabeth, the signals were against us, and our train stopped on a curve. The brakeman went back, as usual in such cases, with a red light to flag any train that might be following us, and he soon disappeared around the curve. Mr. Carnegie and I were seated on the rear platform, and he manifested some concern lest the brakeman fail to stop any on-coming train.

"Watch that curve," said he. "If you see the lights of a locomotive, jump at once; but be sure to jump on the inside of the curve."

"Why the inside of the curve?"

"Because the impact of the locomotive will force this car outward, and if you jump that way you will be killed."

"And what about you?" I asked.

"I can't be moved as you know, and must take my chance here."

Fortunately nothing of the kind happened. His early experiences, when he was superintendent of a division of the same road, had familiarized him with the outward thrust of a heavy moving body when suddenly arrested on a curve. It was his unselfish care for my safety that led him to advise me what to do in a contingency that would have been fatal to himself.

Triumphant Democracy went to press early in 1886. It was a glorification of republican principles as contrasted with monarchial concepts. From data culled by me from old newspapers, magazines and books at the Astor Library in Lafayette Place, supplemented by the encyclopedic knowledge of John Denison Champlin —who supplied the catching title of the book—Mr.

Carnegie had built up an almost sensational comparison of the Republic's rapid march during the preceding fifty years with the slow progress of Europe during the same period; and, of course, this was attributed to the superior political system of America. It was published by the Scribners; and, with his usual generosity, Mr. Carnegie assigned the royalties to Mr. Champlin and me. The book had a very large sale: the comparison, so favorable to the Republic, flattered Americans and foreshadowed the industrial supremacy which they have since achieved.

I went to London in March with advance sheets of the book and sample copies of the American edition. I recall with amusement the consternation of Mr. Marston of the great publishing house of Sampson Low, Marston, Searle and Rivington, when he saw the binding of the American edition. On the front cover was an inverted pyramid labelled "Monarchy" to symbolize the instability of the British constitution, while another pyramid, labelled "Republic" stood on its proper base to mark the solidity of the American political structure! As further emphasis, a broken sceptre appeared under the title on the cover, with quotations from Gladstone and Salisbury in praise of America's Supreme Court. As if this were not enough, an overturned crown appeared on the back!

Mr. Marston, a dignified Englishman of the old school—a veritable Colonel Newcome—disgustedly threw the book on to his desk with the remark:

"The thing is probably as contemptible as its cover is contemptuous!"

He nevertheless allowed his house to publish it, possibly on the theory that the dignity of his imprint would

My Dear Mr Bridge

Charles tells me you sail Saturday.

Success to you !! Make her go —

Mr Morley will be of service & Mr Labouchere should be sent a Copy with print mkd

I hope you will enjoy your visit & return hearty & strong & ready for our next little issue

Yours truly
Andrew Carnegie

Mr Storey will introduce you to him —

Send Copies freely & spend Money where needed

Success is the point aimed at — secure that —

Remember me to Mr Spencer above all —

I hope you will see Matthew Arnold also Julian & Arnold also his great father

A C

offset what he regarded as the undignified character of the work. Yet he had a good deal of sympathy with "The States" as he called them; because his son lived there. And he gave me a copy of a little book entitled *Frank's Ranch,* in which this son had described his adventures in the West.

I have saved several letters which Mr. Carnegie wrote about this time. One, in pencil in his own hand, dated Cresson, April 1st, 1886, reads:

I think we should deluge Britain with T. D. Suppose we let radical clubs, reading rooms and coffee rooms know that copies will be sent (free of cheap edition) upon application. I would send copy of first edition to every library, reading room, &c., free —cheap edition for any who apply. Perhaps it would be best if you engage some young radical to attend to disposing of cheap edition in various towns & give him discretion to distribute gratis to every club &c &c he to give you list of organizations supplied. If sold for a shilling it should go. Scribner told me last week book trade at a stand still—summer—but T. D. *still going.* Busy getting plans for Castle on the Crest—going to have a splendid home—stone castle! Do put T. D. into hands of people—want 25,000 copies at least to go there.

I did better than that, however. No fewer than 60,-000 copies were sold at sixpence each, through circularizing the liberal clubs throughout Britain. I also published translations in France and Germany. The French edition did well; but the German publishers were warned that the book was not regarded with favor by officialdom, and its sale had best be stopped. I, too, was quietly notified that Mr. Carnegie's *Lobgesang* of the Republic did not harmonize with the *Hussarenritt* and other military marches, and that Switzerland had a better climate than Stuttgart's. So I went to Zurich;

and, later in the year, what was left of the German edition was boxed and shipped, without notice to us, to New York, where it remained in the Custom House, unclaimed. It may be there still for aught I know to the contrary.

It was after my return from Europe that Mr. Carnegie fell sick and his brother and mother died. These tragic events, happening all at once, put an end to the plan for a Castle on the Crest. Despite its great natural beauty, the place became distasteful to all of us; and I do not believe any one of that joyous crowd has ever visited Cresson since. The hill-top wood, where we had wandered in happy abandon, was given by Mr. Carnegie as the site of a home for consumptives. But the memory of the glorious rides over the mountains, the stimulating tramps along the trails, the cozy gatherings about the log fire in the evening, when merry quip and jest mingled with music and song and sparkling conversation, will remain with all who were privileged to form a part of that happy company.

Of course, Mr. Carnegie was the mainspring of all our activities, as he was the fascinating center of every circle he entered. Often he would recite whole scenes from Shakespere, changing his voice as he passed from one character to another. Burns he knew by heart, as he did much of his friend Edwin Arnold's *Light of Asia;* and he often joined to the flickering fire-light the glow of his own bright fancy and brilliant imagination, as he talked about his favorite poems. He was a poet himself, as he had shown in a hundred places in his books of travel and coaching. His discriminating selection of the choicest gems of literature, safely locked in

46

his marvelous memory and recited with rare skill, gave
to these impromptu entertainments an unforgettable
quality. He had known everybody of importance in his
own generation; and, in the intimacy of his own home,
his reminiscences had the charm and fascination we
all experience when the lives of the great are opened
to us by one who has known them.

At the breakfast table one morning I spoke of the
death of General Grant, and Mr. Carnegie's mobile
face took on a look of sadness; for the great soldier had
been his friend. I went on, and mentioned several others
of the great world who had recently passed away—
Gov. Tilden, President Arthur, Henry Ward Beecher.
Mr. Carnegie's face grew longer as I slowly proceeded,
and the others at the table grew sad in sympathy. Then,
after a pause, I added "And I am not feeling very well
myself." It was an old joke, but it succeeded beyond its
merit or my expectations. A shout of laughter from
the head of the table, surprised squeals and giggles
from the girls, and a hasty retreat saved me from a
shower of hot rolls. As I peered around the open door
with a mock look of penitence, Mr. Carnegie called:
"You may come back and finish your breakfast; but you
don't deserve it!" He so often made a joke himself
that he was always ready to laugh at one by someone
else, even a poor one like mine.

Just before this I had given expression to a whimsy
which he received with mock seriousness. With some
elaboration, I had maintained that if a person made a
joke, he was entitled, by all the rules of equity, to
receive a laugh in return: that otherwise he would be
giving something for nothing: that the quality of the
joke was immaterial, and that it was the kind intention

behind it that called for payment. Carnegie gravely agreed with me, and said that, in default of such recognition, the joker would be justified in bringing suit against the recipients. He said there was a real ethical principle involved—that the experience of mankind had crystalized around the Latin phrase *Quid pro quo,* with all its implications! It was all delightful fooling, of the kind that gave to these gatherings an ever-present joy.

Which reminds me of a happy visit to the cottage made by Mr. Phipps's cousin, Miss Emma Franks, and her three lovely nieces, eighteen to twenty-three or thereabouts. These young English girls were full of mischief. One night they made a "pie-bed" for their host, and favored me with a like attention. I recognized the joke the moment I got into bed, as I had had similar experiences before. Evidently Mr. Carnegie was unacquainted with this form of English humor; for the next day at lunch he yawned several times, and by way of apology said: "I did not sleep well last night. I could not get my feet down for some reason." The laughter evoked by this confession called for explanations: he had lain all night in the narrow sack which the girls had made by bringing up the lower half of the bottom sheet so that it looked like the top sheet. Despite his remembered discomfort, he heartily joined in the girls' laughter, and so gave the requisite *quid pro quo.*

He liked to see others laugh. When the side-splitting farce "The Private Secretary" was running at a New York theatre, he saw it half a dozen times, each time with a different companion, that he might enjoy her mirth. For it was usually a lady he took with him!

While coaching in England, the girls in the party

made a dummy of a bolster, and put it into his bed. He recognized it at once, and threw it into the bathroom. As he did so, he heard a giggle outside his door. Putting a table against the door and a chair upon that, he climbed up to the transom with a pitcher of water, and poured it—into his own boots which he had placed outside to be cleaned! His laughter at the joke on himself was the loudest.

In those early days he had a half-notion that he could speak in public, but he had never tried. An invitation came from a Mr. Walter Scott, a clergyman in Harlem, to address the children of his Sunday school. Carnegie accepted, to try out his suspected talent. With two ladies I accompanied him. (It may be mentioned in passing that he married one of them and I married the other.) He took as his text his trip around the world. Sitting with the ladies in the front row, I was directly under the speaker's nose. He was ill at ease and spoke with diffidence. "The climate of Egypt is so dry," he was saying, "that you can put a thing under the sand, and after two thousand years you can take it up and find it untarnished." "True," I commented in an undertone; "I have often done that!" The lecturer overheard me, and his ever-alert sense of the ridiculous was touched. He stopped to laugh, and all his self-consciousness left him. Thereafter he spoke easily and often to large gatherings.

These recollections are trivial, no doubt, but they serve to present the gladsome side of one who played a great part in the world, and by his own vigorous personality achieved heights reached by few among his fellows, however grave and serious their outlook on life or deportment in it. His amazing success as an indus-

49

trialist, his books, pregnant with wisdom, his unprecedented benefactions, are known to all. It is only to those who were privileged to be with him intimately that the joyous aspect of his many-sided character is known. He was a delightful playfellow, and as such he had the most winsome manner of anyone I ever knew.

In 1912 I was subpœnaed to give evidence before the Stanley Congressional Committee that was investigating the United States Steel Corporation. Mr. Carnegie testified after me, and denied the evidence I had given concerning a strike at the Edgar Thomson works, which, despite the documentary proof I had submitted, he said had never happened. The clever way in which he evaded the issue, and turned the discrepancy into a joke, excited the admiration of everybody present— except the democratic senators on the bench! And thereafter, for three days he kept this sombre body of investigators in a constant state of merriment. Homer Davenport, the cartoonist, was sent to Washington to cover the inquiry; and the *New York American* came out with a page-wide drawing of a dozen senators, on a bench, in all sorts of grotesque attitudes of mirth, while "Little Andy" sat in front of them with a mock expression of surprise that such dignitaries should be shouting with laughter. The cartoon was not an exaggeration: Carnegie *did* make the senators laugh—laugh uproariously, as he had made many a railroad president or purchasing agent laugh when soliciting a big order for rails.

But there was also a pathetic side to this happy personality. A number of children in New Jersey had been bitten by a rabid dog. The Pasteur treatment had demonstrated its value in Paris; but there was nowhere in the United States a means whereby the most awful menace of all deaths could be removed from these children. Dr. Dennis told Mr. Carnegie of the institute in Paris, where the children could receive the Pasteur treatment and perhaps be saved. "Send them there at once," said he; "spare no expense and charge it all to me." This was in 1885, the year the Carnegie Laboratory was opened as an annex to Bellevue Hospital Medical College; and Dr. Herman M. Biggs was in charge of it. At Dr. Dennis' suggestion Dr. Biggs went to Newark, got the children—there were about five of them—put them on the boat and rushed with them to Paris. There they received the innoculations of anti-rabitic serum from Pasteur himself, and were saved from the most horrible death known. None of the children developed hydrophobia, and one, now a middle-aged man, recently took part in a celebration, instituted by the Park Davis Company of Detroit, to mark the anniversary of this important event. Dr. Biggs brought from Paris a lot of cultures and serum which served to initiate the Pasteur treatment in America. Better still, he had learned from Pasteur himself the technique necessary to renew the cultures and establish their production here.

I recall the anxious interest with which Mr. Carnegie watched this historic enterprise. It was on a Sunday morning that Dr. Biggs, just returned from Paris, came to Windsor Hotel, followed by a colored porter from the Carnegie Laboratory with a large covered basket. On being opened, this was seen to be filled with bottles, test tubes and gelatine plates from Paris. They looked very pretty in their variegated tints and colors and we crowded round to see them. But when Dr. Biggs proceeded to describe them as the germs of a score of deadly diseases, and descant on anti-bodies, prophilaxis, pathogenic therapeutics and the like, those of us who were nearest the table drew back with astonishing unanimity. Like the geni in the flask, they were probably safe in the bottles; but suppose a bottle slipped out of Dr. Biggs's hands? And suppose the anti-bodies didn't anti, or the prophilactics failed to prophilact? There was little knowledge of bacteriology in those days, and we believed in the adage concerning the danger inherent in "little knowledge." So we were content to have Dr. Biggs's colored porter take the basket back to the Carnegie Laboratory, where it would be safer than on the table in the Blue Parlor of the Windsor Hotel.

This Carnegie Laboratory, by the way, was the first institution of its kind in America—or indeed in this hemisphere. It was built, financed and supported year by year by Andrew Carnegie alone. This was seventeen years before the Rockefeller Laboratory was established.

Dr. Fred S. Dennis, at whose instance Mr. Carnegie made this great investment, of which the dividends all accrued to humanity, had an amazing record. He worked in Professor Tyndall's laboratory in London. With Lord Lister, the father of antiseptic surgery and the savior of hundreds of thousands of lives, Dr. Dennis had the high privilege of studying the causes of infection in the Royal Infirmary in Edinburgh and learning the principles and operative technique of antisepsis from the master himself. Returning to America and specializing in the treatment of compound

DR. FRED S. DENNIS

fractures, he was able, by the knowledge thus acquired and his own remarkable surgical skill, to reduce the cases of septic sequelæ from 65 per cent to 1/7th of 1 per cent—practically eliminating a danger which during the civil war had always meant either amputation or death. These percentages were not based on a few isolated examples, but on a full thousand cases in four metropolitan hospitals devoted to the treatment of acute surgical cases. It is doubtful whether Lord Lister himself ever made such a record.

I have often made the rounds of the accident wards of the City with Dr. Dennis, and have seen how his cheerful presence brought comfort, relief and even laughter where, before his entrance, silent suffering and anxiety had filled the wards with gloom. He has just celebrated his eightieth birthday, and from every corner of the country and many places abroad have come congratulations and testimonials from former pupils who are continuing his great work.

Another phase of the Carnegie character may be adverted to, especially as it was the salient factor in his home life. This was his love of and unfailing devotion to his mother. He spoke of her as the Queen Dowager; and, in spite of his aggressive republicanism, he was here a loyal, lowly subject, happy in his subjection. The old lady came into the library at Cresson one day when we were both busy, and began asking trivial questions while she fumbled the papers on the table. Andrew was visibly disturbed, but he carefully concealed it from her. After a while the old lady started for the door, saying as she went: "Well, Andree, I'll go now. I only came in to bother ye." "But mother," he replied, "you didn't succeed;" and placing his arm about her poor old shoulders, he led her gently out of the room. It was a beautiful, almost a sacred, thing to witness. It was better than a sermon.

The Cresson household was extremely modest and simple. Besides the coachman and groom, who slept out, one maid and one cook were kept; though Mrs. Carnegie had an elderly Scotch spinster for maid and nurse. This nurse, Miss Wood, was returned to Scotland after Mrs. Carnegie's death, to spend the rest of her days in the comfort of a life pension. The servants were always treated as courteously as were the guests of the house. I never heard Mr. Carnegie address a cross word to any of them. He invariably thanked them when receiving anything from them, and naturally they responded with a dog-like devotion and service. "Our common humanity" again!

With his partners and managers he was a curious blend of the harsh and the considerate: harsh in urging them to greater effort and considerate in recognition of their successes. One of them—in fact it was his cousin George Lauder—had engaged in an outside speculation—flue-cinder or something of the sort, for which he had borrowed some fifty thousand dollars of Andrew, giving his note therefor. The speculation resulted in failure. When the note fell due Mr. Carnegie asked me to write a letter to his cousin, which he dictated. It was harsh to the point of rudeness.

"But Mr. Lauder will take it badly if it comes in my handwriting," I objected.

"That's the reason I want you to write it: he must be taught a lesson. He'd no right to speculate!"

And so the letter went, and touched a raw spot; for when I next saw Mr. Lauder he made me a labored explanation of his reasons for buying this flue-cinder: it had a large iron content and could be mixed with ore in the blast furnace. He did not mention the sulphur and phosphorus it contained in quantities sufficient to spoil the entire furnace charge. But he did say "Neeg," as he called him, had cancelled the debt. A characteristic touch!

Captain "Bill" Jones, who built and managed the Edgar Thomson Steel Works, occasionally came up to Cresson. He was another mixture of gentleness and harshness. He had the most lurid gift of invective of anybody I ever knew. On his office door was the sign: "Any oil-drummer found on these premises will be promptly bounced." I once witnessed the bouncing of an "oil-drummer." If it had been the oil itself it would have caught fire! A few minutes later when we reached his house—for I was staying with him in his Braddock cottage—he was the gentlest, kindliest man imaginable. His wife was a life-long invalid, and his was a life-long devotion to her. His voice was low and sweet, and full of loving inflections, so that one wondered at his rough exterior. He was honored by his compeers as no one in the steel business ever was—except perhaps dear John Fritz, who was very much like Jones; and he was loved by his men as no other manager was loved.

"You can't realize the abounding sense of freedom and relief I feel when I am sailing away past Sandy Hook," said Andrew Carnegie.

"Nor can you realize the abounding sense of freedom and relief we all feel when you are sailing away past Sandy Hook," echoed Bill Jones.

He died a horrible death through the explosion of one of his blast furnaces. His loss was well nigh irreparable. He did more than any other man to give to America its primacy in steel. Although forty years have lapsed, I still cherish a book that he gave me. It is by Miss Murfree "Charles Egbert Craddock."

There is nothing derogatory in the statement, often made, that Andrew Carnegie was a conceited man. He had ample cause for his vanity. Beginning his American life as a poor immigrant lad, he rose by his own efforts from a dollar and a quarter a week in a bobbin factory at the age of thirteen, to the control and chief ownership of the largest and most efficient steel organization in the world, and in his maturity sold it for close to five hundred million dollars. That alone was some record! Without schooling, he gave himself an education that put him at ease with the brightest intellects of his age. He wrote half a dozen books that would have given him distinction had he done nothing else. The last of these, his *Autobiography*, was described to me by the late Henry Holt—no mean judge—as the finest thing since Boswell. It ought to have sold for a dollar —or even fifty cents—instead of five dollars, so as to become the guide and incentive to millions of American and British boys.

I have just glanced through his contribution to *Liber Scriptorum*, the first book of the Authors Club. It is entitled "Genius Illustrated from Burns." Here are references to the philosopher's stone, to Parnassus, Milton, Shakespere (two), Goethe, President Arthur, Tennyson and to Walhalla. And there are quotations from Carlyle (two), Marcus Aurelius, St. Paul, Matthew Arnold (two), Shakespere and Thompson—a good and creditable array for one without schooling!

Here is something more to be conceited about—a list of his benefactions *during his life,* reaching the impressive total of more than three hundred and fifty million dollars:

Free Public Library buildings (2,811) $60,364,808.75

Colleges:

Library buildings	$4,065,699.27	
Other buildings	4,672,186.92	
Endowment	9,977,588.92	
Other purposes	1,547,535.00	
		20,363,010.11

Church organs (7,689)	6,248,309.00
Carnegie Corporation of New York	125,000,000.00
Carnegie Foundation for the Advancement of Teachers (including $1,000,000 to Teachers' Insurance and Annuity Association)	29,250,000.00
Carnegie Institute (including $13,531,433.67 to Carnegie Institute of Technology)	26,718,380.67
Carnegie Institution of Washington	22,300,000.00
Carnegie Hero Funds	10,540,000.00
Carnegie Endowment for International Peace..	10,000,000.00
Scottish Universities Trust	10,000,000.00
United Kingdom Trust	10,000,000.00
Steel workers' pensions	4,000,000.00
Dunfermiline Trust	3,750,000.00
Church Peace Union	2,025,000.00
Hague Peace Palace	1,500,000.00
Endowment for institutes at Braddock, Homestead, and Duquesne	1,000,000.00
International Bureau of American Republics (Pan American Building)	850,000.00
Engineers' Building	500,000.00
King Edward's Hospital Fund	500,000.00
Church Pension Fund	324,744.87
Simplified Spelling Boards	280,000.00
Central American Peace Palace (Court of Justice)	200,000.00
Study of methods of Americanization	190,000.00
Koch Institute, Berlin	120,000.00

Andrew Carnegie

New York Sociological Society	118,000.00
New York Association for the Blind	114,000.00
American Library Association	100,000.00
St. Andrew's Society	100,000.00
Iron and Steel Institute, London	89,000.00
Pittsburgh Kingsley House Association	79,000.00
Northampton (Mass.) Home Culture Club	77,000.00
Foreign Students' Friendly Relations Committee	70,000.00
Sorbonne (Madam Curie Fund)	50,000.00
Scots Charitable Society, Boston, Mass.	30,000.00

War Grants—

Red Cross	$1,500,000.00	
32 cantonment library buildings	320,000.00	
Knights of Columbus	250,000.00	
Young Men's Christian Assoc.	250,000.00	
National Research League	150,000.00	
National Security League	150,000.00	
Y. W. C. A.	100,000.00	
War Camp Community Recreation Service	50,000.00	
National Board of Medical Examiners	22,500.00	
		2,792,500.00
Miscellaneous		1,050,900.00
Total		$350,695,653.40

In 1904, at a complimentary dinner tendered me by the Boston Iron and Steel Institute, I said:

"The dynamics of self-esteem need an exponent wnen the personality of such a man as Andrew Carnegie is under consideration. For his personal vanity has been the most potent element in his phenomenal success. Honestly holding the belief in his own superiority, he always seized on leadership and kept it imperially to

59

the end. It is a common saying that a man who never makes mistakes never makes anything else. Andrew Carnegie made many; but he never made the mistake of admitting his mistakes. He was much more likely, before speaking of them at all, to convert them into victories. This is the dynamic force of conceit. It was conspicuous in another man of small physique—Napoleon. Indeed, there is a good deal in Carnegie's character as well as his career that reminds one, in a small way, of Napoleon. There is the same imperious demand for precedence, the same dislike of opposition, the same unfaltering faith in himself, the same paternal care for the active units of his army, the same thrusting to the rear of the sick and wounded, of those no longer fit for the first fighting line.* Even the same power to command sleep at any moment is his; and the parallel could be carried down the list of Napoleon's strong points until they trenched upon his weak ones. But no one who has studied the career of either would rank among these weak ones the vanity out of which grew such splendid exhibitions of self-reliance and individual forcefulness."

And speaking of the marvelous success of the Carnegie organization I said:

"Every industrial height reached gave a wider horizon to the young pioneers, of whom the elder of the Carnegie brothers had come to be recognized as leader. His was the speculative instinct, as well as most of the financial strength; but he was ably seconded by his brother and the other partners. As fast as profits were made they were invested in mines, coke-ovens and

* His generous pension arrangements took care of these.

plants for the utilization of products. In them all Andrew Carnegie made it a rule to own at least fifty-one per cent., and saw that the remaining forty-nine came only into the possession of the ablest practical associates. The majority interest represented headship, with its honors and prominence; the minority stood for the technical skill, the power to work, to achieve results, to convert crude stuff into steel ingots, rails, bridges, structural iron and armor plate, to organize and direct armies of laborers, to invent new processes, to devise new machines and cheaper methods. Relieved from the detail of management, the elder Carnegie could take a broad view of the industrial field, let his fertile imagination crystallize into far-reaching combinations for the economical assembling of raw material, the development of new markets for ever-increasing products, the negotiation of advantageous terms of co-operation with other manufacturers, or the devising of measures to defeat rivalry. Here is where his genius developed. Here was a field for the free play of forces that had long been maturing. The masterful spirit developed by uninterrupted success, the ingenuity fostered by early privations, the intimate knowledge of markets acquired on the railroad, the diplomatic training of the self-made man, all combined with the practical knowledge, organizing capacity and inventive genius of Carnegie's partners to build up a business machine so compact and efficient as to place it beyond the reach of competition.

"The greatest single contribution to the success of the giant organization which bears his name was Carnegie's genius for the selection of men, though in this he but equaled his brother, who died young. But his brother left to every man his own individuality. Andrew Carnegie assimilates the best of every one he touches. He absorbs other people as certain of the amebæ absorb each other—by contact; so that one never learns the true character of any man who is closely associated with Mr. Carnegie. If he is strong, his strength seems to become part of Carnegie. If he is weak—but there! Carnegie never has weak men about him. That is one cause of his success. He has jocularly written as his own epitaph: Here lies a man who could get cleverer men to work for him. He has grown great by this selective faculty, this instinct; and he never makes a mistake. Never? Yes, never, if we exclude a bogus lord; but that was not in the line of business.

"This explains why Andrew Carnegie, though head of a great and successful business, could yet know so little of the details of that business. In commercial circles it is considered axiomatic that to direct a huge manufacturing concern to prosperity a man must understand it in every part. Mr. Carnegie knows less about iron and steel than any junior chemist in his laboratory. He despises details, as fit only for the salaried specialist. An amusing instance of his ignorance of the mechanical properties of steel is often laughingly given by himself. The firm was engaged on a Government contract, and, as is usual in such cases, an army or navy officer was on duty at the mill to see that the work was turned out according to specification. One day, while walking in Pittsburgh with one of his partners, Mr. Carnegie was accosted by this officer. 'By the way, Mr. Carnegie,' said he, 'they tell me at the office that they cannot guarantee more than 20,000 modulus of elasticity in that material for the bridge. I must have at least 25,000.' 'That seems reasonable,' replied Mr.

Carnegie, gravely. 'We cannot possibly accept less,' said the officer, and he began to state his reasons technically. 'Yes, yes, I know,' interrupted Mr. Carnegie quickly. 'I'll see that you get the full 25,000. Good day!' As soon as they were out of earshot Mr. Carnegie turned to his companion and asked, 'What on earth is a modulus of elasticity?' The partner, learned in other things, confessed that he did not know. Presently they met Mr. Lauder. 'Dod,' said Mr. Carnegie to his cousin, 'for the love of heaven tell us what is a modulus of elasticity.' And then Mr. Carnegie learned for the first time how the tensile strength of steel is ascertained.

"But the modulus of human elasticity he knew by instinct. No one ever had to tell him how to ascertain the tensile strength of a man, the point to which he would stretch while preserving a uniform diameter. To Andrew Carnegie, the molecular construction of human character, its resistance to pressure and its final fracture point were known in the mysterious way in which fledglings find their nest. Behind the luck that gave him his first capital was an innate power to seize upon the weaknesses and utilize the strength of the men with whom he was thrown. The moral specific gravity of every man was known to him instinctively; and he built up a mighty organization with the human atoms his instinct selected. This is the secret of his success. This is what has made him rich, and he can no more teach the trick to the students he sometimes inundates with advice than these could acquire the homing instinct by eating pigeon-pie."

The simile of the pigeon-pie appealed to Mr. Carnegie, and he joyously quoted it in some article which he published; but he attributed it to "an American humorist," an unmerited compliment—unless it be that by my long and close association with him I had caught the humorous infection from himself!

During his mother's life he never married; but her death left a void in his life that only a woman as sympathetic and gentle as herself could fill. Some years before, he had introduced me to a young lady of such rare personal charm that I found myself drawn into her presence with almost weekly regularity, when, always chaperoned by her mother, she would play accompaniments to my songs and occasionally join me in a vocal duet. She loved music, and we attended many concerts together, especially those of the Oratorio Society, of which Mr. Carnegie had made us both life members. It was a joy, though no surprise, to all his friends when he announced his engagement to this young lady, Miss Louise Whitfield. The marriage took place the next year [1887] at the bride's home in West 47th Street in presence of a few old friends.

Soon thereafter, I moved to California, and there I received a letter from Mr. Carnegie that showed that the delightful simple circle of Cresson days had been transferred to Cluny Castle in Scotland.

Splendid castle here, he writes. Mountain, loch and moors. Just arrived, Saturday eve. Coached from London. All well. Dr. and Mrs. Dennis come to-morrow. I failed to find Mr. (Herbert) Spencer as we passed through London but I heard he was better. I have had too much business to do much literary work, but I expect to begin here soon and work on rainy days: too much fun for bright hours. [How characteristic!] Write me now and then, especially to tell me of your good fortune, for I find that interests and pleases me greatly. Always sincerely yours, ANDREW CARNEGIE.

ANDREW CARNEGIE

And then comes a P. S.

Lou [Mrs. Carnegie] has read your letter and says "Oh, he's going to be married." But that's a woman.

A hit—a palpable hit!

His domestic life was ideal. Mrs. Carnegie, as was to be expected by all who knew her, proved a perfect and sympathetic complement to her many-sided husband, gracefully and tactfully subordinating every ambition of her own to his.* The devotion which beautified his long life with his mother passed over to his wife and daughter. He once wrote a motto for the great fireplace in his brother's home in Florida. It suggests the sanctity of his own home: THE HEARTH OUR ALTAR: ITS FLAME OUR SACRED FIRE.

* Some wives, who put themselves before their husband, have the quality of a decimal point, reducing his value by ten. Others are like a cipher, and coming after, add to his importance as well as his happiness. Thus 1 plus 0 equals 10!

65

Henry Clay Frick

Dec 21st 1917

HENRY CLAY FRICK

A Record of Achievement

To speak of Frick is to bring to mind Carnegie, his antithesis. Col. George Harvey, in 1928, wrote a book, *Henry Clay Frick, The Man*. In it he tells of the first meeting, in 1881, of Carnegie and his mother with Frick and his bride. It was at the Windsor Hotel in New York, the occasion being a mid-day dinner. "It was a noteworthy occasion," writes Col. Harvey. "The two gentlemen, one voluble and hilarious, the other reticent and courteous, eyed each other thoughtfully during the repast," as they were destined thereafter to do for many years to come! The Harvey characterization of the two men, though drawn from imagination, was eminently just and accurate.

My own first meeting with Henry Clay Frick was also in the rooms of Andrew Carnegie at the Windsor Hotel. It was in the early months of the year 1885. Frick, shortly before this, had sold an interest in his coke works to the Carnegies, but had not yet been admitted into the steel business. He was a well-groomed man, not noticably taller than Carnegie, who was pony-built. He wore a full brown beard, which whitened after the Homestead tragedy. His friendly smile was the most noticeable thing about him—that and his extremely courteous, almost deferential manner. One wonders if he had acquired these in his uncle's country-store

67

at Broad Ford, where he had served an apprenticeship behind the counter, or whether they were a "throwback" to his gentle Mennonite ancestry; they could hardly have been acquired in the Connelsville coal fields. He seemed more polished, more refined than the Carnegie partners, who often came to the Windsor to dinner, and had the rough friendliness of western men who do big things. He spoke little, his smile serving as an answer to, or acknowledgment of, Carnegie's jests and habitual enthusiasms.

My last meeting with him was thirty-five years later —just eighteen hours before his death on December 2nd, 1919. He was sitting up in bed, with half a dozen newspapers spread around him.

"Pull up a chair," he said. "Who will be the next President?"

"Nay," I replied, "you are the one to answer that." A week or two before, there had been a great lunch party in the dining room downstairs, at which Leonard Wood had been the guest of honor.

"Perhaps General Wood," I ventured with an inquiring look.

The exact words of his reply I do not recall; but he indicated with emphasis his preference for General Wood, and his belief that he would receive the Republican nomination. Had Frick lived, General Wood would probably have been the Republican nominee in the presidential election of 1920. Boise Penrose, whom I met at the Frick house at this time, controlled the Pennsylvania Republican Machine, but was himself controlled by Henry Clay Frick; and when the hidden force of the latter was no longer pressing the Pennsylvania senator along a reluctant road, he quickly turned out of it. The world knows, and, in the main, has reason to regret the result.

That was an unlucky lunch for everybody, but especially so for General Wood and Mr. Frick; because it was due to the latter's indiscretion at table that his last sickness began. He told me so himself. He knew a great deal about some machines, but very little about the most important machine of all—his own body.

Had he a premonition of a tragic outcome of his indisposition? It seemed so; for he expressed great anxiety that certain works of art, sent on approval and priced at more than a million and a half, should be returned to their owner. As curator of the Collection I was able to assure him that this had already been done, and that his very competent secretary, Naughton, had stood at the door and checked them off as they were taken out of the house. He was relieved.

Eighteen hours later he asked the nurse for a drink of water. Then turning over he said: "I think I can sleep now." Those were his last words—a tired man's epitaph!

He was only sixty-nine, and his mind was functioning as well as it had done years before, when he astonished the industrial world by his spectacular capture of the great steel works at Duquesne without the outlay of a dollar, as described in the *History of the Carnegie Steel Co.* Physically, he thought he was as strong as ever, and, in answer to my inquiry less than two years before, he said he could put up as vigorous a struggle with the assassin Berkman as he had done in 1892. "I expect to live another ten years" he said, "and to spend a million dollars a year on additions to my gallery of paintings." A pathetic crumbling of a noble ambition!

During these thirty-five years, since our first meeting, there were long periods when I saw him almost daily. I often breakfasted with him at Sherry's, Fifth Avenue and 44th Street, where he lived *en garçon* before he rented the Vanderbilt mansion on Fifth Avenue. Yet I never got as close to him as I did to Andrew Carnegie. The characters of the two men were as opposite as the poles, and—although each man tried to conceal the fact from the other—as unsympathetic as oil and water. Carnegie was a "star-spangled Scotchman," with none of the dour attributes of his race: a blithe urchin who never grew up, and ever rejoiced in verbal quips and thrusts that tickled himself as much as they did a responsive recipient. Waving the flag in the sunlight and taking its glitter for his own, he always headed the procession, and did it with joy. Frick was the conscientious toiler, that never gave himself a holiday in half a dozen years and mentioned the fact with pride. If the *joie de vivre* that marked every moment of Carnegie's life formed any part of the Frick philosophy, it was hidden under a constitutional reticence that marked him among his associates as "the silent Frick." He rarely laughed outright, though he smiled easily; and his smile invested his handsome features with a charm that invited the confidences he was so reluctant to return. He scarcely ever volunteered a statement or made a remark that was not evoked by something he had just heard. Questions he asked—even sought opinions, but rarely gave his own. "Shall I wear my heart upon my sleeve for daws to peck at?" He did not say this, but his habitual taciturnity made one think he meant it. I recall two examples of this taciturnity, one serious and one amusing, that illustrate the difficulty of getting at his inner thought.

Returning together on the train from a visit to his summer home at Prides Crossing in 1912, he told me of his plans for the museum he was about to build on the site of the Lennox Library on Fifth Avenue between 70th and 71st streets; and he asked me to call at the office of the architect and report to him my opinion of the drawings that had been prepared for it. The late Thomas Hastings had had made a beautiful plaster model of the house. This he showed me together with a lot of blue prints and the like.

"But Mr. Hastings, this house will not do," I exclaimed as I examined them. "It can never be made into a museum!"

"A museum!" he gasped in astonishment. "That's the first I've heard of a museum!"

"Is it possible you don't know that that is Mr. Frick's intention—his chief thought in erecting this building? Did he not tell you?"

"He certainly did not! He tells me nothing. I go to see him and talk until I am nervous. When I stop talking he gazes at me in silence in the most disconcerting way. Then I make a few more remarks, which are also received in silence; and when I come away I am exhausted of all nervous energy."

Then I told Mr. Hastings what had been confided to me on the train—as though it were a great secret, as perhaps it was; but it was one that ought to have been shared by the architect. The plans were accordingly changed, and the mansion was built to conform to the requirements of a public museum. How perfectly these were met was evidenced many times during the remaining years of Mr. Frick's life, when he allowed, and enjoyed, the presence of two hundred and more visitors at one time, distributed throughout the lower floors of the house, while Mr. Archer Gibson's superb playing of the great organ served to emphasize the owner's happiness in his own hospitality.

It may not be amiss to mention that the beautiful Lennox Library, the masterpiece of Richard Morris Hunt that was demolished to make way for the Frick mansion at Fifth Avenue and 70th Street, was offered by Mr. Frick to the city, to be rebuilt at his cost in any location the authorities might select. They not unnaturally decided in favor of the site of the ugly old arsenal at 63rd Street and Fifth Avenue. Whereupon certain editors set up a clamor against "invading the park," and in the general condemnation of the city officials for this alleged vandalism, Mr. Frick was included. In disgust, he withdrew his offer, and the beautiful Lennox Library was destroyed. It cost $16,000 to demolish the building. It would have cost $200,000 to remove it stone by stone, and re-erect it on another site. The arsenal that it might have replaced, with added beauty to the park and without encroachment on it, was in such disrepair, that some thousands were spent on it soon after Mr. Frick's generous offer had been withdrawn. It was altogether a silly proceeding —on the part of the city government for not ignoring the journalistic diatribes, on the part of the newspapers for indulging in them, and in Mr. Frick for his sensitiveness. Meanwhile, the monument to Richard Morris Hunt, his portrait in bronze, erected by the art societies of the city, looks forlornly across the avenue at the spot where his masterpiece formerly stood!

HENRY CLAY FRICK

The amusing episode I have in mind grew out of an effort on the part of a dealer to sell Mr. Frick a bronze incense-burner, attributed to Riccio. The price was two hundred thousand dollars. I took Mr. Ernest Govett, the well-known expert on medieval bronzes, to see it. It was a very beautiful thing, but not by Riccio or by anyone known outside of Venice. Mr. Govett said it was worth twenty-five thousand dollars and no more. So, of course, it was not bought. Soon afterwards another dealer called me on the phone at my home, and offered me a commission of ten thousand dollars if I could persuade Mr. Frick to buy the bronze for half the price first asked. I called up Mr. Frick and asked him to stay in as I had something of interest to tell him. He waited for me.

"You can have that two hundred thousand dollar bronze for ninety thousand," I reported. "The commission offered me, of course, will come off the price."

At times Mr. Frick's manner was what might be called explosive. This was one of the times. His anger was justified; for the first offer had reached him through a friend. The bronze was subsequently sold at auction for considerably less than ninety thousand dollars.

Soon after this incident I saw a similar incense-burner in Seligmann's store in East 51st Street. I had dropped in casually, and the salesman in charge did not recognize me. When I mentioned this bronze to Mr. Frick he said:

"Jacques Seligmann is coming here this morning. I will see him in the living-hall, and I want you to sit in the library near enough to the door to hear what he says. Don't let him see you."

The comedy soon began. Mr. Seligmann, a charm-

73

ing Frenchman with all the polish and formal polite-
ness of his nation, greeted Mr. Frick with a voluble
suavity that was received with disconcerting curtness.
Then followed a silence, presently broken by a comment on the weather. Another silence. And so on for
several minutes—a casual remark from the Frenchman
and a silent puff from the Frick cigar. Finally Mr.
Seligmann nervously stated the object of his call: he
wanted to serve as the Frick adviser in art! The story
was a long one, told spasmodically, with many spells
of silence. Then suddenly, and with complete irrelevance, Mr. Frick said:

"You have a bronze incense-burner."

"How did you know that?"

"I have means of getting information. I want to
see it."

"Certainly. I'll go and have it sent."

And so the interview ended, no word having been
said by Mr. Frick concerning the real reason of the
Seligmann call. The incense-burner came, was inspected
and compared with its replica—as our memories recalled it—and then returned. The price was about twenty-five thousand dollars.

Incidents like the foregoing seemed to afford Mr.
Frick a sort of tepid amusement. His sense of humor
was latent rather than absent. Quoting William
George Jordan, whose books he admired, I once said
of a conceited person known to us both: "There's only
a limited amount of knowledge in the world, and if
one man has more than his share someone else has to
go short!" At first he looked puzzled; then he said:
"But that's absurd! How can one man have more than

his share?" The whimsy had gone clean over his head
—as did another whimsy, also originating with Jordan.
It was a book about an entirely imaginary personage
—a supposed Russian writer—the "Father of Russian
literature," as we fondly called him. It was the now
famous hoax of the Authors Club—*Feodor Vladimir
Larrovitch: An Appreciation of His Life and Works.*
It contained an exquisite poem by Clinton Scollard, "A
prologomenon" by Prof. Franklin H. Giddings, "Larrovitch's Place in Literature" by M'Cready Sykes,
"Some Translations from Larrovitch" by Richardson
Wright, incidental poems, letters, talks by George S.
Hellman, the late Thomas Walsh, Dr. Titus Munson
Coan, and other well-known writers, together with a
perfectly convincing bibliography by Arthur Colton.
The whole thing was so deliciously done and was such
a complete record of the sayings, doings and writings
of this fabulous personage that even the critics of staid
old Boston were tempted to review it seriously. I
offered one of these books to Frick. "But it's absurd!"
was his querilous comment. "The man never existed!"
And he threw the book back to me! His own imagination expressed itself in industrial and financial consolidations. Here he was a past master, as the world had
occasion to know.

That's how he became so rich, though the element of
luck had its place in his career: he lived with his
grandfather Overholt, in the midst of the Connelsville
coal fields at the time that coke was becoming indis-
pensible in the art of smelting. He was almost the first
in the field, and he grew in importance as the business
grew. And when Andrew Carnegie, with his Midas
touch, took him into partnership, the golden halo,

75

which enveloped the little Scotchman and all about him, also wrapped Frick in aureate beauty and multiplied his wealth many times.

When, in the Fall of 1892, I called on Frick in his Pittsburgh office to get such data as he might be willing to furnish to help me in writing the *History of the Carnegie Steel Company,* he told me he was leaving that afternoon for California, but that he would let me copy a couple of letters from Schwab which might prove of interest; and together we went downstairs to his safety-deposit box. I at once saw that the letters were as explosive as dynamite, and said so. He smiled his quick smile, and waited with me in a cubby-hole while I joyously copied them. He then put them safely back under lock and key. I felt like a journalist who has just achieved a "scoop." Together we then went to see Francis Lovejoy, who had offices in the building on the same floor as Frick himself. Lovejoy I had known years before, when he was assistant to Moore, the Carnegie Steel Company's auditor. Telling Lovejoy to give me all the assistance he could, and let me have the use of any documents he might have retained from his office as secretary of the old Carnegie companies, Mr. Frick shook hands with us, wished me luck, and went to California. When I got to my rooms that evening I found that he had sent me half a dozen fat volumes of newspaper clippings covering the entire period of his connection with the Carnegie interests, including those describing the Homestead strike and his own narrow escape from assassination at the hands of an anarchist. Without these volumes it would have been impossible for anyone to have written an accurate account

76

The deplorable behaviour of Wall-street has sadly ruffled the gaieties of Newport. Indignant wives in that inspiring haunt, where, as M. Paul Bourget tells us, the ladies wear their diamonds at breakfast, have vigorously protested against the heartlessness of the telegrams from New York, warning them to "curtail expenses." Pleasant for a woman who is about to dispense hospitality to learn from a distracted husband that "the bottom has fallen out of Wall-street"! The Newport season was about to close in tears and lamentations when a popular hostess had a brilliant idea. Why not, give a subscription ball? An allotment of five tickets apiece to fifty subscribers at £20 produced a brilliant gathering and a most successful entertainment for the trivial outlay of £1,000. Subscription dinners have been organised on the same plan. Wall-street is much comforted by the Newport finance, and there is talk of a subscription statue of the lady who invented it. Mr. James Howard Bridge, whose "History of the Carnegie Steel Company" has made so great a stir in New York, has no passionate admirer of Dunfermline

London, E.C.

greatest business founded it, in its first issue Mr. Car-

CARNEGIE STEEL COMPANY REVELATIONS.

The Central News New York correspondent says:—Under the caption, "Carnegie Secretly Forges a Weapon against Trusts," the "Herald" on Saturday devoted nearly a page of its issue to the history of the Carnegie Steel Company written by Mr. James Howard Bridge, at one time private secretary to Mr. Carnegie. The writer declares that tariff protection was the lever which forced into existence the business which yielded eighty-eight per cent. of the net profit of the Steel Company.

American & col W Kly

12 · 8 · 03

London

"CARNEGIE SECRETLY FORGES A WEAPON AGAINST TRUSTS."

INTERESTING REVELATIONS.

New York, Saturday.

Under the caption "Carnegie Secretly Forges a Weapon against Trusts," the "Herald" to-day devotes nearly a page of its issue to the history of the Carnegie Steel Company, written by Mr. James Howard Bridge, at one time private secretary to Mr Carnegie. Speaking of his search for material for the history, Mr. Bridge says he found Mr. Carnegie's narrative the least trustworthy. The writer declares that tariff protection was the lever which forced into existence the business which yielded 88 per cent. of the net profit of the Steel Company. He gives in detail the story of Mr. Ca

---

THE AMERICAN MARKETS.

(FROM OUR CORRESPONDENT)

NEW YORK, SUNDAY NIGHT.

To-morrow—Monday—promises to be as critical a day upon the Stock Exchange as any in the recent trying period. This is the moment chosen for the publication of James Howard Bridge's "History of the Carnegie Steel Company." The author is an Englishman, and was formerly secretary successively to Mr Herbert Spencer and Mr. Carnegie. The importance of the book lies not in its revelations of the seamy methods of accumulating wealth and organising a Trust, but in the disclosure of trade calculated to have powerful economic

---

FOURTH EDITION, SIXTEENTH THOUSAND

THE INSIDE HISTORY OF THE CARNEGIE STEEL COMPANY

By JAMES HOWARD BRIDGE

A frank narrative of the growth of a mammoth industry, from its earliest, humble beginning, with a capital of $4 until its sale for nearly five hundred millions ($500,000,000) to the Steel Trust.

"The sensation of the day."—*New York Herald.*

"Essential to an intelligent understanding of the investment value of the steel corporation shares."—*Financial Times.*

"Surprise has given way to amusement as in turning its pages the readers have found all sorts of sensations staring them in the face. The innermost secrets of the Carnegie Steel Co. stand revealed in the light of day."—*Chicago Post.*

"In his 'History of the Carnegie Steel Company,' Mr Bridge has, unconsciously perhaps, given to the world a great epic story. The simple narration of the facts revealed by his patient delving into hidden places makes a story so vile which the wildest flights of romance seem tame and prosaic."—*Pittsburg Gazette.*

"It all reads like a stupendous fairy tale,"—*From the Pittsburg Leader.*

"The author has exploded a bomb in financial and industrial circles with his book, 'History of the Carnegie Steel Co.'"—*St. Louis Ho*

"Mr. Bridge's book is one of immense value to all people engaged in affairs. It is doubtful if any man of large business can afford to get without reading it. To those just entering upon affairs, an important lesson is given in this story."—*John Braham Walker.*

"The Inside History of the Carnegie Steel Company, by James Howard Bridge. This book is founded entirely upon facts and justifies the closest attention of its readers. To understand the situation thoroughly one must read the book which is interesting from beginning to end. The third edition has just been published."—*From the Pittsburg Book Lover Press. New York.*

The Book-Lover Press has secured this great work, and presents a handsomely illustrated edition volume at **$2.00 net.** See the remarkable review of this remarkable book by the editor of the in the October and November numbers of that publication Four hundred and fifty copies of "The Carnegie Steel Company" were sold at $100 each. The $2.00 edition is identical with that

═══ AT ALL BOOKSELLERS, OR ═══

THE BOOK-LOVER PRESS, 30-32 East 21st Street, N

of the important and often tragic happenings of those days.

The Schwab letters, showing that steel rails, selling for $28 a ton, could be made for $12 while the "protective" duty on foreign rails was $4 a ton, attracted universal notice when they were published, and proved quite as explosive as I had expected. They formed the basis of heated discussions in Congress, were read aloud in the British House of Lords, were widely discussed editorially, and translations appeared in foreign journals. Joined to a curious mistake of a writer on the *New York Herald,* to be described, they produced a semi-panic among the stockholders of the U. S. Steel Corporation, who threw their shares on to the market in wild abandon, so that the price of the preferred dropped from $90 to $50 and the common from $45 to $9. This, however, is advancing the story.

Before the publication of my book, Mr. Frick returned from California, and I met him by chance while calling on Mr. Henry W. Oliver at the Waldorf Hotel in New York. It was early in May, 1903. Mr. Oliver was always afraid of fire in a hotel, and his rooms were on the first floor overlooking the sidewalks of Fifth Avenue. There the three of us sat, watching the passing crowds; and I recall that Oliver and Frick "matched pennies" for the twenty-dollar gold pieces each had that day received for attending directors' meetings.

When I got up to leave Mr. Oliver's rooms, Mr. Frick also rose, saying he would walk up the avenue with me. At the Union League Club we stopped and went in. Mr. Frick called for drinks of some sort, and while we sat sipping them he asked me if I really in-

78

tended to publish the Schwab letters. I told him they were already in type, as was most of the book; that my call on Mr. Oliver had been merely to get his consent to the publication of a cablegram from Andrew Carnegie concerning the Mesaba ores, in which there was a slighting reference to himself.

"And what did Oliver say?" asked Frick.

"Print it, damn him!"

Mr. Frick smiled; but after a moment he looked grave and said:

"You ought to have a good lawyer go over your book before it is published. You may get into trouble printing so many confidential documents. If you like I'll send a set of proofs to Mr. Knox (the Hon. Philander C. Knox,) and have him pass upon them."

The compliment implied by this offer, to have the Attorney-General of the United States pass on the legality of my book, was too great to be refused, and a couple of weeks later I sent a complete set of page-proofs to Mr. Frick in Pittsburgh for transmission to Mr. Knox. These came back in due course, with a complimentary letter from Mr. Knox, saying he had read the work "with fascinated interest" and that it would be a distinct loss to the industrial history of Pittsburgh if it were changed in any particular. When Mr. Frick showed me this letter, he asked to be allowed to keep the proofs so that he might read them at leisure. I naturally consented, and he returned them with a compliment that was doubly gracious from one of his habitual reticence.

When the first edition of the *History of the Carnegie Steel Company* was published in July, 1903, Steel

Common was $44 a share and the Preferred $79 a share. Three months later the common was $10 and the preferred around $50. During these months, while I was in Europe, several large editions of the book had been called for—16,000 in one printing—and it was appearing serially in the Sunday supplements of the *Pittsburgh Gazette*. So great was the demand for these supplements that they were repeatedly re-printed.

One of Mr. Frick's financial associates said to me on my return: "Bridge, if you had let *me* see your book ten days before you published it I could have afforded to pay you one million dollars!"

Less astute than this gentleman, whose success in Wall Street justified Mr. Frick in joining his name to the list of financial giants named as trustees under his will, I bought Steel Preferred at $79. After it had dropped to $50 I mentioned my purchase to Mr. Frick. He looked at me curiously, as at a phenomenon.

"Why didn't you speak to me first?" he asked.

"I didn't want to bother you about such a small transaction."

As many will remember, the shares of the Steel Corporation moved rapidly upward in 1904, and, at the instance of Mr. Frick, I had a small part in the movement.

I returned from Europe in November, 1903, landing in Boston; and that morning I read an editorial in the *Boston Herald*, prophesying that Andrew Carnegie would eventually capture the entire possessions of the Steel Corporation by foreclosing the first mortgage which he held on them; and I was quoted as authority for the prophecy. It was one of a series of editorials on the subject. The same day I called on Mr. Holmes, editor of the *Herald,* with a hastily written article, vigorously opposing his dire prediction. This was published next morning in Boston and in New York—in the *Herald,* to which, at my request, Mr. Holmes had telegraphed it. Carbon copies of it were distributed in Wall Street by a news agency, and it was republished in Pittsburgh and several other cities. For the thought of Andrew Carnegie's capture and assimilation of the entire steel industry of the United States had by this time become a national terror. To-day we can smile at the idea; but in those days it seemed not only possible, but highly probable. Mr. Frick read my article, and telegraphed me to come to New York. He was living at Sherry's; and over the breakfast table we mapped out a newspaper campaign to offset a disastrous error into which a writer on the *New York Herald* had fallen in reviewing my book. Learning of my previous literary connection with Andrew Carnegie, this writer had jumped to the conclusion that Mr. Carnegie had inspired my book. His review, largely made up of extracts, covered a page of the *Herald,* and it carried a scare-head in bold-faced type:

CARNEGIE SECRETLY FORGES A WEAPON AGAINST TRUSTS

This was followed by sub-headings equally alarming— one running across the page—and the article indicated that it was Carnegie's plan to capture all the properties of the Steel Corporation by foreclosing his mortgage. As the *Herald* writer had syndicated this startling statement, the scare had become operative in every large city in the country; and this joined to the Schwab

Joseph's Financial News Bureau

TELEPHONE "2201 BROAD"
CABLE ADDRESS DENDALESS, N. Y. Edison Building.
42 AND 44 BROAD STREET, N. Y.

November 17, 1903.

9.30 A. M.

Mr. James Howard Bridge, author of the history of the Carnegie Steel Company, which recently attracted so much attention, has
written the following letter to the editor of the Boston Herald, which
is worthy of repet

From _____ NEW YORK HERAL WALL STR. SUMMARY.

HERALD
Boston, Mass.

dress _____ New York City

ate _____ NOV 16 1903

VAST REVENUES OF THE STEEL TRUST

STEEL TRUST'S VAST REVENUES

James Howard Bridge
Points Out Unlikelihood of Mr. Carnegie Securing the Property by Foreclosure.

Though Net Earnings Were Greatly Cut Investors Could Get Ten Per Cent.

JAMES H. BRIDGE'S VIEW

He Declares It Is Very Unlikely That Mr. Carnegie Can Secure the Property by Foreclosure

U. S. STEEL SECURITIES AND PROPERTIES.

Interesting Deductions Drawn by One Who Has Had Every Opportunity of Knowing the Inside Facts.

In reply to a recent article in the Boston "Herald" on the U. S. Steel Corporation, James Howard Bridge, formerly private secretary to Andrew Carnegie and who some months ago published a history of the Carnegie Steel Co., has written a letter to the editor of the "Herald" in which he gives some interesting statistics bearing upon the intrinsic value of U. S. Steel securities and the value of the properties of subsidiary companies and their earning power.

With respect to the intimation that the earnings of the U. S. Steel Corporation may drop to those of the Carnegie Steel Co. five or six years ago, Mr. Bridge calls attention to the fact that in 1896 the product of the Carnegie Co. was 1,375,249 gross tons of steel. Four years later he...

Gazette

PITTSBURG, PA

Ridiculous Pessimism.

Yesterday The Gazette reprinted a letter to the editor of the Boston Herald from James Howard Bridge, author of the "History of the Carnegie Steel Company," now running in The Sunday Gazette. The letter was in reply to a suggestion by the Herald that Andrew Carnegie, as the holder of first mortgage bonds, might come into possession of the United States Steel Corporation through foreclosure proceedings. Mr. Bridge set forth facts that show the utter improbability of the Herald suggestion.

DUTIES FOR EXTORTION ONLY.

In the "History of the Carnegie Steel Company," by Mr. Bridge, formerly secretary to Mr. Carnegie, just published a letter written by Mr. Schwab, president of the Steel Trust, to Mr. H. C. Frick, dated May 15, 1899, is printed. Mr. Frick was at the time trying

GLOBE
Boston, Mass.

NOV 25 1903

STEEL'S EARNINGS.

They Can be Cut Before Preferred Dividends Are Endangered.

James Howard Bridge, who may be regarded as an authority on the U. S. Steel corporation, in a communication to the Boston Herald commenting on a recent editorial in that paper says: "To suppose that 'the earnings of the present company'—i. e., the United States Steel corporation—could possibly drop 'to those of the Carnegie Steel Company of five or six years ago' is manifestly absurd when it is recalled

THE COSMOPOLITAN

The History of The Carnegie Steel Company, probably ... of a great corporation ever written, is reviewed in the October Cosmopolitan. The book itself has sold — the entire edition — for $100.00 per copy.

On all news-stands, 10 cents

letters, had sent the steel stocks hurtling down on the exchange.

Mr. Frick now wanted this false impression removed; and he represented to me that I was the one to do it. So I wrote a series of articles in defense of the Steel Corporation, and Mr. Frick had them broadcast throughout the country. By the following summer (1904) steel shares had recovered nearly all of their loss; and unfortunately, I promptly sold my stock. Frank Munsey held his, and he made a profit of millions, as did other far-sighted investors.

Eight years later, in 1911, the Steel Corporation was again in a bad way—in conformity with Andrew Carnegie's dictum that "steel was always either a prince or a pauper." Now it was a pauper. Dividends had stopped on the common shares and those of the preferred were in danger. Mr. Frick sent me a message, asking me to meet him in his New York office, this time in the Bankers Trust Building. After a little talk he took up the phone and called up Mr. James A. Farrell, president of the Steel Corporation. To my surprise he said: "Won't you come over to my office to meet Mr. Bridge?" A few minutes later Mr. Farrell came. I was introduced with a statement from Mr. Frick that I was to be "primed" for an article in support of the Steel Corporation, and Mr. Farrell was to do the "priming," that is provide me with the necessary facts. Mr. Farrell took me to his office in the Empire Building, and I spent an agreeable afternoon with this brilliant organizer, who, as courteous as he is capable, has continued the Gary policies of fair dealing and honest publicity. My article was written, and Mr. Frick was so pleased with it that he read it to the Finance Committee of the Steel Corporation. It was duly published, and, doubtless, had a good effect. Among the papers which printed it was the *New York Sun*.

A little later Mr. Frick asked me to write another article in protest against the suit which the Government had brought against the Steel Corporation, concerning which he displayed great indignation, as did many others who ranked the country's welfare as higher than a politician's advantage.

Until the publication of Col. Harvey's book, the old quarrel between Carnegie and Frick had been almost forgotten. But I remembered it. So did both of the interested parties.

After our dispute before the Stanley Committee in Washington, elsewhere described, and before leaving the room of the Congressional Committee, Mr. Carnegie came over to me and, with unexpected cordiality, asked me to call and see him in New York. I did so many times, and we had many pleasant chats about the old days. Of course we talked about Frick, and he seemed to regret the estrangement. It had lasted for more than a dozen years—altogether too long; and I was bold enough to try to bring about a reconciliation. Frick was then in Egypt with J. Horace Harding. On February 3d, 1912, I sent a letter to the latter, telling of my experience in Washington and of my talks with Mr. Carnegie.

"He has told me," I wrote, "that he does not bear a grudge against a soul, and his desire to die at peace with all his old associates is a very natural and pathetic one. Will you pass this information on to our mutual friend (Mr. Frick). If I could be the means of bringing to a reconcilation the two men whose names are now linked only in antagonistic memory, but who are the most prominent in American industry, I should be proud and happy; and I am sure you would be glad to cooperate with me in such a good work. Of course Mr. Carnegie has no suspicion of what is in my mind, and he would probably think me the last person in the world to attempt anything so ambitious. Our friend will recall that this is in line with what Dr. Andrew D. White wrote him eight years ago." *

On his return, Mr. Harding wrote asking me to meet him and Mr. Frick in the latter's office. There I repeated my story, and again urged that a reconciliation was certainly due after the lapse of more than a dozen years. Harding understood the Frick character better than I did, and remained silent. He knew that my efforts were vain; but even he must have been surprised at Frick's outburst of angry denunciation of the man with whom he shared so much of success and fortune. I had never suspected such indignation in this usually quiet and undemonstrative man; nor did I expect such a burst of eloquence from the "Silent Frick." Thereafter he never referred to his quondom partner

---

* Writing from Cornell University, Ithica, N. Y., on October 30, 1903, Dr. Andrew D. White, in a letter referring to my book, and sent me by Mr. Frick, says:—

"It is an amazing revelation of a great creation in the industrial world, one which almost overwhelms me by its magnitude. Of course, the revelations of personal history in it also deeply interest me, but my sincere hope is that by and by as the difficulties are thought over on both sides, they will be minimized and good old kindly and friendly relations be resumed. As I grow older, I feel that, among all the things of this world, old friendships are about the most precious, and that it is worth while to sacrifice something in order to maintain, or if necessary, to restore them."

except as "your friend Carnegie," which only amused me!

Up to this time I had been a literary free lance, writing for magazines when I felt like it, and working on an invention I had made for the purification of municipal water supplies by electricity. Occasionally, when he had an important letter to write, Mr. Frick would send me a draft of it and ask me to put it into shape. Finally he asked me to make a catalogue of his paintings. This was so foreign to anything I had done before that I hesitated over it; but with the understanding that I should not be expected to pose as an art expert, I undertook the work, for which for the first time I was to be regularly paid. My experience with Herbert Spencer had taught me how to use a library; and now, in the Metropolitan Museum reading room I discovered that the portraits in the Frick Collection represented real people who had lived interesting lives, often full of romance. Concentrating my attention on this vital aspect of the paintings, I was soon able to send to Mr. Frick at Prides Crossing a series of biographies of a kind never before made about a collection of portraits by the old masters. The novelty appealed to him, and on his return to New York he proposed that I should always be present when he threw open the galleries to the public, that I might add to the interest of visitors by telling the life-stories of the personages represented on the walls. So in 1914 I became Curator of the Frick Collection, and kept the position until December, 1928.

Sir Joseph Duveen and Sir Charles Allom had invented a remarkable system of illuminating these paintings. Each one had its own spot-light concealed in the glass ceiling, so directed that the light fell only on the canvas, while the frame and surrounding wall were lost in shadow. This gave to the portraits a weird semblance of life; and, sitting alone in their midst, it was easy for me to imagine them as stepping out of the frames and joining each other in friendly talk. The idea pleased me, and I amused myself in jotting down their conversations. In this way came to be written the book *Portraits and Personalities: Imaginary Conversations in the Frick Galleries.* Knowing Mr. Frick as I did, and his great interest in the lives of the painted men and women he had surrounded himself by, I can conceive his pleasure had he been here to see how they had come to life again in this book.

Among the letters I wrote for Mr. Frick I recall one with some pride, because it may survive as long as the Steel Corporation lasts. It accompanied Frick's gift of Massey Rhind's bust of the creator of the corporation, the late J. Pierpont Morgan. Recalling the famous epitaph on the tomb of Sir Christopher Wren in the cript of St. Paul's Cathedral in London: *Si Monumentum Requiris, Circumspice,* I translated and paraphrased it as a tribute to the man who had constructed the greatest and most beneficent industrial edifice in the world, the United States Steel Corporation.

When the late Marshal Joffre visited New York, Mr. Frick let him and his suite have the exclusive use of the house in Fifth Avenue, the entire Frick family moving to a hotel. This act of generosity inspired certain of the Marshal's friends with the idea of purchasing the Joffre home in Paris, and making a museum of it. The leader in this group was Hugues le Roux, a distinguished senator, officer of the Legion of Honor, member of the Colonial Council, Councillor of Foreign Commerce and many other offices of note. M. Le Roux sought my aid in enlisting the interest of Mr. Frick in this enterprise, and greatly to our satisfaction, the latter showed a disposition to furnish all the money required to purchase the property and donate it to the French nation to serve as a Joffre memorial and museum. The house, in which the Marshal and his wife had lived for eleven years, was No. 6 Rue Michel Ange, in the Passy-Auteuil quarter, near the Bois de Boulogne. M. Le Roux wrote me:

"It was from that door that the Maréchal, then General, set out for the war in 1914, and to this home that he returned after the Battle of the Marne. I must say that there was something very moving in evoking such memories at the threshold of this modest dwelling. As I went in I noticed a bunch of mistletoe hung over the iron gate through which all the great people of the war have passed. And what was still more touching was to see the little sign 'Maison á Vendre' blowing in the wind.

"It happened to be the day of the arrival in Paris of the King of the Belgians. Owing to certain political jealousies, the Maréchal had not been invited to meet the King when he came into the Gare at the Bois de Boulogne. But while I was there the King telephoned to ask if he might come at six o'clock to pay his respects to the Maréchal. And Madame la Maréchale told me that the queen had said to her one day when the King and the Maréchal were standing together: 'I like to see them together: they are the two greatest figures of the war!' Well I hope with all my heart that this service may be rendered to this great honest man to whom we owe so much, and also to history. The place could be made a wonderful museum of souvenirs."

The hope was doomed to disappointment; and the

88

reason is almost too comical to tell. It appeared that
Mr. Gompers, the labor leader, was courteously received by Marshal Joffre somewhere—here or in Paris,
and when they parted Joffre kissed Gompers on both
cheeks in the French fashion. Mr. Frick told me of it
in a disgusted tone, and his interest in the Joffre memorial suddenly collapsed! If Mr. Roland Knoedler
ever reads this, he will learn how this effort to immor-
talize a legend, in which he took such interest, was
asphixiated with a kiss! Considering the striking lack of
pulchritude in Gompers, one may perhaps sympathize
with Frick's disgust at the thought of a man's kissing
him!

The correspondence with M. le Roux—he has since
died—reveals the distressing fact of Marshal Joffre's
need. The French government has shown the prover-
bial ingratitude of republics. It rewarded the Victor of the Marne with the pay of an American junior
lieutenant, *"less 2000 francs which are deducted from
his 'retraite'!"*—whatever that may be!

One day, at lunch at Pride's Crossing, I mentioned
that I had brought a book from New York which I
would read to the others at the table, if they wished.

"What's the book?" asked Mr. Frick.

"The Kingship of Self-Control by William George
Jordan," I said.

A gentle ripple of mirth went round the table.

"Just go into the office and look behind the door,"
said Mr. Frick.

"Do you mean now?"

"Yes, now."

I accordingly left the table and went into the room

89

indicated. It is a delightful little den, furnished as an office, with an exquisite collection of original drawings by Millet on the walls. Behind the door was a small table, and on this were four or five piles of books, a dozen or more in each pile. To my amazement they were all by my dear old friend, Jordan. Frick had bought them by the dozen to give to his guests. I had not known him to be a patron of literature, and I wondered at his selection of Jordan's writings. Then I recalled the titles of the several works, and they supplied the explanation. They might have served as a list of the most salient features of the character of Frick himself. Here they are:

> *The Power of Purpose.*
> *Self Control: Its Kingship and Majesty.*
> *The Majesty of Calmness.*
> *The Crown of Individuality.*
> *The Kingship of Self-Control.*

When I returned to the table, I told those present something about Jordan, who had been editor of the *Saturday Evening Post* and the *Ladies Home Journal,* under Curtis, and he had done much to build up their great circulation before Edward W. Bok had completely americanized himself. He had been handicapped from childhood by a shrivelled leg, the result of infantile paralysis, and, as he described himself with a humor that was infinitely pathetic, he was "just a tripod": he walked with a crutch! But his brilliant mind needed no crutch, as his writings eloquently show. On the other hand, he was devoid of what may be called the dollar sense: he sold his books as fast as they were written for a few hundred dollars, and let his publisher make

the large profits that were rightly his. As a consequence
he was always in financial straits.

Soon after my return to New York I took Jordan
to the Frick house and introduced him to the family.

"Do you think your friend could use a thousand dollars?" inquired Mr. Frick after Jordan had left.

"It would be a godsend," I answered.

"Then give it to him with my compliments." This
happened twice; and Jordan was most grateful and appreciative.

At this time he was engaged on an ambitious work
on "Mental Training as a Remedy for Education."
It was to be in five or six volumes, of encyclopedic
range; and, to mark his constitutional impracticability,
he had no publisher, no money and nothing to go upon
but his indomitable enthusiasm and industry. It was a
hopeless job, but I could not get him to see it. Then an
idea occurred to me, which I should hesitate to mention were it not for its success. He wanted to refer to
a book which I thought might be in the Boston Library.

"You go to Boston," I told him. "While there write
to Mr. Frick at Pride's Crossing, and say you would
like to call on him. Take your dinner jacket. You will
be invited to spend the night at the Frick house. Next
morning, you will breakfast alone with Mr. Frick, for
the ladies take breakfast in their rooms. Alone with
Mr. Frick, you will have an opportunity of telling him
about your work on Mental Training. Unless I am
mistaken, he will help you to finish it."

Jordan followed my advice to the letter, and it all
came out as I had foreseen. Frick offered to pay
Jordan a thousand dollars every quarter for three
years, which was the time Jordan thought would be

necessary to complete his work. For three years there-after, Jordan lived in clover, getting his notes together and making huge preparations for the six volumes, now swollen to eight in his enthusiasm. He had rented, and furnished in exquisite taste, a "Little Room" in West 38th Street. This he filled with books bought in London and elsewhere, and the pile of preparatory notes grew ever in size and impressiveness. But nothing was sent to the press. I warned the impractical genius that the money would stop at the end of the three years unless something more tangible than perfunctory notes was forthcoming; but, with disarming sweetness, Jordan kept adding to his pile of notes, and showed me with pride the excellent system of classification he had invented for them. That was as far as he ever got. The money stopped, the "Little Room" was disman-tled and given up, the books were sold, the preparatory notes were wrapped in bundles, and when Jordan was on his deathbed three years ago, he would have been in dire need but for the generosity of Andrew Carne-gie, who had given to the Authors Club a benevolent fund of a quarter of a million dollars to meet such cases.

This system of Mental Training was supposed to fit one to meet any emergency in life, and, in one of its minor aspects, to enable one to make a prompt and ap-propriate reply to any statement. This Jordan could do; but I suspect it was due more to his innate ability than to any artificial system of training. I recall several in-stances of his exercise of this faculty of instantaneous repost. At the Authors Club one night at supper, Jor-dan was being teased by two clever fellows sitting next to him. His retorts were brilliantly witty. They re-minded me of a juggler who could keep half a dozen balls in the air while spinning a lot of plates, or balancing another man on a pole.

"Jove!" I exclaimed to Duffield Osborne, who sat next to me. "Isn't Jordan brilliant tonight!"

"Jordan," called Osborne across the table, "Bridge says you are brilliant. What's the proper answer to that?"

"Why emphasize the obvious?" came back like a shot.

On another occasion a reporter essayed to test Jordan's powers of repartee, after his lecture on Mental Training. Jordan protested, but finally consented to the test.

"You may remember," said the reporter, who had come primed, "that Charles Lamb, finding himself at dinner between two ladies, one of whom was very attractive and the other less so, paid all his attention to the attractive one. The other, somewhat piqued, kept interrupting Lamb's talk, and he too got peeved.

'Madam,' he said testily, 'I have not heard a word you've said. It's gone in at one ear and out at the other.'

"Now," queried the reporter, "what ought the lady to have said?"

"Obvious," answered Jordan. " 'Ah, a vacuum, I perceive.' "

"Good," said the reporter. "And what ought Lamb to say to that?"

"Equally obvious," said Jordan. " 'But Madam, sound will not pass through a vacuum.' "

"Good again," said the reporter. "Now what ought she to say to that?"

93

The Main Gallery

"Look here," protested Jordan; "how much further is this inquisition to go?"

"Just this once," replied the reporter.

"Well, the lady might have said: 'But Mr. Lamb, you have just demonstrated the contrary!'"

This was the sort of thing Jordan could do by the hour. "How would you define a kiss?" asked a wizened old fellow who looked as if he had never had the experience. "It depends," said Jordan, "whether it is a hope or an achievement."

But this is a chapter about Frick, and Jordan has been introduced in it simply to illustrate how the inarticulate Frick silently gave away large sums where he thought they would be helpful, not so much to the individual as to the race. At his death a dozen splendid gifts were made known in Pittsburgh which, up to that time, had been unsuspected even by those who had benefitted by them. His will, distributing five-sixths of his great fortune among a dozen or more public institutions, but put the finishing touch to a career that had always been marked by acts of spontaneous generosity.

Despite his disconcerting taciturnity, his inflexibility so defiantly demonstrated in the Homestead tragedy, his unrelenting enmity towards Carnegie which he carried to his grave and which Col. Harvey, in his book, carried beyond it, despite all this and more, there was a singularly charming, humane and charitable side to the character of Henry Clay Frick. As I have shown, he gave abundantly of his fortune during his life in ways that never became known to any but the recipients.

His will was the crowning achievement of a life

95

marked by an interrupted succession of material gains
—victories in the industrial world, shrewd bargainings,
an imperious demand for recognition of his rights and
an unforgiving remembrance of what he deemed his
wrongs. The courtly manner of his earlier years grew
a protective armor as time went on, and as his growing
wealth attracted schemes and schemers. The materialistic aspect of his life, as seen from outside, was quali-
fied by his love of children and of art. It is in these
gentler phases of his complex character that he is remembered by those who knew him best.

The genial Autocrat of the Breakfast Table would
hold that Henry Clay Frick had a triple personality
—one for each of his three names. I found there were
half a dozen of him. There was the Frick of Col.
Harvey, a chevalier *sans peur et sans reproche:* kind,
gentle, never out of temper, "beyond compare *'suaviter
in modo, fortiter in re,'* " of classical beauty, like a
statue "of Hercules by a student of the master Lycip-
pus," in "nimbleness of movement" quick as the great
god himself, yet not readily responsive to wit, rarely
laughing, but with a "slow understanding smile" that
suggested a resemblance to General Grant. Next was
the Frick known to Judge Gary, somewhat different
from the one just described. Still more unlike Col. Harvey's Frick was the one known to Andrew Carnegie.
Here the *"fortiter in re"* was much more in evidence
than was the *"suaviter in modo,"* as may be seen by reference to Carnegie's pleadings in the famous Equity
Suit. The fourth Frick was the Santa Claus who paid
$170,000 to some thousands of Pittsburgh children
whose Christmas savings had been lost by the failure of
a bank, in which Frick had no interest. This is the Frick

one likes to remember. Frick was human. His appreciation of beauty was boundless. There is yet another Frick—known only to himself—the Silent Frick. Finally, and best of all—the Frick known only to his grand-children. This is holy ground, like that where Jesus sat. "For of such," was also Frick's conception of "the Kingdom of Heaven!"

TERRA-COTTA GROUP
by Clodion

97

"A Lady and Maidservant"
by Vermeer of Delft.

THE FRICK COLLECTION

It is impossible to dissociate in thought the great art collection formed by the late Henry Clay Frick from his own impressive personality. It became the expression of his inner life—the materialization of his ambition—the aim and end of all his later efforts. It is also the visible token of the thoroughness of his own character; for it is one of the few art collections in the world consisting entirely of masterpieces. In this it illustrates the dominant character of the man. He never attempted the impossible; but whatever he undertook he achieved wholly and completely. And this great collection, the crowning joy and glory of a life of successful endeavor in other fields, will ever remain a monument to the intellectual absoluteness of his character. Joined to his other bequests, it is also a perpetual memorial to his splendid altruism.

To describe the Frick Collection of paintings, bronzes and other *objets d'art* as practically unique, in that it includes none but masterpieces, is not a mere figure of speech; there is in it nothing that is not of superlative merit. Nowhere else can be seen more than a hundred paintings of the highest artistic value without a single one of second quality. Nowhere else can Fragonard be seen at his best. The greatest examples of Van Dyck's three periods are here. Velasquez' superb Parma portrait of Philip IV, costing nearly half a million and worthy of a room to itself, is flanked by one of Goya's greatest canvases; and on either hand are Frans Hals' famous "de Ruyter," his "Burgomaster," and the marvelous brushwork in black and grey of the dignified old "Dutch Vrouw." Rembrandt's greatest and most dignified representation of himself is here; while his famous "Polish Rider" hangs in stately dignity amid worthy examples of the work of Rubens, Paul Veronese, El Greco and a dozen ancient masters of portraiture. No fewer than three Vermeers are in the Gallery, two of them of historic interest. In other rooms are Gainsboroughs—including the famous "The Mall in St. James's Park,"—Reynoldses, Constables, five Turners, all of the highest quality. Romney, Raeburn, Hoppner are represented by illustrious examples; and Corot's most radiant work finds itself in the goodly company of his great contemporaries. Troyon, Daubigny, Rousseau and others of their time are similarly honored by association with giants of other days, such as Holbein, Bronzino, Bellini, Titian, and, in their own line, with such masters in landscape as Ruisdael, Hobbema, Cuyp and Van de Capelle.

The catholicity of Mr. Frick's artistic appreciation is further shown by a collection of renaissance bronzes, marked by the same unique quality of excellence. Donatello, Verocchio, Cellini, Giovanni di Bologna, Riccio—of whom are nearly a dozen examples —Bellano, Bertoldo and others famous in the history of Italian Renaissance are well represented, without any admixture of the dubious or the meritricious.

So, too, with two score jewel-like enamels bearing the names of artists who, over three hundred years ago, gave distinction and fame to Limoges. It is said of

Linnæas that he knelt in worship when he first saw the golden beauty of a flowering gorse-bush on the English uplands. A kindred feeling inspires one at sight of these exquisite gems of renaissance art, created as they were for devotional purposes. This collection of Limoges enamels is the finest private collection in the world.

Of Chinese porcelains the selection has been as judicious and painstaking as in the other divisions of the collection. Here are examples of *famille rose* of the Yung Ching and Chien Lung reigns running through a whole gamut of color, from the most delicate shade of pink to the richest ruby, glowing like the precious gems they simulate. Of the lustrous products of the kilns of K'ang Hsi, known as "black hawthorns," the collection is more complete than in any museum; and these alone would lend distinction to any exhibition of Chinese ceramic art, even without the added glory of a set of four blue and white hawthorns of such sapphire brilliance as defy adequate description. One of these is the famous Blenheim vase, which is said to have sold for a sum in six figures a quarter of a century ago.

Mr. Frick was the most modest of men. His success as a great industrial leader gave him prominence —made him indeed famous, while his genius for finance brought him riches beyond compute. The prominence he evaded; the fame he ignored; the riches he spent in secret philanthropy and in the gratification of his artistic tastes. His associates knew him as "the silent Frick." But his smile was eloquent of satisfaction when those who knew commented intelligently on the works of art he was always glad to show to such

MISS MARY EDWARDS
by Hogarth

as could appreciate them. This Collection was his pride; he had none other. And his enjoyment of it needed no witness. He spent hours alone with the beautiful objects he had gathered about him. Often in the early morning, in the deserted gallery, I would find cigar ashes around a chair that had been drawn up in front of some old friend, who seemed ready to step out of his frame to thank the patron who had placed him in an environment of beauty and refinement. And, parenthetically, the palace that Thomas Hastings built to house the Collection is in every way harmonious. It is the joy of architects and artists who have visited it; as artistic a creation as anything it contains. The beauty of its interior is due to the taste and skill of Sir Charles Allom and Sir Joseph Duveen.

It is indicative of the human quality of Mr. Frick's character, that, while he was capable of judging the artistic merits of a painting, he became very keen to know the homely details of the artist's life, or of the life of the man or woman who looked at him from the canvas. Some five years before his death, during a sickness which confined him to his room at Prides Crossing, he used to sit up in bed, to read the life-stories of his portraits, which, by patient delving in libraries, I was able to send him day by day; and on his return to New York, he walked with me round the gallery with a new interest, and with a friendly smile that betokened human fellowship with the personages who, up to that time, had been to him but as great examples of the painter's art. It was amusing to me, to whom the stories were old, to have him tell me of incidents in the life of this or that personage as familiarly as he would have spoken of some event in his own life. In short, the portraits had become his friends and acquaintances, something more than mere paint and varnish.

The Duveen-Allom system of lighting the gallery enhances this illusion of vitality. Visitors have been heard to protest that they have seen changing expressions on the faces of the men and women on the walls, as the lights were altered. There is a portrait by Frans Hals that constantly has this uncanny appearance of life. It is the "de Ruyter." Even without artificial illumination, this face is like that of a living man, with a quizzical look that at times runs over into a smile.

To the art expert who scans a canvas through a magnifying glass and limits his appreciation to technical excellencies, this humanization of an old master is an unworthy condescension. He is apt to forget that a portrait is primarily a biography, and is a great work of art only in proportion as the biography is convincing. No such weakness for the technicalities of art diminished the interest and pleasure Mr. Frick found in close human fellowship with his paintings. His recognition of the amazing facility of Hogarth in the portrait of Miss Edwards was in no way diminished by the interest he took in the romantic events of Miss Edwards' life. Indeed, the strong personality of the portrait is emphasized by knowledge of the fact that to save her fortune from her spendthrift husband, she had recourse to the drastic means of repudiating her marriage and declaring her son illegitimate. Romney's charming portrait of Miss Harford, the natural daughter of the last Lord Baltimore, gains in interest when one recalls the unwritten romance of early American history which has given the lady's name to a county in Maryland. The magnificent full-length Gains

borough, once sold for six guineas and now worth half
a million dollars, evokes keen sympathy for the regal-
looking Francis Duncombe, writing from the Fleet
Prison for aid for her worthless husband. There are
eight Van Dycks in the collection, and romance clus-
ters about each of them. The portraits of Franz Sny-
ders and his wife were sold by Philippe Égalité during
the French Revolution, and became separated. After
more than a hundred years, Mr. Frick brought them
together again, to their mutual satisfaction, as the sympathetic onlooker may readily see. Sir John Suckling,
the royalist soldier-poet and conspirator, like another
English poet of more recent times, fled in disgrace to
Paris, there to die a miserable death. The Earl of
Derby led Charles II to the hiding-place at Boscobel
and the Royal Oak, after the defeat at Worcester; was
himself wounded and captured; escaped, was captured again, and beheaded at Bolton, furnishing material for a romance by Harrison Ainsworth and a sneer
from Carlyle. His wife, who stands by his side in Van
Dyck's great painting, was the heroic and successful
defender of Lathom House, against Cromwell's
troops, and has become a leading character in one of
Sir Walter Scott's novels. The little girl by her side
had also her romance. She married her father's friend,
who fought duels, pulled the Duke of Buckingham's
hair, practiced amateur doctoring, and died by an ex-
perimental dose of his own medicine. Velasquez' great
portrait of Philip IV was painted in an old shanty at
Fraga, the King standing up to his knees in rushes to
keep his feet warm. It was carried in quasi-religious
procession through the thronged streets of old Madrid,
and deposited under a golden canopy in the cathedral.

LE RENDEZVOUS
by Fragonard

To tell how it finally came to America would fill a long chapter, covering a chase of rival dealers over and around Central Europe. The superb series of Fragonard panels, besides their urgent appeal to the technician, could tell of Madame du Barry and her picturesque entourage, her extravagances, her wilfulness, her romantic career ending with the guillotine. A nobler story invests with sympathetic interest the marble bust of Madame Roland, one of the most eloquent products of Pajou's magic chisel. Of the two Holbein portraits of Sir Thomas More and Sir Thomas Cromwell, history itself can furnish veridical details, while tradition embellishes that of More with a scene in which the ill-fated Anne Bolyn, in a paroxym of anger, flings this very panel out of the palace window, to be picked up in fragments in the streets by a passing Italian connoiseur, a member of the Papal legation. The two great allegorical pictures by Paul Veronese were part of the booty of Gustavus Adolphus at the capture of Prague; and his eccentric daughter Christina took them to Rome. They afterwards hung for many years in the Palais Royal as part of the collection of the Duc d'Orleans. The "Arrival of the Packet Boat at Cologne" is the famous painting that Turner himself disfigured with lamp-black at the Royal Academy in 1826, because it outshone two of Lawrence's portraits hanging near. Ruskin says a shiver ran down the artistic spine of England before a false report of its destruction in a railway accident was corrected. The "Man with the Red Cap" variously attributed to Giorgione, Titian and Sebastiano del Piombo, is the painting Sir Hugh Lane brought to America to add to this Collection, and, going back on the "Lusitania," lost his life. Romney's Henrietta Vernon ("Lady Warwick") was the daughter-in-law of Nattier's "Elizabeth Hamilton," in the same gallery, who was the mother of eight children and was locked out of her home by her irrascible husband, according much gossip to that gossipy age. Bellini's magnificent "St. Francis," mentioned by a contemporary diarist in 1525, is the one the British nation was tempted to buy by public subscription half a century or more ago, and failed because of its high price.

Such are a few of the romances that cluster around the various items of this Collection, and such are the incidents that, to one as humanly receptive as was its creator, had an appeal that greatly enhanced his joy in it.

While to-day the world is the poorer for his departure, Mr. Frick has left it enriched with a beauty that will endure for ages. He has shared the treasures of his mind and the garnerings of his industry with unborn generations. Hundreds of years from now, men and women will find joy and inspiration because there once lived, labored and loved, a man named Henry Clay Frick. For his will, distributing five-sixths of his colossal fortune among a number of public institutions, contained the following clause:

"I direct the Trustees, immediately after my death, and during the lives of my said wife and my eldest child living at my death and the survivor of them, to cause to be duly incorporated an institution to be known as *THE FRICK COLLECTION* for the purpose of maintaining a Gallery of Art . . . and encouraging the study of fine arts, and of advancing the general knowledge of kindred subjects; such gallery of art to be for the use and benefit of *ALL PERSONS WHOMSOEVER* to the end that the same shall be a *PUBLIC GALLERY OF ART TO WHICH THE ENTIRE PUBLIC SHALL FOR EVER HAVE ACCESS,* subject only to *REASONABLE REGULA-TIONS* to be from time to time established by the said Corporation."

With affecting pathos he added that this was "a purpose which I have long cherished and which is very dear to me."

He also left an endowment fund of fifteen million dollars, since almost doubled, to maintain and add to this great art Collection.*

How came the poor uncultured lad who served out to the farmers' wives of West Overton their little pounds of tea and sugar, their cuts of bacon and cheese, who, in the rustic forum round the stove, gossiped and talked politics with their men folks, and patted the tousled heads of their youngsters as he leaned across the counter of his uncle's country store —how came he to know the difference between a Romney and a Rembrandt, neither of whom had ever been heard of in the Westmoreland county of those days? According to Col. Harvey he nightly slept on that counter—did this for two long years! Surely there was nothing in this humble environment to foreshadow a great artistic evolution. But it came—slowly at first, and then, with the swelling tide of Carnegie prosperity, it grew with tropical luxuriance, over-shadowing every other interest in life.

* The trustees under Mr. Frick's will were: John D. Rockefeller Jr., George F. Baker Jr., Horace Havemeyer, Lewis Cass Ledyard, Walker D. Hines, J. Horace Harding and three members of the Frick family. Mr. Harding has since died; and his place on the board of trustees has been filled by the Hon. Andrew W. Mellon.

ADMIRAL MICHAEL ADRIAENSZ DE RUYTER
by Frans Hals

His first timid approach to the fine arts was in 1881, when he paid $800 to William Schaus of New York for a little painting by Luis Jimemez, entitled "In the Louvre," or "Une Révélation." Then he got married, and deserted the muse for half a dozen years. In 1887, however, he bought two paintings, one by Tito Lessi, called "Reading the Newspaper," which sufficiently distinguishes it, and one by Meyer von Breman, "The Darlings." This he bought of John Wanamaker, and paid $5000 for it. It is a touching exhibition at this early day of his love of children, which was ever his most beautiful characteristic. These two purchases sufficed for another eight years, when, in 1895, he came under the spell of Roland Knoedler, and bought of him a dozen pictures in one year. Among them was a Bouguereau, two Cazins, a Jacquet and two by Fritz Thaulow, who visited Pittsburgh about this time. Next year he bought, mainly from the Knoedlers, no fewer than seventeen pictures, including several water colors. Of the paintings the most important was a Diaz, "La Mare aux Vipers," for which he paid $15,000, and also a Rousseau, "Dessous de Bois," for a like sum. These are now in the Frick Collection. In 1897 he bought another Diaz, a L'hermitte, a Millet pastel, and a Dupré—"La Rivière," now in the Collection. The following year a full dozen paintings were bought, one by Corot, "Ville d'Avray," costing $25,000, the highest price paid up to that time. This was the year when his attention was attracted to the English portraitists: he bought Romney's "Mary Finch Hatton," for $10,000. Next year he bought a Hoppner, a Rembrandt and a Nattier. These are all in the Collection, and, of course, are now worth many times what they cost. In 1901, the Carnegie companies having been absorbed by the Steel Corporation, he bought Turner's "Antwerp, Van Goyen in Search of a Subject"; and paid $26,00 for Vermeer's "Music Lesson," worth to-day at least $200,000. This year he also acquired Jacob van Ruisdael's "A Waterfall," which used to hang over a mantel in his Pittsburgh home, where he showed it to me in 1902 with great pride. For by this time he had been badly stung by the collectors' bee. During 1902 he paid $75,000 for a Hobbema; $40,-000 for Cuyp's "Herdsman," both now in the Collection, and acquired three paintings by Lawrence and Reynolds that happened to be at Prides Crossing when he died. These three are not in the Collection, because his bequest to the public covered only the things in the Fifth Avenue house. In 1903 he paid $30,000 for Romney's "Miss Francis Harford," now worth $200,000; and $115,000 for Gainsborough's "Mrs. Hatchett," which he never liked and which is worth no more than it cost. Having garnered his golden sheaves through the sale of his steel stocks, he spent $267,000 on paintings in 1904—Romney's "Lady Hamilton," now worth three or four times as much as he paid; Lawrence's "Lady Peel"; and a Turner, for $45,000, that to-day would fetch twice or thrice as much at any auction. In 1905 he bought paintings by Van Dyck, El Greco, Raeburn, Cuyp, Titian and Metzu, thus showing the widening field of his artistic interests. The following year he made his greatest purchase, the famous Ilchester self-portrait of Rembrandt. Its cost was $228,000, yet it is price-less. After Bellini's "St. Francis in the Desert," it is the greatest painting in the Collection. It is vain to speculate what it would bring at an auction sale, which, happily, is impossible, but a million dollars would not be an unreasonable guess. I asked Lord Ilchester why he sold it. "Death duties," was his reply! That year Frick's expenditures on four paintings exceeded half a million dollars. They were, besides the great Rembrandt, a Reynolds, a Frans Hals, and a beautiful Van de Capelle. The following year Mr. Frick paid $120,-000 for a Van Dyck that had been smuggled out of Italy in an automobile. It is the half-length portrait of Marchesa Giovanna Cattaneo which hangs near the superb full-length portrait of her cousin Paula Adorna in the Main Gallery.

This portrait of Paula Adorno is the greatest Van Dyck in the Collection, and it came within an ace of being ruined by the treacherous winter climate of New York. I have told the story of its rescue in *Portraits and Personalities in the Frick Galleries*. It came from the collection of the Duke of Abercorn.

During the succeeding years Mr. Frick seemed not to hesitate at any price asked for the masterpieces to which his interest was now confined. Fifty thousand dollars was a commonplace; $200,000 for a single painting by no means rare; and when Rembrandt's "Polish Rider" was offered to him he gladly paid $308,651 for it. If it could be sold to-day it would bring twice that hugh sum! The year he bought this great work his total payments for paintings amounted to nearly $850,000. This total was almost equalled in the following year, when he bought his most costly portrait—that of Philip IV of Spain by Velasquez—$475,000. This year he also bought another Hobbema Landscape, almost like the one acquired nine years

LOUISA GEORGINA MURRAY
by Sir Thomas Lawrence

before. For the first one he paid $75,000; for the second, $135,000. The difference in price marks the change in values in nine years. These paintings are so much alike that Mr. Frick spoke to me about getting rid of one; but he never could make up his mind which one to surrender.

At first he was guided in his purchases by Mr. Roland Knoedler and his partner the late Charles Carstairs, with both of whom he established the closest of friendships. Later he conferred almost daily with Sir Joseph Duveen, through whom, at a cost approaching five million dollars, he acquired the famous Du Barry *Panneaux de Grasse* of Fragonard, the Boucher panels, painted for the Pompadour, the J. P. Morgan collections of renaissance bronzes, Limoges enamels, Chinese porcelains, and some furniture.

It was in 1911 that the conception of a great public gallery of art, like the Wallace Collection in London, assumed definiteness in Mr. Frick's mind, although there had been suggestions of it before, which had largely determined the high character of his purchases. He wanted nothing but the best, and was willing to pay any price to get it. Thus he paid $350,000 for the great Clarendon Van Dyck, "James Stanley Earl of Derby, his Wife and Child"; almost as much for the same artist's "Paula Adorna"; $200,000 for the Veronese allegorical paintings; $125,000 for El Greco's "Knight of Malta"; $195,000 for the three Whistlers that had belonged to Canfield, the gambler; $325,000 for the two large Turners, now hanging in the main corridors; and finally the large sum already mentioned for the Boucher panels, the Morgan Fragonards, bronzes, porcelains and enamels. In all, he must

have spent on his Collection during the last ten years
of his life close to twenty million dollars, which sum
is to be added to several millions expended on art
works during the preceding nine years, when, the Carnegie company having been absorbed by the U. S. Steel
Corporation, and Mr. Frick, relieved from active business, first began seriously to lay the foundations of
his great art collection. Had he lived a few years
longer he might have achieved his ambitious purpose
—to have the greatest obtainable masterpieces under
a private roof. Even with a fifteen million dollar
endowment fund and its increment, it is doubtful that
the trustees may complete his work, for unfortunately,
more than millions are necessary to reach results of
the kind aimed at by Mr. Frick: he, specializing in
art for more than twenty years, and ever receptive to
expert advice, was in a class by himself.

In the eleven years since his death nothing of importance has been added to the Collection, if we except
two interesting but unbeautiful primitives, acquired for
half a million dollars. One is a historic panel by Duccio
and the other a small Berna da Siena. Two large pieces
of sculpture, representing the Annunciation, were also
obtained in Rome in the belief that they were genuine-
ly antique masterpieces. They were not beautiful, and
had no appeal except that of supposed antiquity—the
least of all valid reasons for including them in a Collection in which every piece had been selected for its
intrinsic beauty and complete harmony with its environment. The gentlemen on the board of trustees declined
to accept these sculptures, even before it was discovered that they were a recent product of the now-famous
factory operated by the clever Dossena.

The *London Times* credited me with the discovery of the fraud, and I received congratulations from England. But that was a mistake. I do not know who first recognized their spurious character. Their falsity was, however, known to me months before any mention of them was made in the public press. That the gentlemen on the board of trustees rejected them is an encouraging sign. Their responsibility is a great one, and this Dossena incident demonstrates that what Mr. Frick, in his will, defined as "a public duty" is now being seriously interpreted as such. "Not for an Age, but for all Time" is their watchword!

MARBLE GROUP
by Falconet

117

ELBERT H. GARY
Portrait by J. Philip Schmand

ELBERT H. GARY

"A VERAY PARFIT GENTIL KNIGHT."

J UDGE GARY was a personality to be remembered almost with reverence by those who had the inspiring privilege of his friendship. I first met him in 1902, when he sent me an unsolicited compliment through Walter Hines Page, in acknowledgment of *The Trust: Its Book,* which Mr. Page's firm had just published. This was a symposium on industrial consolidations by the men who had been chiefly instrumental in forming them—Charles R. Flint, known as the "father of trusts," James J. Hill, the "empire-builder," S. C. T. Dodd, of the Standard Oil Company, Francis B. Thurber, with opinions on this modern economic development by President Roosevelt, Mark Hanna, Thomas B. Reed, President Hadley of Yale, Samuel Gompers, Roswell P. Flower, Professor Sumner, Chauncey M Depew and many other leaders of thought. Judge Gary had been impressed by my application of the Spencerian doctrine of Evolution to this modern phase of industrialism, which he characterized as a new and helpful concept of a tendency that was becoming increasingly effective in the business world. "For," said he, "if it is shown that the Trust, as we know it, is the product of natural law, such as governs the growth of organisms in general, the efforts of man-made laws to discredit it will prove vain."

MILLIONAIRES AND GRUB STREET

President Roosevelt, always sensitive to the effect of public opinion and ever ready to bestride a popular movement and ride it as his personal hobby, seized on the "Trust," threw his saddle on it, and became again the "rough rider." Which prompted the following letter from Walter Hines Page:

THE WORLD'S WORK

DOUBLEDAY, PAGE AND COMPANY, PUBLISHERS

34 UNION SQUARE, NEW YORK

WALTER H. PAGE, EDITOR

Sept. 6th, 1902.

My dear Mr. Bridge:—

I have an ambitious idea for an article for "The World's Work," which it occurs to me might interest you. The President, you see, is going about the country very vigorously preaching his doctrine of publicity about corporations, particularly the big ones, and making mention of the possibility of a constitutional amendment to give the Federal government control over them. I really don't believe that he ever expects to see this amendment, but, nevertheless, he keeps talking about it and I think he uses it as a rather rhetorical method of giving emphasis to his earnest position about publicity.

It has occurred to me that a real magazine article (not a mere newspaper article) might be made that would be of wide interest, expressing the corporations' view of the President's attitude. I think that the best way to get at this is to get expressions of opinion from a large number of men who manage great corporations. The men who give these opinions need not necessarily be quoted in the article, and, of course, we should not wish to use anybody's name who had any objections to his name being used, but a concensus of opinion might be got without using names. Then, I imagine, there are some men who would not mind being quoted.

ELBERT H. GARY

In other words, out of a lot of interviews of this sort, using the interviews as raw material, could not a most admirable article be constructed? Would you care to undertake it for us? Please let me hear from you at your very earliest convenience about this. I want to get such an article in the number we are now at work upon.

Sincerely yours,

WALTER H. PAGE.

J. H. Bridge, Esq.,
    New York City.

Judge Gary was, naturally, the first one to be interviewed, and thus commenced an acquaintance which lasted till his death, nearly thirty years later.

The high standing of the *Worlds Work* secured me a courteous reception from the heads of the great corporations I visited—with but one exception, Mr. H. O. Havemeyer of the Sugar Trust. His single contribution to the discussion was to the effect that he didn't "give a damn what the President said or thought!" This was in keeping with the character of the organization he headed, and his own unethical conception of his rights as chief of a great industry whose shares he was using at that time as a football in Wall Street.

Some years before this I invested in a couple of hundred shares of "Sugar," and as I was leaving the broker's office I ran against my friend John S. Beach, whose large fortune grew out of the success he had carried to the firm of Bridge and Beach of St. Louis. Mr. Beach occupied a sort of paternal relation to me, and now, at lunch in the Lawyers Club, he scolded me for buying such a speculative stock as "Sugar." I offered to sell the stock forthwith.

"Wait a little," he said. "I am going to dine with Mr. Havemeyer to-night, and I'll try to find out whether your purchase is safe."

The next morning before I was up, his butler came to the Windsor Hotel with a note, to the effect that "Sugar" would go to 125. It was then 85. "Don't let this lead you into a fool's paradise" was the closing sentence of the note. But it did. I bought enough more shares to make a profit of $50,000, before the stock dropped from 127 back to its original figure. Mr. Havemeyer probably "made" a million or more by this move, and doubtless congratulated himself on his shrewdness.

With this experience in mind, I was neither surprised nor chagrined to learn that Havemeyer did not "give a damn" what the President of the United States said or thought about Trusts!

With Judge Gary this sort of thing was anathema. He considered it worse than robbery; and it was largely because of his vigorous denunciation of stock-gambling presidents and directors that I closed my article in the *Worlds Work* with the following statement, which is as valid to-day as it was thirty years ago. More so, indeed, if the current revelations of the secret payment of $5,497,684 to the president of a great steel company for five and a half years' services, is any indication of prevailing conceptions of directors' duties to their shareholders!

There is one aspect of this subject which is deserving of emphasis, and that is the tendency everywhere visible among what are called trust magnates toward a more elevated moral plane. The evils and abuses of corporate power are being reme-

ELBERT H. GARY

died by the demands of the higher industrial life which we are reaching. The position of the man who directs an army of workers and controls the collected savings of thousands of his fellow-men—and women—is so lofty that even if his natural inclination were to dishonesty, he is too conspicuous to indulge it. A sensational rumor that such an industrial leader has been seen at a roulette table is cabled to the ends of the earth and brings an avalanche of protest from investors. The kings of finance and the lords of industry live in as fierce a light as that which beat on Tranby Croft. Moreover, they are subject to the sleepless scrutiny of each other. In no place is commercial integrity valued more than in Wall Street; and there is rarely room on the directorate of any great corporation for one whose record is not clean. The grosser forms of dishonesty are fast being eliminated from American commercial life; and although stock-jobbing presidents and directors are not extinct, they are ever growing less numerous. Mr. James B. Dill, the great legal authority on trusts, says that at a recent directors' meeting of one of these great corporations, a resolution was passed "that it was the consensus of opinion that no director or officer of the company should avail himself of this advance knowledge (of the increased value of the company's property) to purchase any of the stock of the company on the market, before the statement was made to the public." And in further illustration of the higher conception of the duty of directors now becoming general, he quotes the following statement from the recent report of one of the large corporations, published and signed by the executive officer:

"The total number of stockholders of the company, immediately after its organization, was about 1,300. The total now is 5,153, of which 1,860 are women. Trustees as we are for this large and constantly increasing body of stockholders, many of them women, some of them the widows and children of former associates, all of them entitled to the best service we can give them, we must and do feel that the administration of this great property is a trust of the highest and most sacred char-

123

acter, and while it is in our charge we shall ever strive to administer it in this spirit."

As the world knows, it was the late J. Pierpont Morgan who created the great organization known as the United States Steel Corporation. It is almost as well known that it was Judge Gary who endowed it with a soul. Miss Tarbell has told the story in her book; and the Judge, inscribing a copy for me "with warm regards," vouched for the truth of it in every particular, not excepting his conflict with stock-jobbing directors and gambling managers. A friend of mine had the same name as one of the high officers of the Corporation, and occasionally received, by mistake, brokers' notices which told a sorry tale of this official's gambling in the shares of his company!

In contrast, I am tempted to mention a fact that came to me on unimpeachable authority. It happened that the Judge had a large balance in his bank just before an extra dividend was to be declared by the Corporation. One of his associates who was aware of both these facts, suggested to the Judge that he use this balance to add to his holdings in his company's stock. He refused until after the extra dividend had been publicly announced: he was unwilling to profit by his advance knowledge. And he was right. His fortune was already ample. His conscience was more to him than a few thousand dollars. It is amusing to read in Miss Tarbell's book how his directors chafed under his "Sunday-school homilies," which apparently were not entirely supererogatory!

A year or so before he died—he was in his 78th year—Judge Gary came to the studio of Emil Fuchs in the Hotel des Artistes to have his portrait painted.

Hearing that I was president of the building and lived in it on the next floor, he asked that I be sent for, so that we could talk over old times while he posed. The posings were numerous and long; and the Judge and I had many intimate talks about the growth of the steel industry and the men who had been most intimately associated with it. Sometimes I would preface a question with "You need not answer unless you like"; and he would invariably reply: "Your caution is needless!" And we would both laugh, to the discomfiture of the artist, who asked for immobility in his sitter.

There was one little matter that I wanted cleared up. Mr. Frick had held President Roosevelt responsible for some breach of faith following the purchase of the Tennessee Coal, Iron and Railroad Company by the Steel Corporation; and he cherished an ill-will towards Roosevelt up to the day of the latter's death. Personally, I held Roosevelt in the highest esteem, almost in veneration, and said so that morning; which led to a testy retort from Frick.

Judge Gary admitted that there had been an apparent breach of faith, but it was due to the act of some minor official who was unaware of an understanding made direct by Frick and Gary with the president and with Mr. Elihu Root. The Judge joined his encomiums to mine as we talked about the country's loss in the untimely death of this great man. Despite my respect for Mr. Frick's judgment, I still think of Theodore Roosevelt as the greatest American of his generation. As a member of the Authors Club, I knew him long before he became prominent, and my admiration for him grew as he grew in greatness.

The Judge's portrait by Fuchs was not a success,

and, after his death, I asked my friend J. Philip Schmand to paint the portrait which accompanies this chapter.

Judge Gary was a lover of art and had a keen sense of values. He came up to the Frick house several times while I was in charge of the Collection, and I found his talk about pictures as entertaining and illuminating as I had found his talks about steel. In his own home, which he had filled with beautiful things—paintings, porcelains, rare Polish rugs, all of the highest merit— he was a delightful host. His was a winning personality. He made you feel that his own joy in living—which was always in evidence—was augmented by the simple fact of his meeting with you, however casually. Thus I have met him at the opera, and been made to feel that to him the entertainment up to that moment had been incomplete! He had a genius for friendship. It is not possible to say more in fewer words, and Chaucer would have dubbed him "a veray parfit gentil knight."

GEN. SHERMAN AND THE STUARTS

A Beautiful Friendship

General Sherman's own *Memoirs* are so complete that I hesitate to add to them. But my meeting with him was under unusual circumstances, and illustrated his loyalty to an old friendship in a way that gave the incident an interest worth recording.

Brigadier General David Stuart, who commanded a division in several of Sherman's battles, had always been deservedly held in high favor by his great leader, whose affectionate interest in General Stuart's lovely daughter Marion—my cousin by marriage—lasted as long as he lived, and showed itself in many charming ways. For instance, he went from New York to Chicago to meet Marion as she came from Colorado with the body of her husband, a naval officer named Terry, who had died of consumption; and he accompanied her, with his consoling presence, all the way to Annapolis.

In February 1889, Marion was visiting Mrs. Stuart, my wife's mother, at the Windsor Hotel; and as General Sherman was in New York, she invited him to dine with us. His response was immediate:

General W. T. Sherman has this moment learned that Marion Stuart Terry is at the Windsor Hotel and will be sure to avail himself of her kind invitation to meet him at the Windsor at 6½ P. M. of Friday at dinner, though he will thereby violate an invariable rule not to dine out more than four days

DAVID STUART
Brigadier-General

a week. His youngest sister, Mrs. Moulton, is very sick, has summoned her children from Ohio, and himself has obligatory engagements for every night except Friday of this week.

Should Mrs. Moulton be claimed by that old man with the scythe, he will nevertheless come to see one for whom he feels such profound respect.

No. 75 West 71st St.,
    New York, Feb. 19, 1889.

Two days later came another letter, written close to midnight, as follows:

No. 75 West 71st St.,
New York, Feb. 21, 11:20 P. M.

Dear Mrs. Terry,

My sister Mrs. Moulton died this 9:30 P. M. I had an engagement to dine with Elliot Shepard Esq. at 7:30 P. M. At the last moment I begged to be excused, and tomorrow I have with you an engagement for 6½ P. M. at the Windsor. Notwithstanding I will keep this engagement with you, although I may have to come to the Windsor in my funeral carriage.

I have been for hours, making telegraphic messages to places at the West, announcing this death, and the funeral next Sunday from Glendale, Ohio. I must accompany the funeral train to the cars and may be a little late. Therefore keep a place for me, and I will fill it before the dinner is finished. I always want to see you, and please do not think me unfeeling—for Fanny Moulton was always a bright welcome guest everywhere. She was our youngest sister—No. 11 in a family of that number. She married early in life and has children and grandchildren who will love her memory even more than her brothers and sisters. We have done all that was possible to alleviate her suffering, but when I come to the Windsor tomorrow please make all allowances.

Her son, Sherman Moulton, will make all arrangements tonight for the funeral at Glendale, Ohio, Sunday, P. M., and he will report to me tomorrow the exact time when the train will start. After which I can come to the Windsor.

Of course I ought to have died years ago. Now I find myself in New York, with hundreds of promises, weddings, dinner parties and funerals, that I may have to escape to the Rocky Mountains where an old veteran may live in comparative peace.

Of course as yet I know not the exact hour when the train leaves the depot, but I suppose it about 6 P. M. In which case I may be a little late.

Always affectionately,
W. T. SHERMAN.

129

In spite of his kind intentions, he found that it would not be possible to keep his engagement, and he wrote the next day that "there are so many questions which I alone can settle that at this last minute I must beg you to excuse me. My brother the Senator," he writes "is *en route* from Washington, and my sister Elisabeth is here, 77 years of age, and insists on going out to Glendale—almost certain to be fatal to her at this inclement season of the year. Please excuse me tonight. Send me word if you will stay over Sunday, when I may find you in. Truly your friend, W. T. Sherman."

On Sunday he came and stayed to dinner. I met him at the hotel door and went up in the elevator with him; and I remember how the throng in the office made way for him; and many men, recognizing his tall figure, respectfully raised their hats as he passed.

The simple family dinner, in Mrs. Stuart's apartment, was just what the general wanted, after the excitement and worry attending his sister's death and funeral. I was the only other man present. Mrs. Stuart tactfully led the conversation away from painful subjects, and so heartily did the general join in the talk that we all forgot that he had arrived at the hotel just as his sister was being buried. With the coffee the general wanted a special little cigar to smoke, and I was happy to find that they had his particular brand at Tyson's down below.

After all these years it is hard to remember what we talked about. California, certainly, where he had spent several years in the early days. Indeed, General Sherman was in San Francisco before and during the excitement following the discovery of gold—first in 1848 as a young officer in the army, and five years later as an official in an important banking concern. His first trip was around the Horn; mine, the previous year, had been by way of New Orleans, by sea. And I had recently been with General Nelson Miles and his wife—who was Sherman's niece—at the only hotel in the little town of La Ciudad de Nuestra Señora la Reina de los Angeles, which boasted some forty thousand inhabitants! (Now a million and a half!) This leading to further reference to General Miles, I mentioned his less distinguished namesake, General Dixon S. Miles, who commanded a division at the first battle of Bull Run and was later killed in his sadly incompetent defence of Harper's Ferry; and I told a story which I had heard Colonel Waring tell. General Sherman listened with interest. Then he gravely remarked "General Dixon S. Miles is dead. He died on the field of battle." That, the last great sacrifice, absolved him from every sin—of commission or omission! And so the talk got back to California and the mid-west, where his nephew had campaigned against the Indians.

I recalled that Mrs. Miles had accompanied her husband on one of these marches, with the thermometer at thirty below zero; and she had told me how the smoke of the camp-fire had gone straight up, and, with the absence of wind, she had not noticed the cold. Which led General Sherman to talk about the joys of camp life in the invigorating climate of the west, as contrasted with the blighting effects of such eastern weather as we were then experiencing on that bleak day in February. He longed to get away from it all—the social allurements that did not allure, the damp cold that penetrated old bones, the smokey haze of the city atmosphere that got into one's lungs and gave a murky

131

tinge to one's outlook on life. But despite his com-
plainings it was evident he enjoyed New York, with
first nights at the theatres and dinners never "more
than four nights a week." His longing for western
solitudes was not as keen as he would have us believe.
All he really wanted was to have the bands stop playing
"Marching Through Georgia" whenever he appeared
in public. He said he sometimes felt like taking refuge
in the South, where he would be free of the nuisance!

He stayed till late, smoking the little cigars, and
swinging his crossed knees in homely comfort as he
rambled from one topic to another. The memory of
that night is one of the high lights in a long and varied
career. It was a nugget of fine gold I had from
William Tecumseh Sherman when he said to me "the
beacon-lights of life are its friendships!"

General David Stuart, the life-long friend of General Sherman, was the eldest son of Robert Stuart, a
partner of the first John Jacob Astor and one of the
founders of Astoria. Washington Irving has immortal-
ized the deeds of this hardy young Scot. He had three
other sons, one of whom named John, entered the navy,
and died of consumption when only twenty-eight years
old, leaving an infant daughter Frances, who became
my wife.

On May 13th, 1930, there was sold at the American
Art Galleries in New York, for $2,700, a manuscript
described in the fac-simile, copied from the auctioneer's
catalogue, which appears on the following page:—

MANUSCRIPT JOURNAL OF THE
THIRD OVERLAND EXPEDITION IN THE UNITED STATES
MADE BY ROBERT STUART
ONE OF THE PARTNERS OF JOHN JACOB ASTOR
IN THE FOUNDING OF ASTORIA
THE VALUABLE AND IMPORTANT SOURCE OF
IRVING'S DESCRIPTION OF THIS EXPEDITION IN
"ASTORIA"

192 [IRVING (WASHINGTON).] Stuart (Robert, Commander of the Expedition). MANUSCRIPT DAY-BY-DAY JOURNAL OF THE EXPEDITION FROM ASTORIA TO ST. LOUIS, 211 pp., 4to, half sheep (broken). June 29, 1812 to April 30, 1813.

THE VALUABLE AND IMPORTANT SOURCE OF INFORMATION ON THE THIRD OVERLAND EXPEDITION IN THE UNITED STATES, AND THE SECOND EXPEDITION FROM WEST TO EAST, FROM NOTES TAKEN ON THE ROUTE. This manuscript appears to be the completed copy of the journal written and extended from the rough notes of Robert Stuart jotted down from day to day during this long and terrible journey, for the use and information of John Jacob Astor; and by Mr. Astor turned over to Washington Irving, who, with certain deletions, practically transcribed it in Vol. II., pp. 84-184, of the first edition of "Astoria". Mr. Irving wrote on the fly-leaf of the journal: *"Retour de l'embouchure de la Colombia jusqu'a au Missouri par——& six personnes."* This journal was found in a cupboard at Sunnyside by E. M. Grinnell, grand-nephew of Washington Irving, and has remained in possession of the family till now. It is also the Journal from which the route of the expedition shown on the map in "Astoria" was compiled as indicated by the pencilled directions and distances in the margin.

THE JOURNAL IS ONE OF THE MOST REMARKABLE ACCOUNTS OF EARLY WESTERN EXPLORATION FOR MINUTE DETAIL AND CLEAR AND VIVID DESCRIPTION. Mr. Astor had been without news of his colony on the Pacific for over two years, and in April Reed started overland with despatches but was robbed by the Indians and forced to turn back. Robert Stuart then volunteered for the mission and on the 29th of June, 1812 set out from Astoria accompanied by Ramsey Crooks and Robert McClellan, dissatisfied partners who wished to return East, John Day, Benjamin Jones, Andre Vallée and Francois Leclaire. The first 26 pages of the journal describe the Indian tribes on the Columbia river, their mariners and customs, numbers, etc., in detail; and indeed, throughout the journey every tribe encountered is as thoroughly described as circumstances permitted, and these, in many cases, are THE FIRST DESCRIPTIONS OF THE INDIAN TRIBES. On the trip up the Columbia, John Day, the hunter, became insane and was sent back to Astoria. On July 31st the party purchased horses from the Walla Wallas and directed their course into the Snake River region. They followed the course of the Snake River to its source in the Rocky Mountains, where on the 19th of September the Crow Indians robbed them of all their horses. Thence on foot they started across the Rocky Mountains, and apparently DISCOVERED THE FAMOUS SOUTH PASS, which discovery was claimed by Ashley eleven years later. With practically nothing to eat for days, it was finally proposed by Le Claire to cast lots that one might be killed to supply the others with food; an opportune old bull buffalo saved them from this extreme measure. On Nov. 2nd they pitched camp for the winter and stocked it with provisions, but were driven out by the Indians in December, and finally camped on the head-waters of the Platte River. Breaking camp in March, they proceeded down the banks of the river on foot to the Indian trading station and thence by canoe to St. Louis.

[DESCRIPTION CONCLUDED ON NEXT PAGE]

[NUMBER 192]

Washington Irving made almost a verbatim cópy of this journal in "Astoria", leaving out some gruesome details and embellishing it with a few highly dramatic but fictitious incidents. It is not strange, therefore, that the London Spectator in reviewing "Astoria" states that Irving "has retained the raciness of his authorities".

IMPORTANT AS A SCIENTIFIC RECORD. The direction and distance of each day's march is recorded in the margins; the animal life is described in detail, especially the fur-bearing animals in which Mr. Astor was interested. He notes the character of the soil; the kind and amount of timber; the numerous mineral springs, salt basins, and other natural characteristics.

THERE ARE BUT FEW OF THE OVERLAND JOURNALS THAT RANK IN IMPORTANCE WITH ROBERT STUART'S, AND NONE THAT EXCEED IT IN ACCURATE, VIVID DESCRIPTION.

[SEE ILLUSTRATION]

This manuscript of 211 pages, in a beautiful Spencerian hand, without any erasure, was an elaborated transcript of a journal which Robert Stuart kept from day to day as he led his expedition through the uncharted regions of the Great West. Lacking ink, he had recourse to the juice of wild berries for his writing; and it is emblematic of his heroic devotion to duty that, despite the attacks of Indians, the hardships of travel, often without food or shelter, he kept this record until he reached civilization. Washington Irving, in his great work *Astoria*, tells how Stuart met a proposal to cast lots that one should be killed to supply the others with food:

As they were preparing for the third time to lay (sic) down to sleep without a mouthful to eat, Le Clerc, one of the Canadians, gaunt and wild with hunger, approached Mr. Stuart with his gun in his hand. "It was all in vain," he said, "to attempt to proceed any farther without food. They had a barren plain before them, three or four days journey in extent, on which nothing was to be procured. They must all perish before they could get to the end of it. It was better, therefore, that one should die to save the rest." He proposed, therefore, that they should cast lots; adding, as an inducement for Mr. Stuart to assent to the proposition, that he, as leader of the party, should be exempted.

Mr. Stuart shuddered at the horrible proposition, and endeavored to reason with the man, but his words were unavailing. At length, snatching up a rifle, he threatened to shoot him on the spot if he persisted. The famished wretch dropped on his knees, begged pardon in the most abject terms, and promised never again to offend him with such a suggestion.

Quiet being restored to the forlorn encampment, each one sought repose. Mr. Stuart, however, was so exhausted by the agitation of the past scene, acting on his emaciated frame, that

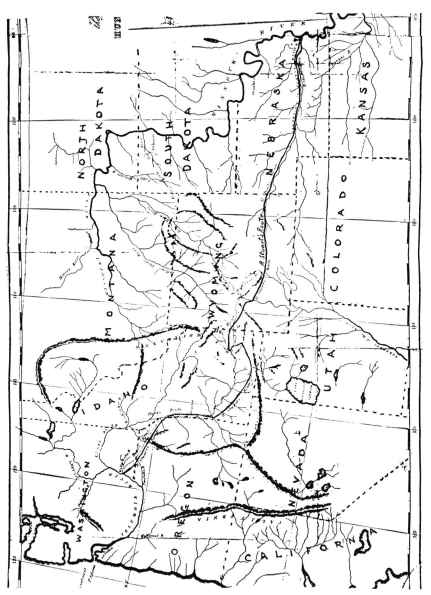

MAP OF ROBERT STUART'S ROUTE FROM ASTORIA IN 1812

he could scarcely crawl to his miserable couch; where, notwith-standing his fatigues, he passed a sleepless night, revolving upon their dreary situation, and the desperate prospect before them.

The route traversed by this heroic little band is indicated on the accompanying map, made for me by my friend Frederick S. Dellenbaugh, who accompanied Major Powell in his remarkable trip through the Grand Cañon of the Colorado in 1871-2-3.

Soon after his adventurous return to civilization, Robert Stuart married and took his wife to Mackinac Island, where he continued as one of Astor's partners in the Southwest Fur Company, successor of the American Fur Company. Here David was born, in 1815. In the '30's the Stuarts removed to Detroit, to a home on Woodbridge Street, between Hastings and Rivard Streets; and later, Robert Stuart built the Stuart mansion on Jefferson Avenue. He was an influential whig and was State Treasurer in 1840-41. Later he was appointed Indian agent, succeeding H. R. Schoolcraft, whose writings occupied much of my time and attention while working with Herbert Spencer. Stuart thus served from 1843 to 1845 and was then appointed to supervise the construction of the Joliet Canal. He died in Chicago about 1848.

Old David Stuart, who had accompanied him on his trip around the Horn and joined in founding Astoria, lived in the Jefferson Avenue mansion as a member of the family; the west wing, afterwards used as an office by Dr. Morse Stewart (no relation) being built expressly for his accommodation. He died in the house a few years before the death of his nephew Robert.

David Stuart, Robert's eldest son, is described by a contemporary as "one of the most brilliant lawyers that ever pleaded before a Detroit court. He was also a popular democrat politician and represented Wayne County in the Thirty-third Congress. He was nearly five feet eleven inches in height and weighed about 165 pounds, with a symmetrical, vigorous frame and elastic step, grey eyes, bushy brown hair, and handsome features—graceful in action, dashing in carriage, magnetic in manner, and distinguished in appearance. A gay fashionable man, he had the entree of the best circles in society and was also popular in all classes." When the war broke out, he was the leading lawyer of Chicago. He immediately gave up his lucrative practice, organized two regiments in Cook County and took the field with one of them. He was lieutenant-colonel of the Forty-second Illinois and Colonel of the Fifty-fifth. At the battle of Shilo he commanded a brigade, and was wounded, but refused to leave the field. He was brevetted as brigadier-general, and Sherman, who admired his courage and skill as a soldier, recommended him for the full grade. President Lincoln nominated him, but political enemies interfered and prevented his appointment. He died in Detroit in 1868, and was buried near his father and mother in Elmwood cemetery, in a lot adjoining that of Lewis Cass.

His two brothers, John and Robert, both joined the navy. John, my wife's father, was sailing master of U. S. S. Lexington in 1853, and his record of a voyage around the Horn and back has recently been placed among the archives of the Explorers Club. Robert resigned from the navy after John's death, and when the war broke out volunteered his services and joined the Ira Harris light cavalry. While on duty in Virginia, he was drowned in Acquia Creek and his body was brought to Roslyn, Long Island, where his widow erected the imposing clock tower that marks the place. His daughter, Virginia, because of her beauty and wealth, was the toast of the young bucks of Washington in the early seventies; but she disappointed them all by marrying a poor clergyman, Alexander Mackay-Smith, who reached episcopal honors as the bishop of Pennsylvania. Their daughter in turn became the bride of the German naval attache Boy-Ed, whose activities in the interests of the Fatherland during the Great War resulted in his expulsion from the United States.

General Stuart had also a sister, who married the founder of Baker City, Oregon, to which he gave his name.

Byron is said to have compared great families to growing potatoes, the best part being usually under ground. This seems to be the case here. The male members have died off, the name has become only a tradition; but the son of Admiral Blue, who married one of Stuart's granddaughters, may continue its gallant history in the American navy.

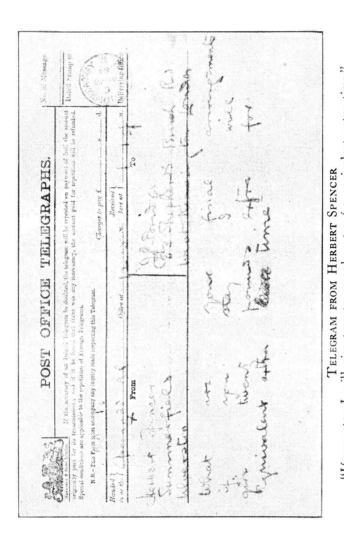

TELEGRAM FROM HERBERT SPENCER

"If you stay I will give twenty pounds extra for equivalent extra time."

EDWARD L. YOUMANS AND
"SOCIAL STATICS"

WITH AN UNUSUAL LOVE STORY

J OHN FISKE has written an excellent life of his friend, Edward Livingston Youmans, founder of the *Popular Science Monthly,* and its editor until his death in 1887. The great influence of Youmans on the scientific thought of his day cannot be overestimated. Nor can the charm of his personality. To me he was always a gracious and inspiring friend, and did much to make my early days in America, where I landed without friends or even acquaintances, far happier than I had been while serving Herbert Spencer. It was with actual pain, therefore, that I learned I had been the unwitting cause of some embarrassment to him.

Coming home from the Century Club with Henry Holt, I mentioned Spencer's discontent with the Appletons for republishing his book, *Social Statics,* without his consent; especially so as he had changed his opinions concerning some of the matters discussed therein. Mr. Holt evidently repeated this talk, which I had immediately dismissed from my mind. To my surprise and chagrin I received a letter from Prof. Youmans, which is worth preserving because of its intrinsic interest. It is dated from Thomasville, Ga., March 10th, 1885.

Dear Mr. Bridge,

. . . A letter from my brother yesterday contains a reference which moves me to send you a few words of explanation. My brother says: "Mr. Willie Appleton alluded for the second or third time to a report, which comes from Mr. Bridge, to the effect that Spencer had often objected to their publication of *Social Statics* and was very indignant about it."

The facts of the case are these. Mr. Spencer declined, for wholly sufficient reasons, to bring out a second edition of *Social Statics* in England, and he certainly objected to its being done in this country on the same grounds.

But there was a constant and an increasing call for the book both in England and here; and it was perfectly certain that it would be republished in this country by somebody. The practical question was, therefore, whether the book should be brought out in a creditable and reputable shape, uniform with his other works, and on the same terms of payment, or whether it should be picked up and pirated by some unscrupulous publisher, probably in a cheap and shabby form, and thus set the precedent for American theft of his publications. Nor was this all. A thoroughly disreputable publisher of Nassau St. named * * *, who ran a line of skeptical publications together with a line of literature as erotic as the law would allow, and which he advertised under the stereotyped heading "Those Delicious Books"—a man of notorious bad reputation and a stench in the nostrils of the decent community—was after *Social Statics* to reprint it, and came within a hairsbreadth of getting hold of a copy which I had presented to a friend in Brooklyn. I got it away; but there was no other way to block his game than to bring the book out ourselves. If * * * had got it there would have been an end of Herbert Spencer on this continent. It was in the time of the war, with strong anti-British feeling. Spencer was known only as an English infidel and materialist, with suspected leanings to laxity in the sexual relations, and * * * would have advertised the worst side of the case, while the simple fact of the association of his name with that of Spencer would have been fatal to the influence of his books and the future of his reputation here. I therefore raised $1100 to pay for the stereotyping, and, without asking Spencer's consent, brought the book out. He wrote a preface to it and imported American editions for English use. I always regretted the necessity of doing this, because I foresaw that he would be more and more annoyed as time went on with being pinned to the old text of this book. But I hold this to have been but a serious inconvenience and a small evil in comparison with what would have resulted had I not taken the responsibility of acting in the matter.

Excuse me for troubling you with these details; but I thought you might as well be aware of the circumstances.

Yours very truly,

E. L. YOUMANS.

I immediately wrote back, regretting that my thoughtlessness had caused him embarrassment, and explaining my action as best I could. Whereupon I received from Youmans this further letter, also dated from Thomasville, March 16th, '85.

Dear Mr. Bridge,

Your letter is this moment received. I was glad to get it and reposted it immediately to Mr. Willie Appleton, as it will set him at rest howsoever he got his impressions.

But I regret that you should have been annoyed at the rumor as I reported it. In writing to you I cared chiefly to inform you of the facts, for the reason that there is actual ground for Mr. Spencer's dissatisfaction. Of course he made the best of it, and as the new edition of *Social Statics* was creditably executed, was permanently on sale in the U. S., and constantly called for in England, he arranged for an English edition of the reprint. But none the less has he regretted, and I presume increasingly regretted as his views have advanced, that the book was not left to the time and circumstances that produced it. You have no occasion to disturb yourself for having stated to anybody that Spencer objected to the reprint, for that is what I have been in the habit of saying to everybody, and have written it again and again in the *Popular Science Monthly,* when Spencer has been charged with inconsistency and held to the ideas of the old book.

We continue very well down here in this much milder climate; but it is very monotonous and we shall be glad when the time comes to get out of it. My sister asks to be remembered kindly to you.   Very sincerely yours,

E. L. YOUMANS.

I have deemed it worth while to reproduce these letters because, apart from the incident that called them forth, they have some bearing on a later event. I refer to the unpleasant controversy which Henry George started over the revised edition of *Social Statics,* from

which were omitted certain parts which he had urged
as supporting his theories concerning land nationaliza-
tion and the single-tax movement; and he falsely attributed Spencer's change of heart to an unworthy desire to placate the land-owning classes of England. So
he published a book entitled *A Perplexed Philosopher*,
aimed directly at Spencer, quoting from Browning

> "Just for a handful of silver he left us,
> Just for a ribbon to stick in his coat!"

Nothing could have been more unjust, for there is nowhere in Spencer's life or writings any warrant for the
implied parallel. Large numbers of Henry George's
book are still being sold, or given away by the society
that is engaged in single-tax propaganda.

Spencer did a thoughtful act shortly before Youmans died in 1887. Fearing that neither would last
much longer, Spencer sent to Youmans, in advance of
its publication, a paragraph from his *Autobiography*.
In this he acknowledged his great debt to his American
disciple and friend, through whom the *Synthetic Philosophy* had been brought to the attention of thousands
of Americans, who would never have heard of it but
for Youmans's unselfish devotion. Here is the paragraph:—

Prof. Edward L. Youmans was, of all Americans I have
known or heard of, the one most able and most willing to help
me. Alike intellectually and morally, he had in the highest degree
the traits conducive to success in diffusing the doctrines he
espoused; and from that time to this he has devoted his life
mainly to spreading throughout the United States the doctrine
of evolution. His love of wide generalizations had been shown
years before in lectures on such topics as the correlation of the
physical forces; and from those who heard him I have gathered

that, aided by his unusual powers of exposition, the enthusiasm which contemplation of the larger truths of science produced in him was in a remarkable degree communicated to his hearers. Such larger truths I have on many occasions observed are those which he quickly seizes—ever passing at once through details to lay hold of essentials, and, having laid hold of them, he clearly sets them forth afresh in his own way with added illustrations. But it is morally even more than intellectually that he has proved himself a true missionary of advanced ideas. Extremely energetic—so energetic that no one has been able to check his overactivity—he has expended all his powers in advancing what he holds to be the truth, and not only his powers but his means. It has proved impossible to prevent him from injuring himself in health by his exertions, and it has proved impossible to make him pay due regard to his personal interests. So that toward the close of life he finds himself wrecked in body and impoverished in estate by thirty years of devotion to high ends. Among professed worshippers of humanity, who teach that human welfare should be the dominant aim, I have not yet heard of one whose sacrifices on behalf of humanity will bear comparison with those of my friend.

How great was Spencer's need of Youmans's help is indicated in a letter which the latter wrote to his sister in August 1862, describing his first meeting with the English philosopher:

His health is bad. He has not had a night's rest since he wrote the Psychology. He can't sleep, and if he does he wakes ten or twenty times during the night. He is very excitable, and when excited cannot sleep at all, gets alarmed at the state of his brain, and flies from the scene of danger. He undertook to attend to some Derby ladies at the exposition, and had to fly from the city before his time.

As respects his business the poor man has had a troubled time indeed. His books have never paid him anything, but, on the contrary, have weighed him down like a millstone. Five hundred copies of the Psychology were published; three hundred remain on his hands. The Social Statics has done better. Seven hundred and fifty were published eleven years ago, and the edition is nearly exhausted. None of them are stereotyped, and so the several editions will shortly be out of print, and he says he shall not try it again. Five hundred Education were printed, and two hundred are sold. He was desirous of doing something to circulate them, so he bound up some cheaper, to be sent by mail to teachers if they desired. Twelve copies were thus disposed of, with the result of giving mortal offence to the book trade, who are down upon the work in consequence of this informality. To crown his experience, his publisher, George Manwaring, has failed within three months whereby he loses everything from the Education, and enough more on his other publications to make his loss five hundred dollars. As respects the First Principles, notwithstanding all the efforts, the whole thing would have been exploded and abandoned this summer but for some means which he obtained from the death of an uncle. By using that little capital he has been enabled to maintain the project and live. He did not say much to me about his experience, but alluded to it two or three times in a very simple and touching way in connection with the assistance he had received from America. That is all the profit he has ever yet had from his work, and he said it was as grateful and opportune as it was unexpected. . . . When I looked upon the man, with his health broken and nerves shattered, and remembered that his is the foremost intellect of our civilization, and that he is a man beyond all other men of his age to control the thought of the future; when I thought of him hampered and harassed for want of means to publish his great thoughts—as having to think for the world and then having to pay the expense of instruction, I confess I thank God that I had had a little opportunity to do him service. Dear sister, let us respect ourselves more that we saw through the obscurity of distance the genuine and exalted claims of this unheralded man, and were led to help him in a way that he most needed help.

147

John Fiske, quoting this letter in his Memoir, says:

The publication of these books (in America) was an experiment entirely due to Youmans's urgency. As soon as they were ready for the market he wrote reviews of them, and by no means in the usual perfunctory way. His reviews and notices were turned out by the score, and scattered about in the magazines and newspapers where they would do the most good. Not content with this, he made numerous pithy and representative extracts for the reading columns of various daily and weekly papers. Whenever he found another writer who could be pressed into the service, he would give him Spencer's books, kindle him with a spark from his own blazing enthusiasm, and set him to writing for the press. The effects of this work were multifarious and far-reaching, and—year in and year out—it was never for a moment allowed to flag. The most indefatigable vender of wares was never more ruthlessly persistent in advertising for lucre's sake than Edward Youmans in preaching in a spirit of the purest disinterestedness the gospel of evolution. As long as he lived Mr. Spencer had upon this side of the Atlantic an *alter ego* ever on the alert, with vision like that of a hawk for the slightest chance to promote his interests and those of his system of thought.

Youmans told me of a somewhat romantic event— it was more than an incident—in his life. During his boyhood he was almost blind. Living on a farm, his experiments were made with great difficulty until he enlisted the aid of a young farm-hand, who mixed various chemicals as instructed, and described the results to the blind boy sitting near. At times Youmans's sight would return, and then, in the enthusiasm of discovery, he would overwork his eyes and drop back into sightlessness. The young farm-hand was intelligent, and apt in learning from these experiments. When the Civil War came, the boy volunteered for service; and the slight knowledge of chemistry he had acquired with Youmans caused his selection as apothecary's assistant. After the war, some of the officers of his regiment, who had become attached to him, subscribed enough money to pay for his passage to Europe and for his studies at a medical school. On his return to America with a degree, he called on Youmans, who had partly recovered his sight, but was always subject to its loss if he used his eyes to read or write. The young doctor, on hearing this, exclaimed "I think I can help you," and rushed away to his lodgings. He presently returned with a leather case, which on being opened revealed a lot of round glasses in little partitions. Fitting a pair of these into a frame, he put them in front of Youmans's eyes and asked "Can you see now?" "No, not as well as before," was the reply. "How now?" asked the doctor as he substituted another pair of lenses. And so he went on, applying one set of glasses after another, until Youmans, growing excited, exclaimed that he could see! And that is how he got his sight, and was able thereafter to read and write. But he never learned to spell. He used to say that our system of spelling was so illogical that no one could learn it without doing violence to his reasoning faculties—if he had any!

This was the first time the now-familiar apparatus, used by opticians on nearly all of us, was seen in America: the young protegé of Youmans introduced it.

Another romance is associated with Youmans, or rather with his wife, a gracious and sweet little hostess, as I always found her. As a young girl she had an admirer, the brother of her most intimate friend; but she was uncertain of her own feelings. This young man, whose name was William L. Lee, having received a negative to his proposal of marriage, decided to migrate to Oregon, where he thought his opportunities as a surveyor would be greater than in a little New England coast-town. The trip, in the Forties was a formidable one, round the Horn and up the South American coast. Great was the excitement in the village; and the young lady, whose uncertainty had inspired the voyage, grew less uncertain as the day of sailing grew near. Woman-like she hesitated until the very morning of her lover's departure, when she wrote and sent a letter accepting him. Too late! The ship had sailed; and months must pass before she could reach him with any message.

The ship stopped at Honolulu, to take on provisions and water. Young Lee was tempted to stay there, having received an advantageous offer from the king, Kamehameha III., to assist in surveying and laying out roads throughout the islands. Informing his family of his change of plans, he asked, in his letter to his sister —which she naturally read to her friend—to have sent out to him certain of his belongings, including a long tin cylinder of drawings. This cylinder was about to be sealed by the sister when her young visitor said: "Don't close that for a few minutes." Running home, she soon returned with the letter which had come back to her after the sailing of the ship several months before. This letter, in its unopened state, telling the story of a young girl's regret and disappointment, was dropped into the tin cylinder and sent on its weary way to Honolulu. The ship that carried it was lost, as were all of the things sent to Lee—all but the tin cylinder, which being sealed, floated, and was picked up after the wreck. In

the course of time, a long and anxious time as we may
believe, the cylinder and its priceless contents reached
young Lee. Imagine his feelings, if we can—dismay at
what he deemed his needless departure from his home,
anxiety over the lapse of time since the missive was
despatched on its long voyage, and the possible change
of heart that his inexplicable silence in regard to it
might have occasioned, mixed with the joy of learning
that his love had finally met with response in the maiden
herself! And now the difficulty of profiting by it! There
was no four-day mail service between Honolulu and
America in those days. Ships occasionally stopped at
the Sandwich Islands on their way from the Horn to
the upper coast of America; but there was no regularity about them, either coming or going. The position
Lee held under the king was, for a youngster, a lucrative one. He was torn between conflicting desires. It
fortunately chanced, however, that a missionary friend
and his wife were about to return to New England; and
with these he despatched a letter, telling the young lady
of his difficulties, but offering to return to America, and
give up his hopes of preferment in Honolulu, if she felt
she could not make the journey in the company of his
missionary friends, when they came back to Owyhee
after a brief stay in their home town.

Here again were mingled feelings, this time in the
breast of the maid. The trip around the Horn was not
to be lightly undertaken, to say nothing of the unusual
course suggested, that she leave her home to take a long
and dangerous voyage to a lover whom she had not
seen for two years, and to whom she had not been formally plighted. After what we may believe was her
own indecision, augmented by contradictory advice of

friends and family, she ended the suspense of those about her by deciding to take the long voyage to her lover. The news of her intended departure on such a romantic mission spread throughout the country-side, and caused great excitement in a simple community, in which a voyage to Owyhee (Hawaii) was like a trip to the moon. Some years ago, I met an elderly lady in New York who told me how she had stood, a little girl at her mother's side, as they traced on a map the course which the bride-to-be would have to take to reach her savage destination.

The ship arrived in due course. It was Sunday morning, and the entire population was at church. But the service was cut short, and everybody, including of course young Lee, hastened to the beach. Lee was unwilling that his bride should land until the marriage ceremony had taken place; and so he hastened on board, and there the lovers were married.

Lee stayed in the islands and prospered, becoming known in their history as Judge Lee, and having an important part in their development. He died there in 1857 a wealthy man; and years afterwards his widow married Prof. Youmans. They lived in what I believe was the first cooperative building in New York—the Knickerbocker, at the corner of Fifth Ave. and 28th St. where I often enjoyed their hospitality, and where Mrs. Youmans told me this story.

Dr. Titus Munson Coan, whose father was one of the first American missionaries in Hawaii, told me that Mrs. Youmans—who survived her second husband— intended to leave a part of her fortune to his children for their education; but on her death, nothing of value, except the furniture, was found in her home. And he always wondered what had become of the riches she was known to have had. Perhaps another romance, if it were known!

JAMES HOWARD BRIDGE
Photo by M. J. Boris

THE ELEGANT EIGHTIES AND THE GENIAL NINETIES.

SOME RANDOM RECOLLECTIONS

ALONE and friendless, but full of hope and a spirit of high adventure, I landed in New York in October, 1884. It was a bright autumnal morning. The harbor scintillated and smiled in the golden light like a benediction. Fussy little steamers with splashy paddle-wheels and grotesque "walking-beams" swinging above their decks, moved laboriously hither and thither over the shining water. Having seen, at the Paris Exposition in '79, the gigantic head of Bartoldi's Statue of Liberty, I looked for her gracious welcome, but in vain: Bedloe's Island was bare except for a few shabby buildings. The city itself, seen from the harbor, was in no way impressive. The highest building was the red tower of the Produce Exchange, recently built, vying with the steeple of Trinity Church, soon to be dwarfed by the sky-piercing towers of Commerce.

We were put ashore at the Barge Office at the Battery, where, before Ellis Island, so many millions of immigrants, seeking a new country and fresh opportunities, first pressed the soil of the Land of Hope. For some reason that day, cabin passengers were transferred to a tender in the bay, and put ashore in the huge shed usually reserved for steerage passengers. This made me one with them!

THE BLIZZARD OF '88
Note the network of telegraph wires.

Knowing no one in the great city, I left my modest
luggage at the Barge Office and walked up Broadway.
It was crowded with omnibusses, cabs, trucks and other
horse-drawn vehicles. There were no horse-cars, for
Jake Sharp had not yet got his unpopular charter to

build tracks along its narrow length. The side-walks were rough and uneven, often purposely made so to keep people from slipping in winter weather. On every block was a giant telegraph pole, holding aloft a net-work of wires that almost hid the sky. The buildings were all of three or four stories in height, being mostly private houses converted into offices and shops.

As I neared Wall Street I heard a great hubbub in a basement, and I went down some dirty stone steps to see what it meant. It was a sort of exchange, where a shout-ing, pushing crowd of men was dealing in oil or some such thing in ways I did not understand. The pulling, struggling mass of humanity was a shocking and de-pressing sight to one who had just come with high hopes of a career along intellectual lines; and it was not until I reached the serene beauty of Grace Church that I recovered my normal hopefulness.

There I turned off Broadway. In Eleventh Street, encouraged by a paper sticker fastened to a door-post, announcing "vacancies," I found a hall bed-room that met my modest needs, and engaged it pending develop-ments. I then walked back to the Battery to recover my little box.

The next day was Sunday. Drawn as by a lodestone, I walked up Fifth Avenue to the Windsor Hotel, where Herbert Spencer had stopped while in New York two years before. Little did I think, as I stood fascinated before its red-brick splendor, that it was to be my New York home for many years—until, in fact, it was de-stroyed by fire on St. Patrick's day in 1899.

Fifth Avenue was then a badly paved street, lined with high-stoop houses of brown stone, all looking alike. And they were alike inside, as I soon found: a front parlor separated from a back parlor by curtains or folding doors, and as gloomy as heavy draperies, plush furniture and dark woodwork could make them— "mass production" in domestic architecture and furnishings, bereft of beauty. But the cloudless sky, the exhilarating autumnal air, the prosperous crowds that peopled the streets, gave a zest to my explorations that freed me from loneliness and filled me with hope.

Spencer had given me, better than a purse of gold, a letter to Professor Youmans, who had long served as his American *alter ego*. This is it:

> 38 Queens Gardens,
> Bayswater, London,
> Sep. 25/84.

My dear Youmans,

The bearer of this, who is also the writer of it to my dictation, is one whose hand you are thoroughly familiar with, as being presented to you in my letters of several years past.

Mr. James H. Bridge, who has been my secretary during these years, has decided to push his fortunes in America. I have on more than one occasion endeavored to dissuade him, for the reason that stress of life with you, especially in all the higher occupations, is so great that none save those with very strong constitutions are likely to stand it. However, he has various reasons for making the attempt to find a career in the U. S. which outweigh all the deterrents which I have put before him— reasons which he will probably communicate to you himself, and which I am in thorough sympathy with.

He has served me very well as secretary; having besides his ability as a shorthand writer, a good knowledge of French and a considerable knowledge of German and Spanish; add to which he has been able to further my work in such ways as I have pointed out by inquiries intelligently pursued. He will, I think, be a desirable assistant to anyone having literary undertakings on hand.

158

Perhaps if anything falls in your way likely to be suitable you will keep him in mind.

P. S. Let Mr. Bridge have this back again when you have read it. It may serve other purposes.

Ever yours,
HERBERT SPENCER.

When I went early on Monday morning to present this letter at Appleton's big building in Bond Street, which they shared with the Waltham Watch Co., I found that Professor Youmans—as he was called to distinguish him from his brother, in the same office, who was called Doctor—was absent in the country. But Doctor Youmans greeted me as an old friend, and advised me to call on Andrew Carnegie, which I immediately did.

Mr. Carnegie received me and my Spencer letter with a characteristic burst of friendliness. I was just the man he was looking for, he said; he was about to write a history of the material development of the United States during the preceding fifty years, and I was to go forthwith to Mr. John Denison Champlin, at Scribners in Broadway near Grace Church, who would take me to the Astor Library in Lafayette Place, and show me just what researches I should make for use in the forthcoming book—not yet started! It was like a fairy story, for I was to fix my own salary! Thus began a life-long friendship with John Denison Champlin, whose son, thirty years later, married my daughter, and whose grandson, the fourth of the name, is also my own. I may say, by the way, that although I did not know it at the time, I fixed my salary higher than that Mr. Champlin was himself receiving from the Scribners! His astonishment was mixed with admiration!

When Professor Youmans returned to town he was gratified to find that I had already found a niche for myself in the New World; and thereafter he set himself to make that niche more agreeable than the one I had left by the side of Herbert Spencer. He gave me a seat at his home table, had his dear wife take me out to social functions, got a guest-card for me at the Century Club, then conveniently near in East 15th Street, and introduced me to his many friends in the Authors Club. I wish he could have known that forty years later I should be elected to the presidency of this club; he would have been gratified.

All this of course was very surprising to me—and very delightful; and in my youthful exuberance I tactfully suggested to Spencer that again his induction was killed by a fact when he urged me to give up my idea of leaving him to seek wider opportunities in the New World. His reply was prompt:

38 Queens Gardens W.

Decr. 3rd. 1884

Dear Bridge,

I am glad to learn from your letter that you had so quickly met with an opening so favorable as that you describe.

I did not give you a letter of introduction to Mr. Carnegie, because he would have felt put under pressure by it in a way I did not wish. As it happened, however, in the absence of Youmans, your call upon him served equally well if not better. You ought to make your position with him one satisfactory to both; and I should think it not unlikely you will do so.

I am glad that you named to me the fact about the duty paid by Youmans on the bust. It was stupid of me not to think of the probability that he would be taxed in that way and had I hereafter learned the fact when too late, I should have been very much vexed. As it is I have put the matter all right by sending him a check for the amount.

160

It was fortunate also that you were able to tell Youmans the facts with regard to Tylor. The circumstance that you yourself found the second volume uncut was of course conclusive.

I shall be glad to hear from time to time how you are getting on.   Truly yours

HERBERT SPENCER.

The reference to Tylor had to do with a controversy in which Spencer had been charged with borrowing something, without acknowledgment, from *Primitive Culture,* or some other of Tylor's books. The bust was one of Spencer, a replica of that now in the National Portrait Gallery.

At Youmans' hospitable board I met George Iles, who, after a lapse of nearly half a century, remains one of my dearest friends. He, as well as our host, was engaged in popularizing in America the writings of Spencer, Huxley, Tyndall and others of the great English scientists who have revolutionized the thoughts of mankind the world over. His gift of lucid exposition of the new conceptions of the universe was almost as great as that of Youmans himself; and had he followed Huxley's advice, he would have made this his life work instead of subordinating it to more profitable activities that have given him leisure and comfort in his old age. In this he was wiser than either Huxley or Youmans, who shortened their lives by excessive altruism.

At the Century Club I met many men of mark who alas! are almost if not quite forgotten amid the present giddy-paced rush and bustle. I recall an interesting talk with Professor Marsh of Yale, who discovered the three-toed horse in the fossil rocks of Wyoming. I got to know and like Professor Rood of Columbia College, whose work in physics laid the foundation of many later discoveries which have had important commercial uses. He always wore a red tie. Then there was Calvert Vaux who, with Frederick Law Olmstead, had much to do with the making of Central Park; Paul du Chaillu, the great African explorer, who endured so much ridicule because of his Munchausen-like stories of gorillas, which no one believed; Edgar Fawcett, the poet; Hamilton Wright Mabie, who has left a dozen books of essays that are read to-day; Gordon Hammersley a rich episcopalian of ritualistic tendencies, who gave me an elaborately printed book he had written on Chemical Changes in the Eucharist! And many others who have escaped my memory. Somehow it seems as if the men of that time were more important, more interesting than those of to-day: they had fewer interests, but they concentrated on them.

Distance usually diminishes the apparent size of objects seen. The contemplation of remote personages has the opposite effect. There were giants in the Authors Club in those days. The Executive Committee in 1884 contained the names of Oliver B. Bunce, author of a little book of apothegms, *Don't,* which everybody and his wife quoted; H. C. Bunner, whose witticisms filled the room, escaped through the open window, billowed across the city and flew all over the world; S. S. Conant, editor of *Harpers Weekly,* who mysteriously disappeared between his office and his home in Staten Island, and has never been heard of since; George Cary Eggleston, Richard Watson Gilder, whose patronimic fittingly described his function, George Parsons Lathrop, Brander Matthews and E. L. Youmans. These were my gracious hosts in the little hallowed rooms over the Fencers' Club, at 19 West 24th Street, where I reverently watched them absorb mysterious salads and bottled beer just like any common mortals.

I spent most of my evenings in the cosy rooms of the Century Club during that first month or two, for my guest-card was courteously renewed. One night as I walked across Fourteenth Street on my way to my solitary room, I saw the horses taken from the carriage of Adelina Patti and, amid a wild scene of enthusiasm, ropes were fastened to it and a hundred men and boys ran shouting with it to the Brevoort House, where the Diva was stopping. The Academy of Music in Fourteenth Street was the home of opera in those days. Then there were ten-mile processions of curiously-garbed men carrying torches up Fifth Avenue, and shouting in unison that "British gold would not wash in that crowd," or vociferating inquiries as of "Ma" to the whereabouts of "Pa"! They were thus advocating the election to the presidency of James G. Blaine instead of Grover Cleveland. A night or two later came another procession, equally noisy and equally solicitous about certain Mulligan letters which Mr. Blaine was said to have written, and the crowd marched with military step urging those who watched them to "Burn, burn, burn this letter!" They also called in unison upon a "dear, dear, dear Mrs. Fisher!" It was all very confusing, but apparently "a good time was had by all."

In London I had sung in a choir under the direction of Sir Joseph Barnby, known everywhere for his graceful quartette "Sweet and Low" and many other more pretentious compositions. I thought to do the like in New York, and joined the New York Choral Society, consisting of three score or more of fashionable young

163

folks, who met for practice in Steck Hall in East 14th Street, and gave several concerts during the winter in Chickering Hall, at the corner of Fifth Avenue and 18th Street. Some of these singers came from up-town to the rehearsals in carriages attended by footmen. Steck Hall, if it exists, is a long way from the Mecca Temple, both in time and space! And Chickering Hall, where fashion gathered, is but a memory—and not much of that!

Heloïse Durant, daughter of Doctor Durant, the railroad builder of that day, wrote an operetta, "Kismet," which was given at Chickering Hall to a large and fashionable audience. It was repeated at the University Club, near Gilmore's Garden in Madison Square —where Diana later dwelt on a lofty tower, copied by Stanford White from the Giralda in Seville. I was captain of Janisseries in this operetta; Mrs. Fremont, the beautiful daughter-in-law of the "Pathfinder," was the Sultana. Miss Edwalyn Coffey, a veritable thistledown of fairy movement—later Mrs. Charles de Kay and mother of half a dozen or more handsome children, now men and women, with children of their own—executed an oriental dance with Willie Grinnell and Lorimer Stoddard, son of the poet. Stoddard, a serious-minded youth, trod the measure with a solemnity that made the part funny by contrast with Grinnell's roguish playfulness. He afterwards dramatized "Tess of the D'Urbervilles" with much success, but died before his high promise reached fulfilment.

Grinnell lived with his parents in a large ornate mansion overlooking the river at Audubon Park, where the new section of Riverside Drive now curves under the magnificent buildings forming the Medical Center. This was then all open country; and what is now the extended drive was a narrow lane, hardly wide enough for one buggy to pass another, with high hedges on each side. At dinner, we used to watch through the open window the "Mary Powell" as she passed up the river at the foot of the lawn. Grinnell *père* was the son of Moses Grinnell, the famous banker and founder of the Union League Club. He financed an expedition for the search of Sir John Franklin, lost in the Arctic, and Grinnell Land was named for him. Willie Grinnell died a few years ago, leaving to the City a large and valuable collection of *objets d'art* he had made.

At the New Year's party of 1885 at the Windsor Hotel, Mr. Carnegie asked me to come and live with him, so that there would be someone to look after his mother during his frequent absences in Pittsburgh. She was approaching her seventieth year, a kindly, sweet but somewhat dominant personality. I naturally accepted the flattering invitation, and thereafter lived as a member of the Carnegie family until Andrew's marriage in 1887. During his absences from home I took his place with his mother. Invariably as she took my arm to go in to dinner, she would notice that I was dressed as for a party, and smilingly comment on the fast life I was leading. "Going out again," she would say with the quaintest of Scotch burrs, "My, but ye're a gr-reat gadaboot!" And finding some lady to spend the evening playing cribbage with her, so that she would not be lonely, I would hurry away to some concert or rehearsal of the Choral Society, or a meeting of the Piano Club. This was what she thought a fast life!

Just round the corner in East 47th Street was another club, which met weekly. It was held in the home of a

Russian countess, Madam Neftel, and was known as the Drawing Room Club. There I met the younger set of New York fashionables, most of whom I have forgotten. I recall Alexander Lambert, who became a central figure in the musical life of the city, Maud Morgan the harpest, George Edgar Montgomery, a poet, whose works have not survived him, Dr. John S. White, head of the Berkeley School, who afterwards bought the old Columbia College buildings in East 49th Street, where Mrs. Barnard and her two beautiful nieces, daughters of General Barnard, used to hold Monday receptions. Dr. White got one of the Gould boys, who had been his pupil, to join him in the purchase of the Columbia property; and he told me that young Gould showed his heredity by capturing all the profits of the transaction!

Those receptions of Mrs. Barnard were characteristic of the period—a mixed crowd in the restricted space of the front and back parlors, moving about with tea-cups, mutual elbowings and apologies, greeting old acquaintances and, in my case, making new ones. Munroe Smith, Hjalmar Hjorth Boyesen and his charming American wife, Stephen H. Thayer, the banker-poet, Mrs. (General) Custer, Calvin Thomas, Professor Rood, Bronson Howard and his wife—of whom more anon, Mrs. Youmans and many other delightful people who have left a fragrant memory with me. President Barnard, who was almost deaf, usually came in for a few minutes, and embarrassed those of us who were not accustomed to an ear-tube by thrusting the end of it at us, and bidding us pour into it the joke at which we had been laughing. Having a contrary purpose, it was yet as destructive of conversation as were Herbert Spencer's ear-pads.

166

At one of these functions Boyesen and I exchanged a few words in German, which led his pretty wife to remark that she had tried to learn that difficult language and had given it up. I thereupon offered to send her directions that would facilitate the study of it; and I have found the draft of them in my Scrivener's Wallet:

A few simple rules for beginners in German.

To properly pronounce this beautiful language, you must clear your throat—not before speaking, but while speaking.

At first carefully rinse your mouth before resuming English. Later you may get to like the flavor of German, and season your English with it. Nothing is prettier than English with a German flavor.

Practise the sound of Ch alone—and beyond the reach of missiles.

Remember that a maid has no gender, that a table is masculine and masculine things often feminine. You may thus correctly say: The maid, it takes a potatoe and peels him and on the table him places; him (the table) it (the maid) then already in the corner (feminine) sticks.

"Already yet" (noch schon) is one of the three things not verboten in Germany.

Whenever you get involved in a long sentence and don't know how to end it, ring in "bin geworden sein." Literally it means "am become to be," and to German minds is logically correct.

Learn a few starting phrases to give yourself time to think of what's coming. Thus: Bitte; Können Sie mir sagen? or Darf Ich fragen, sagen u. s. w. "Und so weiter" is a good thing to end with. It means etcetera, and is written U.S.W. but in small letters.

Get your verbs as far away from your nominative as you can; and split them up into fragments whenever possible. This gives great relief, and may enable you to avoid the use of unladylike

167

expletives. This breaking up of German verbs is about the only injury you can do to the language, and at times you will be glad to smash things even to this extent.

In some parts of Germany they begin some words as if they had an ill-fitting dental equipment in the mouth and it is a sign of breeding. Thus sp is pronounced schp, or st, scht. Get this at any cost; it is very beautiful when you are hardened to it.

"HELL!" That only means "bright."

Gewiss, wirklich, wunderbar, colossal; a few exclamations of this sort will easily enable you to carry on a conversation.

Gemütlich is something the Germans think peculiarly theirs, and they are very proud of it. They pretend no other language has its equivalent and no other race the virtue it describes. You, my dear lady, have unconsciously been it ever since I have known you.

Sing "Lorelei" when you are very happy. It begins: Ich weiss nicht wass soll es bedeuten dass Ich so traurig bin. Helen Keller once recited this to me. She is deaf and blind. But really healthy Germans in their happiest hours sing: "I don't know what it means that I am so sad!" I could tell them, but they might not like it!*

"DU BIST" is not what its sound would indicate.

The sun is feminine, the moon masculine. That's because only men should go out at night.

W is sounded like V, and V like F. Germans speaking English, for some reason valid only to the Teuton mind, reverse this habit and pronounce V like W, and F like V. I suspect it's because they hate the English.

Don't try to conjugate "pfeifen." Whistle it.

Here endeth the first lesson!

Another club—they were the fashion of the day— was the Nineteenth Century Club, founded by Court- land Palmer. It first met at his house in Gramercy Park,

---

* Just as Americans, in their expansive moments, joyously carol: "All the world is sad and weary!"

but outgrowing this, he moved it to the Art Auction rooms at the corner of Broadway and 23rd Street over-looking Madison Square. In a little book, *Uncle Sam at Home,* published in 1888, I described this club:

It is a curious amalgam of fashion and intellect. Writers of repute from other cities and members of the club read papers or make speeches on all conceivable topics, while the members and their friends to the number of about five hundred, sit around on camp-chairs in all the glory of swallow-tails and decolleté dresses. Here intellectual gems vie in brilliancy with diamond bracelets, and shapely necks and heaving bosoms divide your attention with glowing thoughts and well-turned phrases. It is a heavenly combination! The club has no constitution. Its motto, "Prove all things; hold fast that which is good," indicates the width of its hearth. Round it in friendly converse, gather Cath-olic priests, Unitarian and Baptist ministers, Free-thinkers, Agnostics, Positivists, Socialists, Cremationists, and thinkers of every possible type, but always of good calibre. It is indeed a microcosm of the world—except that grumblers are excluded. Round this center of light and leading gyrate smaller social systems, with all their attendant orbs and satellites, spreading far across space—from Madison Square to Harlem and Hobo-ken—and dotting the intellectual firmament with an infinitude of lesser lights.

Through Mr. Carnegie's influence and the friend-ship of Mr. Courtland Palmer I was privileged to belong to this exclusive club almost from its formation. With the late John W. Alexander, who became one of America's great painters, and Mr. William Travers Jerome, whose militant activities when district attor-ney of the City of New York made him famous, I proudly served as official usher at the club receptions. We were all three very young, and bore our duties seriously and our ribbon-boutonnières with dignity.

Millionaires and Grub Street

When Courtland Palmer died in July, 1888, I was in California, and Colonel Robert G. Ingersoll was thoughtful enough to send me a number of newspaper cuttings descriptive of the beautiful way in which this brave spirit met his end. From these I select a short editorial from the *New York World* of Friday, July 27, 1888:

AN AGNOSTIC'S END

The brave and even cheerful manner in which that pronounced free-thinker, Courtland Palmer, met his end cannot fail to attract attention.

"The general impression is," he said, just before submitting to the operation which he was assured would almost inevitably be fatal, "that free-thinkers are afraid of death. I want you one and all to tell the whole world that you have seen a free-thinker die without the least fear of what the hereafter may be." The doomed man conversed cheerfully with his friends, bade the members of his family an affectionate farewell, provided for the cremation of his remains, hummed a tune from "Tannhäuser" which he asked should be sung at his funeral, and then faced what he believed to be an eternal sleep—like one

> Who wraps the drapery of his couch about him
> And lies down to pleasant dreams.

It is not necessary to share Mr. Palmer's agnosticism—for he only said, "I don't know there is not a heaven, but I don't know that there is"—to admire his philosophic courage in the face of death.

His life had fitted him for the ordeal. A rich man, he sympathized with the poor and sought to ameliorate their condition. He felt deeply and thought strongly on social questions. If his theories were air castles he at least tried to materialize them. Like Abou Ben Adhem, he "loved his fellowmen."

Col. Ingersoll's eloquent tribute to his friend will rank high among the best specimens of mortuary eloquence.

I was instructed by the whole family to thank you for each and all,

Yours always

R. G. Ingersoll

At Colonel Ingersoll's home I was a frequent and appreciative guest. It was an atmosphere of love, and no one could breathe it without absorbing some of its divine quality. If a church service is helpful in proportion as it confers a spiritual uplift on its votaries, then a Sunday evening spent in the radiant presence of this great man, whose sunny optimism gave a warmth and comfort to all who came within its range, was at once a *sursum corda* and a benediction. Not he alone, but every member of his great family gave to the "stranger within his gates" all that was best in them.

It was in truth a great family. There was the gentle grandmother, the serene mother, the two beautiful and talented daughters, the sister and her husband and child, all vying to make the visitor feel for the moment that he was a part of themselves. I deem it no small privilege to be able to recall five generations of the family of Col. "Bob" Ingersoll, as he is still affectionately remembered by many.

Nor was it a small privilege to meet with the great ones of earth who gathered there on a Sunday evening. Carnegie was a frequent guest. I recall that he took Miss Eva Ingersoll to hear Henry Ward Beecher, and after the sermon, which she enjoyed, Carnegie introduced her to the preacher, saying "This is the first time she has heard a sermon in church."

"Well, well! you are the most beautiful heathen I have ever met," as Beecher took both of her hands in his. "Tell your father I am glad to believe that we have both been working for the same good ends, though on different platforms."

And Ingersoll on hearing of this, made the retort courteous that "the world had waited many centuries for a Beecher and would probably wait many more for another!"

At these Sunday gatherings John W. Mackay, of cable and telegraphic fame and John D. Crimmins, who, I believe was a good Catholic, would sit in silence listening to the witty persiflage of their host and Maurice Barrymore, the drolleries of little Marshall P. Wilder, the vibrant voices of Julia Marlowe, Viola Allen, Agnes Booth, or the charming placidities of Amos R. Eno, whose dying efforts to leave a rich endowment to Columbia University were thwarted by the absurd claims of nephews, nieces, cousins and other distant relatives, who successfully contended that a man had no right to leave his fortune to whomsoever he pleased. Then, of course, there was Walston H. Brown, who modestly hung in the background, and finally carried off as his wife the greatest prize of all— Eva Ingersoll, whose classic beauty was a theme for poets and painters alike.

A short time before he died I was seated at the bedside of Henry Holt, whose friendship I enjoyed for nearly forty years; and we talked about the possibility of a future life. I said: "Have you received any further evidence since you wrote your two volumes *On The Cosmic Relations* that conscious life persists after what we call death?" He answered with great assurance: "Lots of it! I *know* it does!"

Col. Ingersoll gave his family his solemn promise to communicate with them after death, if it were possible. He has remained silent. Mrs. Holt, on the other hand, believes she is in daily communication with her husband and that he is directing the completion of a book he left unfinished. His own belief in the intercommunion of the living and the dead never faltered during his eighty-odd years. At his death, the Authors Club inherited his large collection of books on Spiritism and kindred subjects, with a fund for its upkeep. As I approach the time when I shall join the Silent Majority, I confess to something more than curiosity as to whether I shall meet and know the many friends whose memory I am now recalling.

To use an expression that has almost become a vulgarism, it is "intriguing" that so many men of the highest mental caliber and of great intellectual diversity have become more or less enthusiastic believers in spiritism. Sir William Crookes, the physicist President of the Royal Society, whose discoveries made possible the X-ray and the miracle of Radio, his great successor Sir Oliver Lodge, whose speculations concerning the ether are epochal, Lombroso the criminologist, whose materialistic writings leave one astonished over his spiritism, Maeterlinck, his intellectual antithesis, a poet and a dreamer, Schrenck-Notzing the great German psychiatrist, Flammarian the French astronomer, Charles Richet, the physicist, Sir Conan Doyle, doctor of medicine and creator of great detective stories, Alfred Russell Wallace, who shared with Darwin the discoveries which revolutionized the thought of the world, Professor Schiaparelli, whose name has been given to the Martian canals he was the first to see, Richard Hodgson the psychologist, whose originality as an undergraduate challenged the attention of Herbert Spencer while I was with him—all these men of great intellectual capacity and of widely-divergent interests have committed themselves openly to the belief in the inter-communion of the living and the so-called dead. It is puzzling, to say the least!

Andrew Carnegie gave a dinner in '85 to a dozen people. There were present William C. Whitney, Secretary of the Navy, Brayton Ives, railroad magnate and banker, Lawrence Barrett, the famous tragedian, Courtland Palmer, their respective wives, and, of course, Mr. Carnegie and his mother. There were also Miss Mary Clark, an old friend, and myself. I am the only survivor of them all! Melville E. Stone and I attended together the funeral of Aaron Naumberg, the philanthropist, with whom a short time before we had sat in the Lotus Club, swapping stories, Stone telling of his weird experiences in the Chicago fire. His wonderful memory, graphic powers and keen sense of humor, made the occasion a memorable one. Now he too is gone. All but the youngest of the Carnegie partners I knew have passed on. Of a hundred and fifty members of the Authors Club when I joined, a mere half dozen remain, and these are no longer able to attend its fortnightly dinners.

There is much to be said for Osler's fanciful idea. After fifty, friends drop into the void with painful regularity; and after sixty it is hard, impossible to replace them with others.

In ancient Sparta the older men alone went into battle during important crises, the younger ones being sent back to their city to stimulate the birth-rate, and so prolong the life of the nation. It was a fine idea! The Kaiser and I both were old enough to go—he was studying in Bonn the year I was there. With his litter of sons he would never have been missed! But I might have preferred to be sent back to help to save the nation in more peaceful ways!

The world and his wife came to the Windsor, and I met them both. Abner McKinley and his family lived there, and his brother the Senator, afterwards President, visited them with frequency. Leland Stanford often sat at a table near the Carnegie's, with relatives of his wife from Albany or somewhere "up-state." Pullman stopped at our table to exchange greetings with Carnegie and shake his mother's hand. George Westinghouse spent most of his winters at the Windsor, with his somewhat eccentric wife. Long before it had the authority of fashion, she wore her blonde hair "bobbed" and prettily curled. Her little boy was dressed in velvet and lace like Lord Fauntleroy, and he looked so pretty, thus garbed, that his mother, who put him to bed herself, often let him sleep in his day clothes. At his invitation I once went down town on the elevated with Mr. Westinghouse, who wanted me to tell about an invention I had patented for the production of ozone by a dielectric placed across the path of a brush discharge. His quick understanding of my new technique and his familiarity with the patent situation were noteworthy in one who might be thought to have no time for such minor details of his vast businesss.

"Dick" Croker lived at the Windsor for a time, and was as modest in his demeanor as if he had not been the real ruler of the city. The habitual residents of the house looked at him with curiosity, but made no friendly overtures. He responded in like manner.

The creator of the Metropolitan Life Insurance Company, John R. Hegeman, was also a member of our mixed company. He was a big man—as well as a great one; but, with his long oily hair, he did not look the part: he was more like a patent medicine vender, or a Buffalo Bill. But he had a gracious manner when, as rarely happened, he or his wife was accosted by any of the close circle of old residents, who naturally formed a friendly group among themselves.

Frank A. Munsey lived at the Windsor while he was trying to make a success of a little publication, most of which he wrote himself and called *The Argosy*. His habitual seat in the dining room was with three other bachelors, one of whom was very rich, and the general belief was that Munsey received considerable financial aid from this gentleman, who died before Frank achieved the great success which followed the conversion of the weekly into a monthly magazine. In Paris in 1900 Munsey told me that his net income from his publications then amounted to more than a million dollars a year! He invested largely in the securities of the Steel Corporation when they were at their lowest price, and his profits in them were enormous.

Josh Billings (Henry W. Shaw) made his home at the Windsor when not lecturing. He wore his hair long, and had a curl at his ears like an ear-trumpet. He was almost deaf; and I frequently used this curl, as we sat at lunch, to transmit to him the jokes that invariably kept us all in a roar when Andrew Carnegie was present. I remember a mild jest of Josh Billings whenever we had a new waiter. "Half a dozen oysters on the half shell." Then calling the waiter back "Not all on one shell!"

Which reminds me that Joe Jefferson was similarly deaf, similarly wore his hair long, and, similarly, I used that long hair as an ear-trumpet. He was a member of the Authors Club, and had written me about some prophecies I had made in a book, published by Henry Holt in 1886, describing a trip across the Atlantic in an air-ship in which was the now-popular talking-picture. I had even invented the now common word "photophone" for it, and used it freely in my book. But Joe Jefferson had never heard it; neither had anybody else; and, naturally, he had never seen a "Movie-Talkie." We attended together a performance of a "tabloid" play about "Ophelia," given by the Twelfth Night Club; and so vociferous in his excitement did Joe become that I led him out of the hall: being nearly deaf, he had not realized how loud his voice had sounded. He insisted on having a copy of the book and he wrote me a nice letter about it on January 8, 1897. "Your prophecy is most interesting" he wrote, "as it has come to pass. I congratulate you." But it had not all "come to pass" even at that late day! As one of the vice-presidents of the Radio Corporation has informed me that the word "photophone" was also invented in his office, I feel justified in printing, as an appendix to this book, my description of a "talking-movie" which I called a photophone, in a book published in the Spring of 1886, but actually written between 1880 and 1884.

Of the Windsor family group was Mrs. Gilchrist, the sister of D. O. Mills who used occasionally to come and see her and her friends, of whom Mrs. Carnegie was one. Mrs. Gilchrist was lame, and, anticipating the fire which we all knew would occur sooner or later, her rooms were on the street level, and she and her husband, Dr. Gilchrist, escaped unhurt. Not so with Mrs.

Lucy Carnegie's sister, Mrs. Bradley, who was one of the forty-odd who died in the fire.

Let me record an act of heroism on the part of Warren, the elevator operator. He had been there many years, and everybody liked him. On the day of the fire, he brought a group of refugees to the ground floor and started up for another. Firemen tried to stop him, saying the cables would give way, and that the so-called safety devices would clamp and hold the elevator between floors. "My God," he answered, "I can't let those people burn! You should see their faces through the glass doors on the upper floors!" So up he went, and coming back, the elevator stuck between floors when the cable was burnt through. He was a brave man. He knew the danger better than did the passengers who perished with him.

A little while before the fire, a new-fangled contraption had been installed in every room in the hotel, to enable the occupant to escape in case of need. It was a belt and a thin rope that passed through some sort of brakeing apparatus, and was screwed to the wall near the window. One was supposed to fasten the belt around one's waist and jump out of the window, when the brake would let one slowly down to the street. It worked perfectly for them that understood it; but most of those who died threw the rope out of the window and tried to slide down it. Being no thicker than a clothes line, it cut their hands and made them let go, to fall to their death on the pavement.

Arriving from California the day before the fire, my wife went to the Windsor to engage rooms, and was warmly greeted by Warren, who, through long acquaintance, had the respectful freedom of an old

THE WINDSOR HOTEL FIRE

servant. Fortunately for us, there was no vacancy in the
front of the house as we required, in order that our
Stuart cousins, connected with the navy, could witness
St. Patrick's parade from our windows. We therefore
went to the Hanover Hotel at Fifteenth Street, and

got rooms with a balcony overlooking Fifth Avenue, where we waved flags to the navy men we knew as they marched towards the tragedy we so narrowly escaped.

During the Civil War a group of young girls gathered around a piano in Baltimore and sang new words to an old German song, "O Tannenbaum." It became the Confederate song "My Maryland," commemorating the "gore that flecked thy streets O Baltimore." One of these girls married Jefferson Davis's secretary, and became Mrs. Burton Harrison. She lived first in Irving Place and then in lower Madison Avenue, where she edited, from time to time, an unprinted magazine called *The Ephemeron*. This was read aloud by its contributors, before a select audience of the intelligentzia of the city during Lent. Chauncy M. Depew was the critic, and well he filled the place. Mrs. Harrison, who had written, amongst many other things, a "best seller" for that primitive day, entitled *Sweet Bells out of Tune*, contributed a witty paper to *The Ephemeron* I attended. She called it "Forty Days on a Camp-stool," which was how we spent most of our afternoons during the Lenten season—listening, in. private houses, to lectures and the like. I remember that Frank Stockton contributed a "Story of Assisted Fate" in his characteristic vein, afterwards printed in the *Atlantic Monthly*. There were other papers, all clever and full of sparkle.

After the meeting Mrs. Harrison told how her young son—afterwards governor of the Philippines—had paid her a pretty compliment as he stood with his arm about her waist. Mr. Carnegie, with his ready wit, at once said: "who would not pay you a pretty compliment if he had his arm about your waist?" She was an attractive woman, and the comment was as appropriate

181

as it was well received. Carnegie's alert mind never missed a chance like that.

Young Francis Burton Harrison married, as his first wife, one of the Crocker heiresses whom I used to meet when dining with the family of Mr. Wm. H. Mills in San Francisco. Her father was one of those who held the *Overland's* note for a thousand dollars.

The nearest approach to a literary salon in the America of those days was assuredly that of Mrs. Anna C. Lynch Botta, author of the *Handbook of Universal Literature,* which, notwithstanding its ambitious title, really justified itself by its excellence. At her home in West 37th Street, between Fifth and Sixth Avenues, one met every important literary man of the time, whether native or foreign. Her receptions were always crowded with interesting people; and her lovely niece, Miss Lynch, gave a bright note to what might otherwise have been what the "flapper" of to-day would call a "high-brow party." Mr. Carnegie, paying one of his usual compliments to a pretty woman as we were leaving one afternoon, was met by the embarrassing query: "But why don't you get married yourself?"

"Ah madam" he instantly replied in mock despair, "the ladies I would marry are either, like yourself, already married, or they have higher ambitions than mere matrimony."

William C. Whitney, afterwards Secretary of the Navy, lived in a house at the corner of Fifth Ave. and 57th St. where the Hecksher Building now stands, with its thirty-storied tower. Mrs. James Brown Potter had just created a sensation in Washington by her recital of a poem called "Ostler Joe," thought in those sober days to be a bit *risqué.* So Mr. Whitney had her give, at his

house, a private performance of a play with Kyrle Bellew
—a private performance attended by two hundred people! I went with Mr. Carnegie, Miss Whitfield, and
the beautiful Mrs. George Place, and again the question was asked of Carnegie, "But why don't *you* get
married and have a home like that?" I forget the
answer, but the question soon received a practical
reply: he married Miss Whitfield, the other lady of the
partie carrée.

I have mentioned Mrs. Bronson Howard in connection with the Monday afternoon receptions of Mrs.
Barnard at the old Columbia College in East 49th St.
I knew her before I came to America, and the manner
of our meeting was in this wise:

As a schoolboy in Germany I used to throw amorous
missives across two walls to a pretty blonde English
girl of sixteen as she and her school mates walked about
their garden. Her answers were hidden in the ivy of the
wall, and stealthily taken by me after dark. The innocent correspondence being discovered and reported to
the girl's mother, I received a less tender missive from
England, advising me to pay more attention to my
studies and less to the girls in the school next door but
one. Naturally, this was but a slight obstacle to the
course of true love, and the correspondence continued
through an intermediary, a cousin. When I left Bonn
to enter the French Lyceé, where Pandia Ralli was—
though I did not know it then, nor dream that he would
be a contributor to the *Overland* under my editorship
—I got the mother's consent to write to the young lady
—not oftener than once a week! This continued until I
returned to England, and became a reporter on the
Hastings Times. Mother and daughter were staying

at Brighton, near by; and having to report the Lewis Assizes, I took the opportunity of running over to Brighton and calling on the ladies. There I found that the father had heard of my attentions and had telegraphed his wife to bring the young lady back to London forthwith. "My Lord!" he had exclaimed, "what would the public think if I should become a grandfather!" Or so it was told to me by Arthur Matthison, who was playing the "ghost" in Henry Irving's "Corsican Brothers." For the father was no less a person than Charles Wyndham, who was playing juvenile parts in Bronson Howard's plays! But mother and daughter ignored the command and stayed in Brighton. So did I; and later I went up to London, and with youthful courage called at 3 Marlborough Road, St. Johns Wood, where the Wyndham family at that time made their home. There I met Bronson Howard, who, as I learned much later, was engaged in a quest similar to my own. But his interest was in Wyndham's sister, whom he afterwards married.

One night, many years after, Bronson Howard and I walked home through the park from the Authors Club. We were talking about the Wyndhams. "What became of Miss Edgewood, Sir Charles's sister?" I asked. "She is Mrs. Bronson Howard" was the unexpected answer. "No!" I exclaimed. "Yes!" said he. We had both stopped walking in mutual surprise. "No!" said I again. "Yes!" said he with emphasis. The following Sunday, Mrs. Howard and her distinguished husband called on my wife and me at the Dakota, and we all had a good laugh over what they were pleased to call my "puppy-love affair." Maybe so! It was very sweet—while it lasted!

New York in the "Elegant Eighties" and the "Genial Nineties!" It is hard to realise that this of 1931 is the same place! The highest building was the tower of the Produce Exchange, where visitors were taken to get a birdseye view of the city. Later this distinction was won by the *World* building, where my old friend Don C. Seitz held out under the Dome. Upper Broadway was known as the Boulevard. Riverside Drive had not more than a score of houses in its entire length, all of ancient lineage. One, belonging to Cyrus Clark, where I occasionally went to Sunday tea, was a cottage, like a farm house, in a hollow just north of where the Soldiers' Monument now stands on a rock overlooking the river. It had a splendid row of elm trees in front of it. Looking east from here across the fields, the Ninth Avenue Elevated stood like a huge lonesome caterpillar, and the Dakota at 72nd St. loomed large across the vacant lots. Sprinkled about were the shanties of squatters, made up of odd pieces of timber, old boxes, and the like, while goats cavorted about the rocks near by. "Goatville," as it was called, reached as far south as 72nd St. on the west side, and quite as far on the other side of the park in the streets leading off Fifth Avenue.

In the Windsor hotel gas was the only illuminant; although when I went to Europe in 1886, to bring out the English edition of *Triumphant Democracy*, I found the electric light in common use. Indeed, in Milan, that year, I found Edison's incandescent lamps in many buildings; and in my room at the hotel there was one on a movable stand like those of to-day.

At the Opera House, as in all the theaters, the footlights were of gas; and I recall how Madam Calve, at the Metropolitan, bravely continued her Habañera as she placidly watched the flames shoot up from a broken rubber-tube in the orchestra, while her frenzied audience seized their wraps and many fled towards the exits. She often came to my apartment to play with my little daughter and sing lullabies to her. She remembered the incident, and confessed that her bravery had been but superficial. It served its purpose, however, and prevented a panic.

The Fifth Avenue stages were new, and fashioned largely after the one-horse cars that ran across the town with straw-covered floors in winter, and sputum-soaked floors in summer. Broadway was free of car-tracks until the middle of the eighties, when Jake Sharp got a charter from the boodle aldermen of that period, and some of them went to jail for their share in the so-called civic improvement. Jake Sharp, too, fared almost as badly for his frankly bought charter. To enter a Broadway stage, one, if sufficiently agile, ran behind it and gave a tug to the rear door. This jerk was transmitted by means of a leather strap to the driver's leg as he sat on the box seat, and the signal was answered by a pedal relaxation which allowed the door to open. A forward movement of the driver's leg tightened the strap and closed the door. The passenger, if he were wise, would drop his nickel into a glass box behind the driver as soon as he got in the stage. If he did not, the driver would tap on the glass and tell him to "hurry up!"

The Windsor Hotel had a Turkish bath annex in the house next door, in East 46th St. to the roof of which I had planned to escape whenever the fire occurred which we all anticipated. A fashionable lady of my acquaintance inadvertently sat upon a hot pipe in this Turkish bath, and, when she had dressed, astonished her waiting coachman by sending him home. As walking was painful, she got into a Fifth Avenue stage, and every man in it at once rose and offered her his seat. Men were more polite in those days than now. Of course, she smilingly declined their courtesy. Presently, as people left the stage, there were several empty seats; but she steadfastly clung to the overhead strap, and remained standing and swaying to the movements of the vehicle, much to the mystification of the other passengers.

Elliot Shepard, a son-in-law of W. H. Vanderbilt, was the chief owner of these stages. One winter day when the streets were glassy with ice, Miss Ingersoll and I, from the window of her home on Murray Hill, watched the pitiful struggles of the stage horses laboring and slipping as they pulled the heavy vehicles up the hill; and I called on the Society for the Prevention of Cruelty to Animals and lodged a complaint. Shepard responded, not by adding an extra horse, but by taking the stages off altogether. He referred inquiring reporters to me at the Windsor, and I soon had an excited group of them there. I placidly told them to see Col. Ingersoll, who made an amusing statement to them, saying that the sight of Elliot Shepard's horses always reminded him of the story of the rib in Genesis!

Elliot Shepard owned the *Mail and Express,* and every day he printed as a caption to his paper a text from the Bible. He was very religious. When he went abroad one summer, Foster Coates, whom he left in charge, did not like these texts and day after day printed the same one—the shortest he could find. It was "And Jesus wept!"

The Vanderbilts controlled the New York Central,

and they started a rate war when the West Shore road was opened; so that I was able to go to Niagara Falls for a dollar and a half. This I did during the Christmas holidays; and walked across the river below the falls on the ice. Others doing the like, were caught when the ice-bridge broke, and were carried down to the rapids and drowned. The foolish exploit has now been legally banned.

Fred May, who fought a duel with James Gordon Bennett for insulting his sister—who later married W. C. Whitney—struck a policeman, and nearly killed him, for May was as big and strong as John L. Sullivan the prize fighter. He fled to South America and lived there until the indictment for the assault was quashed, in recognition of his bravery in swimming out to a wreck and saving a troup of American chorus girls on the coast of Brazil or some such place. But he was debarred from New York, and for a time in Washington I was with him almost daily. He and Buffalo Bill quarreled about some woman, but mutual friends arranged a meeting of reconciliation. This was at Chamberlins. The year was 1892. Fred advanced, as he told me the next day, with outstretched hand to Cody, who grasped the extended hand with his left hand, and with his right delivered a frightful blow at May's face and knocked him under a table. Cody quickly left the place and took the first train to New York, while May was hunting for him with a gun. This was an aspect of Buffalo Bill which I should not have believed if May himself had not told me of it. At the grave of Cody, on a mountain top near Denver, I have not felt that spiritual uplift which the deeds of the valiant dead are supposed to inspire in us.

These were the days of the peach-blow vase, sold at auction for the dower of a princess; of Salvini and Edwin Booth in *Othello* at the Academy of Music, when the herculean Italian tossed Desdemona from one arm to another like a little sack of bran, and Booth's exquisite Shakesperian diction was smothered in what sounded like quotations from Dante; of Ada Rehan's creating a tradition in American drama which has remained but a tradition since her day; of Dixey's beautiful legs in "Adonis," when they were the wonder and admiration of the little town of New York; of the titanic battles in Wall St. between Jim Keene and Addison Cammack, the "nigger-driver from New Orleans" as Keene called him; of Jay Gould held by the scruff of the neck and his "pants" over a railing near Exchange Place by the infuriated Morisini—afterwards promoted to the position of personal body-guard of the little black-bearded pirate of Wall Street; of the receptions of J. G. Brown, John La Farge, Jasper Conant in the old Tenth Street studios; of similar artists' receptions in the old University Building in Washington Square; of dear old Mrs. Sherwood's ample figure at every social function and her book on etiquette; of Mrs. Paran Stevens, whose house has just been pulled down to make way for a sky-scraper, and who, tempted into the Madelaine to witness a French funeral cortege, took a seat fronting the mourners with a huge wreath designed for a home-going compatriot, and labeled "bon voyage"; of New Years' formal calls, when Carnegie's youthful partners from Pittsburgh astonished his mother by appearing in her apartment at the Windsor in full evening dress at half past nine in the morning; of Col. Fellows, district attorney, a confederate vet-

eran, vaulting over the turnstiles on the elevated railway platforms, to mark his disapproval of these new-
fangled machines for forcing passengers to collect their
own fares; of corpulent Dr. Robert H. Lamborn, in
whose office the city of Duluth was born, riding a bicycle
up Fifth Avenue into Central Park at the head of a
procession of similar enthusiasts of the new sport; of
the all-star revival of the "Rivals" at the Union Square
theatre in 14th Street, with a caste of John Gilbert, Joe
Jefferson, W. J. Florence, Mrs. John Drew, mother of
the later idol of the stage, and others long forgotten;
of Harriet Beecher Stowe, on the platform of the Metropolitan Opera House, reciting the "Battle Hymn of
the Republic"; of Paderewski in the supper room of
the Windsor, arousing the wonder of those at the next
table by his skill in catching in his mouth chunks of
bread dexterously thrown by himself; of Simeon Ford,
mine host of the Grand Union Hotel, with his clever
signs in the wash-room, inviting guests of a literary bent
to refrain from writing on the walls, but to inscribe
their lucubrations "on this board: poetry here, prose
there"; of Major Pond, in the Everett House, surrounded by autographed portraits of all the great and
near-great who had visited these shores in search of the
festive dollar that haunts the purlieus of the Lyceums
of the land. All these, and many more than I can now
recall, gave to New York a character that it has since
lost, and regretfully so. That I witnessed these varied
scenes and knew most of the actors in them is a somber
sort of happiness that I hope will remain with me until
I, too, sink into the Great Silence and join my friends
there.

THE OVERLAND MONTHLY

Bret Harte's Legacy.

K ATE FIELD was a vivid personality. She lived at a time when few of her sex reached, as she did, a prominence equal to that of the best-known public men of her generation. Her activities covered every field—from the domestic drama to international politics, and ran over into scientific and industrial promotion. She founded the first Sorosis Club. She introduced the Bell telephone to Europe. She did more than any one person to bring about the annexation of Hawaii. She owned and edited *Kate Field's Washington*, the most frequently quoted publication of her time. And with it all, she never lost the feminine charm that made all men her willing slaves. That she should be forgotten so soon is a pathetic commentary on the bustling egotism of the present generation.

It was characteristic of her liking for the unusual, and what may be called her unexpectedness, that she made a formal call on me in a wild camp in the mountains of Mexican California. Travelling almost unattended in the Peninsula, where roads are often the dry bed of winter streams, where habitations are few and barren of comfort, where the people, though hospitable and kind to the stranger, are chiefly Indians, who live God alone knows how!—this dainty lady, finding herself in primitive quarters at Real del Castillo, and hearing that I had a camp a few miles away, rode over to see what I was doing, and if it was worth while to tell about it in the articles she was writing for a San Francisco paper. She thought it was; for a little while later, I received, with her compliments, the printed story of her visit. But to my annoyance I found myself described as a "protegé of Andrew Carnegie!" I did not mind the Carnegie reference, but I disliked the thought of being any one's protegé.

It is curious what seemingly insignificant things sometimes give an unexpected direction to our lives. This unimportant incident affected my life and changed its current for many years. Across the mountains, now pink in the setting sun and calling forth ecstatic admiration from Miss Field, I knew of hundreds of acres of rich placer ground, and, with a lariat, I had lowered myself down a primitive shaft that showed a vein of glittering gold-quartz as far as I could follow it. Only three of us knew of it, the others being natives; and, despite her pleadings, I was forced to refuse Miss Field's desire to take her there. Moreover, the trail was impossible to any woman except an Indian. So she returned to San Diego, and soon after I followed, and saw her at the Coronado Hotel, which had just been built. Here our acquaintance ripened into an enduring friendship.

Other interests called me east, and I never went back to the fortune lying in the rocks and soil of Mexican California. Instead I spent one in an attempt to revivify a moribund publication that had had a glorious history, but was now, literally, a "back number."

In Washington, the following winter, Miss Field took me to hear a lecture by Rounsevelle Wildman on "The Malay States," in which he was or had been U. S. Consul. Some years afterwards Wildman came to the Authors Club in New York, and, with Bronson Howard we walked home together across the park. He had just been appointed by President McKinley to the consulate at Hong Kong; and now proposed that I take his place as editor of the *Overland Monthly* in San Francisco. I was absentee owner of a ranch in the central part of California, and the suggestion of living again in that beautiful state, with a congenial occupation, appealed to me very strongly. In short, I accepted the offer, which as chief stockholder in the Overland Publishing Co., Wildman had the right to make. I thereby took upon my shoulders a task for which I was financially unfitted. For it was money, and plenty of it, that was needed to enable that dignified old magazine to compete with the cheap publications of Munsey and McClure. That it was founded by Bret Harte, that Mark Twain had been one of its early contributors, that Charles Warren Stoddard, Noah Brooks, Martin Kellogg, Ina D. Coolbrith, Henry George, Prentice Mulford had joined to give it a prestige in places far remote from San Francisco, was literally ignored by the sons and daughters of the Golden West. To the sturdy literary products of their own rugged land they preferred the gruel-thin pabulum of the dime picture books, that came from the east in tens of thousands; and advertisers, both east and west, naturally gave their patronage to the magazines that had the largest circulation on the coast. As Wildman had reduced the price of the *Overland* from 25c to 10c in order to compete with Munsey and McClure, and paper, printing and binding costs were fifteen to twenty per cent more than in the east, I fought a losing fight from the start.

Ambrose Bierce, whose bitter tongue had the quality of a whip-lash that could draw blood, disliked Wildman—whom did he like?—and he had sneeringly written and spoken of "the warmed-Overland!" The contemptuous phrase stuck to it like a splash of mud. There were others who had carried their antagonisms to Wildman to the magazine he edited, and I inherited them. One of these had an amusing outcome.

The city of San Francisco owed the Overland Company a sum of money for magazines supplied to the public schools. The city controller refused payment, for some reasons that did not seem valid to me; and meeting Gavin McNab, the local political boss, in Montgomery Street, I told him about it. Assuring me that the debt would be paid without further delay, he asked me if I was willing to serve as a delegate, from the district in which I lived, to the coming State Democratic Convention in Sacramento. If I had any political leanings they were Republican; but I thought the experience would be interesting, if not actually profitable to the magazine, and I readily consented to accompany the mayor, the late Senator J. D. Phelan, to Sacramento. And so, without having a vote myself, I represented some thousands of voters who lived in the district in which the California Hotel was situated, and helped, as

194

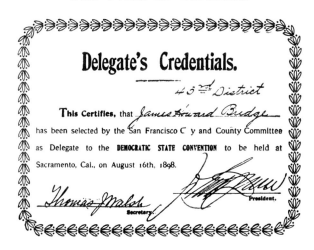

Delegate's Credentials.

45ᵗᵈ District

This Certifies, that *James Howard Bridge*

has been selected by the San Francisco C y and County Committee as Delegate to the **DEMOCRATIC STATE CONVENTION** to be held at Sacramento, Cal., on August 16th, 1898.

Thomas Malsk
Secretary.

President.

directed by the boss, to nominate to the governorship a politician named Budd, who, so far as the *Overland* was concerned, never reached either blossom or fruit-age. The experience was interesting, but not profitable.

Some years before I took charge of the *Overland Monthly* I was living on my ranch near San Luis Obispo. It was part of an old Spanish grant; and I had for neighbors several other Englishmen. One of these rode over to my place one morning as I was about to drive to Paso de Robles, to take the train for New York. He surprised me by handing me a parcel containing, as he told me, the manuscript of a book he had been writing, and he asked me to read it on the train and throw it away if I thought it was not worth offering to a publisher. He had always impressed me with his ready wit, his nice, precise habits of speech, his questioning interest in things literary; but I had no thought of his aspiring to authorship. I accepted his parcel with misgivings, and read the tale on the train.

It was amazingly clever—beautifully written, well conceived and constructed, and leading to a logical, natural climax. It was *The Romance of Judge Ketcham;* its author was the now well-known Horace Annesley Vachell!

He has since published a score of excellent novels, and has had the rare distinction of having two plays running at one time at leading New York theatres— one, "The Chief," with John Drew in the leading part. "Quinnies" was equally important as a book and as a play; and, curiously, it was recommended to me by Henry Clay Frick, whose literary taste differed so greatly from my own. Vachell became a regular and prized contributor to the *Overland* in Wildman's time, and continued as such in my own. But long before I took the editorial chair, Vachell and I collaborated in a picture-play, "Cupid in California," a somewhat rollicking comedy acted by a talented company in front of a camera. This was before the day of moving pictures. Major Pond paid me a hundred dollars a night for reading this play, while, to illustrate the story, two hundred or more "dissolving views" were successively thrown on a screen. Vachell did the like in England, but soon tired of the platform and gave it up in the interest of fresh creations, which he produced with a clock-like regularity. His descriptions of our ranch life and the amazing growth of California are sprinkled through his stories with inimitable skill and accuracy, and one of them, *Bunch Grass,* is a near-classic. His story *The Hill,* descriptive of a boy's life at Harrow, where Vachell spent his youthful years, is not inferior to Kipling's account in *Stalkey and Co.* of his own school-days at "Westward Ho" in Devonshire.

HORACE ANNESLEY VACHELL

In '98 or thereabouts San Francisco had one of its habitual earthquakes—a bit worse, however, than the usual interesting tremor. The day before, Major Pond and Marion Crawford had called on me, and I returned their call the next morning at The Palace Hotel. I found them both in a state of mild excitement. It seems

197

they had been seated in the large court around which the hotel was built, when tables began suddenly to rock, chairs to shed their occupants, walls to creak and sway and swear, as is their habit in earthquakes, and shouting people to run for the nearest exits. Crawford started to join the terrified throng, when Major Pond pulled him back by his coat-tails.

"Sit still," he cried. "You are safer here than outside!" Which was not entirely true, for the glass roof was breaking, and bits of glass were falling around them. But Crawford obeyed, and at once became observant, perhaps to use the experience in his next novel. For the psychical reactions of an earthquake on mere man are not to be studied every day, and they differ in every individual. Caruso, for instance, was seen standing in the street holding on to a lamp-post and singing scales. His first fear was for his voice. A group of men playing billiards in the top floor of the Call Building ran around the tables like rats in a trap, shouting at the top of their voices: the elevator, which was their only means of escape, had stuck between floors. A man sitting in a bath tub at the Palace Hotel with a glass of hot grog at his side—which he was taking for a cold—reached for the teetering glass and emptied it down his throat—the ruling spirit strong in death!

I was reading manuscripts in bed, on the top floor of the California Hotel, and near an open window that came to the floor. The bed was suddenly tilted three times towards the open window, and I looked down into the street. There I saw two men under a corner lamp, apparently watching to see me thrown out of the window to their feet. "Two more jerks like that" I was saying to myself "and I am gone!" The unwonted

FROM THE PICTURE-PLAY: CUPID IN CALIFORNIA

noises—the metal weights in the window sashes swing in their sockets and sound like bells—the creaking walls, the drunken reeling of furniture, the thumping movements under the mattress—all combine to produce a paralysis, akin to fascination, that makes quick rational motion impossible. So I lay, half reclining,

199

looking at the two men under the lamp in the street, until the movement stopped. Then I quickly slid off the bed and ran into the corridor. I found that everybody on the floor had done the same. All were talking, some shouting, and quite heedless of their appearance in various states of dress and undress. Then the ladies suddenly realized how they looked, and scurried back into their rooms to find a shawl or other covering, in which to wait for the second shock, which all knew would follow. In this way we waited, all talking hysterically, all asking questions as to what had best be done, whether to wait where we were or run down stairs. But amid the confusion and conflicting opinions, there was unanimity in this: that no one wanted to be left alone in his room with an earthquake. If we were to be killed, let it be in good company! As a matter of fact a number of people were killed by falling walls. And this was only a baby-earthquake compared with that which came a few years later.

One day, toward the end of '98, my assistant Green came into my office and said there was a man outside who had a story to sell, and wanted an immediate decision as to its acceptability. I went to the outer office and greeted him. He said his name was Jack London. "You mean 'John,' " I said. "No, just Jack," was the reply. He looked like a tramp, and nothing like a man who could have written an acceptable story for Bret Harte's old magazine. But when he said he had just come down from the Klondike, I said "Give me your story and come back tomorrow." I took the manuscript home with me that night and had the surprise of my life. The story was called "To the Man on the Trail; A Klondike Christmas." It was the first of the Mama-

OFFICE OF THE *Overland Monthly* IN 1898

J. H. Bridge seated; Roscoe L. Eames; Charles S. Greene with Fred Stocking at the rear.

lute Kid stories, and one of the finest things Jack London ever did. I understood that he had never published before, and that he had come into the office because he needed money—was in fact "dead-broke." Of course there was no hesitation when I saw him next morning.

"We will accept your story, and pay our maximum price—$25—for it. If you will write us a series of six stories, I will pay for them as you bring them in, have Maynard Dixon illustrate them, and feature them in other ways, so that you will be able to get into eastern magazines, and get what your work is worth. For I am free to say that your work is worth more than we can pay for it."

London gratefully accepted my offer, and within the next two or three weeks finished the series and brought them in. "The White Silence," was the next, and was copied by the *New York Evening Post*. Thereafter Jack London never had need to hawk his stuff in any editorial office. He told me that he needed money very badly for "a mother and child." I did not ask what mother or what child, as it did not seem to be any of my business, and he did not tell me. The series included "The Son of the Wolf," "The Wisdom of the Trail," "In a Far Country," and "The Men of Forty Mile."

An interesting outcome of this chance call of his was his marriage. Our manager, Roscoe L. Eames, had a niece, an unusually bright and attractive girl, named Charmian Kittredge, who came occasionally to the office. She was an amateur photographer and competed several times in the prize competition we held. Once she and I went by invitation to the vineyards of the Swiss-Italian Colony in Sonoma County; and I recall

Just to show you what a good time we are
having, I am inclosing a photograph for you
and your wife.
        With kindest remembrances from us
both,
        Sincerely yours,

Charmian Kittredge London

"On the Beach
at Waikiki" 1915

with amusement that while there she inadvertently sat in a puddle of rain water, and assured me that "it had gone all the way through!"

Roscoe, her uncle, had a little sail boat with which he used to explore the shores of San Francisco bay. On the strength of this, Jack London, after his marriage to Charmian, got Eames to help in building the "Snark," and afterwards in navigating it; but Roscoe's experience in the safe waters of the bay was insufficient to qualify him to take a boat across the Pacific, and at Honolulu Jack is said to have "beat him up" and sent him back to Oakland. I hope it is not true. Roscoe is dead, so is Jack. I liked them both. Jack and Charmian did not take Roscoe with them into Southern Pacific waters where they had adventures enough to fill a book, and did so.

Before Rounsevelle Wildman persuaded me to take his place on the *Overland*, he had borrowed for the magazine various sums of money, giving the Company's note as security; and soon after I had taken hold, these notes were presented for payment. They were for a thousand dollars each, and were held by Lloyd Tevis, Claus Spreckles, Collis P. Huntington, Wildman's uncle "Billy" Foote, the well-known lawyer, and Colonel Crocker who had died. Mr. Foote agreed to cancel his note if I could get the other gentlemen to do the same. So I went first to Mr. Huntington. As I entered his office, following my card, he looked up from his desk and gave me a piercing glance that seemed to reach my innermost thoughts. Frick had the same appraising look; and I was conscious of a like effect the first time I met James J. Hill. Mr. Huntington was a very large man who quite filled the big chair at his desk. He wore

ROUNSEVELLE WILDMAN

a skull-cap. After the first analytical look, his eyelids drooped, and he arranged himself easily in his chair, to give me the impression that we were to have a pleasant time together. Mr. Hill did the like. It is a pose that has a protective use; for these men of large affairs are constantly playing a game of bluff with each other, and have developed what is appropriately known as a "poker-face." I did not then, nor now, play poker. I put all my cards on the table, and the old gentleman liked it. He paid me a nice compliment covering my efforts to improve the magazine, and showed his familiarity with them. He forgave the debt, and tore up the *Overland's* note in my presence. I left with a comfortable feeling that I had a friend in this great man, and that he would back me up in anything I did to make the *Overland* interesting. I did not know. I was soon to find out!

My next call was on the western Sugar King, Claus Spreckels. This time I had to go to Paso de Robles to see him; but that was a pleasure, as I had an annual pass over all the Southern Pacific lines, and my ranch was within a few miles of the Springs. With this shrewd old German I found my task no easy one. He was willing to extend the note, but not to cancel it. So I stayed over a day or two, at the big hotel which had taken the place of the primitive wooden structure which I had known ten years before. Then the only way of reaching it was by stage coach, drawn by six horses, and occasionally held up by highwaymen. It was kept by a cousin of Jesse James, and the rustic landlord seemed proud of his namesake's exploits as a bandit. The first time I got there, having ridden from San Luis Obispo, and taken a board from a fence, belonging to my friend Pat Murphy, to make my camp-fire, I had to call Mr. James out of bed to have him throw down the key to a room. It was very late—after ten o'clock at night!

Mr. Spreckles and I had several long talks on the hotel porch, and Pat Murphy joined us. Spreckles had lent money to Murphy, who, having two of the most beautiful ranches—the Santa Margarita and The Atascadero—in one of the finest valleys in southern California, comprising thousands of acres, was unable, by sheer ineffectiveness, to make a living for himself. He now wanted Spreckles to finance him further, so as to develop a sugar-beet industry. Spreckles refused, and poor Pat almost wept on my shoulder. He eventually lost his fine properties, and now the ranches where I used his fence to cook my steak, are filled with prosperous farms and two or three goodly towns.

Mr. Spreckles proving equally obdurate with me as he had been with Murphy, I had recourse to a trick which he himself might have taught me—for he had become confidential when relating his experiences with the Havemeyer Sugar Trust in the east: he had got the better of Havemeyer—no small feat! In a casual way I told Mr. Spreckles that I would have to call for an assessment on the shares of the Overland Publishing Company.

"Well, what of it?" he asked.

"I want your approval."

"How does that concern me?" he asked.

"You are one of the biggest shareholders," I smilingly replied.

"Ach Gott! take your note and your stock too, I vant neider of dem."

And so I came away, as happy as I hope I left him.

I do not remember how the Tevis note was arranged. Hugh Tevis, Lloyd Tevis's son, had married the daughter of my old friend, Judge Boalt, and maybe it was managed through him.

Wildman had such a gracious manner, was indeed such a winning personality, that he probably had no difficulty in persuading these cautious business men to lend the *Overland* large sums of money. He was many kinds of a genius. Having my account in a New York bank, he showed me how to keep a check in the air long enough for it to fly across the continent and back— a trick that was afterwards very useful in times of financial stress. I recall with amusement that one day as we stood with a group in Montgomery Street, he saw approaching the paper manufacturer's agent to whom the *Overland* was heavily in debt. "He is going to strike me for a payment on account" said Wildman. "I'll make him buy us a drink instead." And this he actually did! It was his unwise habit to endorse the company's notes, and this led to the seizure of his baggage as he was on his way to the steamer that was to take him to his post as U. S. Consul-General in Hong Kong! Occasionally I made the same mistake; and years after I had left the *Overland* I was arrested in Boston, and had to settle a claim for paper supplied to the Overland Company to avoid spending a night in jail!

A year or so after his appointment, Wildman got leave of absence from his post in Hong Kong, and with his wife and two beautiful children took the steamer for San Francisco. The ship ran on a rock just inside the Golden Gate and hung perilously on it long enough for some of the passengers to take to the life-boats. Wildman got into one of these, and with a child in his arms was helping his wife and the other child from the ship's ladder into the life-boat, when the steamer gave a lurch, turned over as it slid off the rock and crushed the life-boat and all in it. The whole family of four perished, and the bodies were never found. The tragedy happened almost within a stone's throw of the home of Mrs. Wildman's mother, who as she waited in holiday mood for the return of her loved ones, could have heard the syren cry of distress that came up through the fog as the steamer struck the rock. A sad, sad ending of a promising career!

Another straggler into the office with a story to sell

was Pandia Ralli, who looked like a tramp, and was one. Recognizing the name as Greek, I asked him where he had learned English. He told me he had been in the Royal Mounted Police Force in Canada, but that he had first learned our language at the Grand Lycée, Marseilles. He named a year. I inquired who had been the Proviseur of the Lycée that year—1878, and he answered correctly; who was the Censeur, the Professor of English? His answers were correct. For it happened that that was the year I had myself been a student in the same institution, which is a division of the University of France. It was a striking coincidence, and I was pleased that the character of his work justified its acceptance. He afterwards enlisted in the American army, and went to the Philippines to fight Aguinaldo. He sent back a number of articles descriptive of army life, which I published. Then they stopped, and I heard he had been killed. Many years afterwards, when I was Curator of the Frick Collection, several members of the great banking house of Ralli came to the galleries, and I told them the story of Pandia, as I have told it here. Then I learned that Pandia was the wild sheep of the family, and that they had not known what had become of him.

Another coincidence is deserving of mention. A young naval officer became attentive to a cousin—by marriage—of Rounsevelle Wildman, while the latter was editor of the *Overland*. The young lady was named Stewart and her mother's maiden name was Foote— the sister of the famous lawyer previously mentioned as the holder of one of the *Overland* notes. The naval officer removed to the east about the time I took Wildman's place; and here he met another young lady named

Stuart—my cousin by marriage—whose mother's maiden name also was Foote! This young lady he married. He was Victor Blue, whose gallantry in Cuba during the Spanish war made him the youngest admiral in the service. The only variation in this triple coincidence is in the spelling of the ladies' name—Stewart and Stuart!

Franklin Lane, a young lawyer of no great prominence, brought to the office an article he had written on the political situation in California in 1899. It was a timely subject, excellently treated; and I was impressed with its importance. Its chief motif, however, was: "Shall the Southern Pacific Railroad be permitted to continue in control of the destinies of the State?" The *Overland* held several valuable advertising contracts with the Southern Pacific, and I feared to jeopardize these by antagonizing the railroad. I therefore held Mr. Lane off until I had had an opportunity of consulting Mr. William H. Mills, with whom I was in the habit of dining about once a week. Mr. Mills occupied a high position in the inner councils of Southern Pacific Railroad, and controlled its advertising and other forms of publicity. He read the article, admired it, and thought I ought to publish it, provided I got another writer to take the opposite side. To this end he recommended the editor of one of the Fresno papers. Accordingly, the Franklin Lane article duly appeared, and was copied more or less in its entirety by almost every newspaper in the State. The resultant storm swept the *Overland* out of Southern Pacific Railroad favor: the advertising contracts were cancelled, and my annual pass was recalled. Mr. Mills was as greatly chagrined as I—except that his share of the responsibility was

not known to those in the higher realms of the corporation. But it gave Franklin Lane a prestige which
eventually carried him into a cabinet position. So that
it was not all loss.

Another undistinguished caller who became famous
was Robert Ingersoll Aitken, the sculptor. He invited
me to go with him to see a cover design which he had
made for the *Overland*. His description interested me
and I went with him to his studio, a simple shack in the
backyard of his mother's little house. At this time
Aitken was a rough looking boy of eighteen, brightly-
smiling, strongly-featured, dressed with real or simulated artistic carelessness, and with a manner made up
of a fascinating mixture of assurance and modesty. He
was equally conscious of the latent talent within him
and the need for outside recognition of it. A youthful
Columbus, at the head of his class, he had visions of
undiscovered lands across uncharted seas; and these
visions he has nobly realized: the list of his achievements and the honors that have come to him is a long
and distinguished one. I have always been proud that
his first commission came from me; for, of course, I
immediately bought the plaque he had made. It was in
clay and represented the spirit of war, flying with blazing torch and drawn sword across the American continent. The war with Spain had just begun.

While we were standing in front of the easel carrying the design, his little sister came in, and stood ex-
pectantly near a square stone block near the door. She
had been told that a beautiful lady lay imprisoned inside
this stone, and she was hopeful that my visit portended
an order to her brother to release this beautiful lady,
whose harsh imprisonment had caused her much child-

ish pain. It is a pleasant thought that the lady has since been released from her stony prison—as have many others by the magic of Aitken's chisel.

The clay plaque had to be photographed, so that a half-tone could be made to print on the *Overland's* cover; and I engaged a local man to do this work. When the photographer brought the print into the office it was wider at the bottom than at the top: he had not allowed for the slant of the easel, to keep the wet clay from sliding off its board. So I had it photographed again, this time by a Japanese, who brought a spirit level to the job and succeeded where the American had failed. The latter was not satisfied with the partial payment which I decided his useless print was worth, and he became so abusive that I had literally to pick him up and throw him out of the office.

We were always short of funds. I often took a book to the top of Telegraph Hill and sat there until some process-server had grown tired of waiting for me at the office door, which I could see from my perch! The editing of a California magazine in those days called for cash and muscle rather than for literary skill!

Douglas Tilden, a deaf-mute of great talent, was the head of the Mark Hopkins Institute of Art in San Francisco, where Aitken studied at this time, and Tilden won an *Overland* prize for a "best story." I got Aitken to illustrate this story in clay, reproducing his tablets photographically. This had never been done before, and the novelty attracted much attention from other publishers. Indeed it was not long before Aitken's original way of making a cover design was copied by eastern magazines, and the fad lasted quite a while.

In July 1898 was celebrated the thirtieth anniversary of the founding of the *Overland;* and I was able to get several of those who wrote for the first number to contribute articles to this one. Bret Harte in London did not think it worth his while to favor my invitation with a reply. But Anton Roman, the first publisher was still alive—very much so when he talked about old times. He often came to my office, and nearly always referred to Bret Harte's fanciful story of the modest lady proof-reader who had found indecency in "The Luck of Roaring Camp," which appeared in the second number, and not in the first as so often stated. This seems to have been a very trifling affair, and I got Mr. Roman to tell about it in this anniversary number. This is what he says:—

The particular incident connected with the first year of the *Overland* that has been oftenest and most widely told is the first reception of "The Luck of Roaring Camp" and the trouble it made. My own recollection of the incident differs a little in particulars from Mr. Harte's. As I remember it Mr. Harte and I had both gone with our wives to Santa Cruz for Sunday. We often took such trips in those days. On this Sunday I found in my mail, when the stage from San José came in, duplicate galley proofs of "The Luck of Roaring Camp." Harte had told me the story before. One proof I gave to him and took the other to my own room, where I asked my wife to read it aloud to me. As far as she could go she did, but the story so affected her that she could not finish it aloud and went on reading it to herself. Then I took it and finished it too. Neither of us had a word of objection to make; we were simply delighted with it.

On the following day we all went back to San Francisco. On reaching the city Harte went to the printer's and I to the store. My chief clerk, Joseph Hoffmann, greeted me with the statement that there was a great hullabaloo at the printer's over the immorality of the "Luck." They were saying that it would kill the magazine.

To this I replied that if it killed the magazine it could do nothing more.

Then Mr. Harte came in from the printer's with the sharp demand to know what I meant to do about it.

"Nothing," I said, "but go ahead."

Even this account of the affair differs somewhat from the story I so often heard from Mr. Anton Roman's lips. He maintained that the lady proof-reader was as insubstantial as was Mliss, or any other of the creatures of fancy born in the fecund brain of his first editor!

In his later work Bret Harte seems to have forgotten his California. Which prompted my assistant Green, in default of anything from the real "Truthful James," to contribute to our anniversary number the following verses, based on the actual mistakes of the London Bret Harte:

PLAIN LANGUAGE TO BRET HARTE
With apologies to Truthful James.

Which I wish to impart,
    And I hopes not in vain,
That I think that Bret Harte
    Should come back again
To the land that is called California,
    And the reasons I now will explain.

Which he says that the woods
    On the Carquinez grow,
And he likewise alludes
    To Mendocino
As being just north of Bonita,—
    Oh Bret, you knew better than so!

But what kills me plumb dead
    Is to see where he's writ
That our poppies is red,—
    Which they ain't red a bit,
But the flamingest orange and yellow,—
    Oh Bret, how could you forgit?

Which is why I impart,
    And am free to maintain,
That I think that Bret Harte
    Should come back again,
If he's going on writing about us,
    And I won't take it back, not a grain.

One afternoon, taking tea in Alameda with Mrs. Shafter Howard—the sister of General Shafter—I met a school-teacher, who charmed us with his delicate fancies and exquisite phrasing of them. He had prematurely white hair and beard, and looked like a prophet

215

To Julia Ward Howe.

Lady and Lyrist, your sweet fame
Is but the sound of love's acclaim;
Your larger home, secure and strong,
The nation lifted by your song!

Edwin Markham

of biblical times. I did not at first catch his name; but his great personal charm prompted me to ask it of himself. He was Edwin Markham, soon to become famous with his "Man with the Hoe," and many other delightful poems since. In appearance he has changed but little. Mentally he has ripened much. May the riches of his genius long endure!

In 1900 I was at the Paris Exposition with Mr. Mills, who was there in the interest of the Southern Pacific Railroad, when I received from Roscoe L. Eames a request for more money to keep the *Overland* going. I had already sunk a small fortune in it, and had had nothing in return except the office-file of the magazine from its first issue—a quite valuable security, but not readily turned into cash. This I fortunately still

216

have, as otherwise it would have been destroyed in the big fire.

Mr. Mills, who had been familiar with the financial difficulties of the *Overland* in Wildman's time, advised me to let it go into bankruptcy. I was unwilling to let the old magazine, with its honorable history, fall so low, especially under my direction; and Eames, having written that a possible purchaser had appeared in the "offing," as he expressed it in his nautical phraseology, I cabled him to accept any terms by which the publication might be kept going. The purchaser was Mr. Marriot, owner of the *San Francisco News Letter,* who was competent, financially and in other ways, to infuse new life into the moribund publication. The price has since been put back to 25c a copy, from which it ought never to have been taken. May it long endure!

THE AUTHORS CLUB

A LATTER-DAY WITENAGEMOT*

A CRACKLING log fire; above it a lofty mantel bearing busts of Keats and Shelley, backed by a Parthenon frieze. On an old Turkish rug in front of the fire, the tall handsome figure of Francis Hopkinson Smith, mildly gesticulating, telling a story to a group of half a dozen listeners, seated in easy chairs and on a wide cushioned bench. One of them, George Cary Eggleston, is smoking a long clay pipe of the kind known as "churchwardens." Frank R. Stockton, on the bench, with head thrown back against the cushions, is gazing at the high ceiling, mottled with years of tobacco smoke, occasionally interjecting a comical comment on the narrative. Richard Watson Gilder, slight of figure, long straight hair framing his pale face, and looking like a twin brother of Robert Louis Stevenson, is all attention, his dark eyes dancing in appreciative mirth. At his side, Laurence Hutton gives vent to a subdued chuckle that presently breaks into a resounding laugh. Edmund Clarence Stedman, a miniature Santa Claus, hovering on the outskirts of the group, comes forward

*Witenagemot: "No ancient record gives us any clear and formal account of the constitution of that body. It is commonly spoken of in a vague way as a gathering of the wise, the noble, the great men." Freeman's *Growth of the English Constitution,* Page 17.

218

to join in the merriment. He adds an amusing note;
and presently there is a rapid fire of fun from those
on the bench, and echoes of it from other parts of the
room, where Will Carleton, Charles Ledyard Norton,
John Denison Champlin, Duffield Osborn and others
have foregathered, and stayed their own talk to hear
this new story of "Hop" Smith's recent trip to the
"Eastern Sho'," where he is again building a light-
house. Rudyard Kipling, a visiting guest, in a nearby
nook, is taking it all in with the clear intention of

making use of it—perhaps in a set of verses or, twisted around, in another story "from the hills."

Soon a gong sounds, and the several groups coalesce about the supper table. Here is John Fiske, his face hidden in a flagon of beer, looking like Falstaff, or some ancient Viking, blowing the froth from his beard and beaming good nature and the joy of life on his smiling companions. The gentle Henry Abbey, whose poem "To Baffle Time" is brought to life line by line and hour by hour on occasions such as this; the genial James Creelman, who has seen everything and known everybody; Doctor Thomas R. Slicer of the silver tongue, whose homeliest prose is like the singing of birds; Hamilton Wright Mabie, who looks the gentle spirit his writings suggest; Charles Battell Loomis, who keeps his best jokes for his friends and prints only those of second worth; William George Jordan, who talks in epigrams and, although a bachelor, writes convincingly of the "Little Problems of Married Life"; Moncure D. Conway, who can drop like an eagle from the loftiest flights of metaphysics to the commonplaces of boiled beef and cabbage; Noah Brooks, the hero of every boy in the land and the devoted friend of every man in his wide circle; Colonel Thomas Wallace Knox, his near competitor in both these fields; Colonel George Edward Waring, a hero of Bull Run, the creator of "White Wings," and an all-round good fellow; Daniel Greenleaf Thompson, the lawyer-orator-philosopher, who rarely makes a joke himself or misses one by another; William Hamilton Gibson, who has translated the beauty of his own character into his books and his pictures; all these are there, and more, equally interesting, no less joyous, no less full of the high spirit of good fellowship. For it is one of the fortnightly meetings of the Authors Club. Mark Twain, belying his solemnity with quaint drolleries, comes occasionally to these gatherings. So does Percival Lowell, poet-astronomer; Walter Hines Page, sage-editor-great ambassador; Ripley Hitchcock, god-father of *David Harum* and a dozen other "best sellers"; Henry Mills Alden, patron-saint of Harpers; Calvin Thomas, as witty as wise; Will N. Harbin who writes a book a year and sometimes two. Joyce Kilmer too, comes in late, in the glory and pride of his new uniform; and we wish him the safe return from the red fields of Flanders which he has failed to make. Of course Stephen Henry Thayer, the banker-poet of Sleepy Hollow, is here. Without his gentle presence our joy would be incomplete.

Is it possible that all this is only a dream—a sweet memory?—that these bright spirits are now no more than the smoke-rings they were wont to mingle with their happy thoughts? Surely not! Their thoughts are here, in the books in those cases, their portraits on those walls; and if we listen, with the ear of devotion, we recognize their familiar voices, their cheery greetings, catch their response to the merry quip and jest that ever marked our happy gatherings. If Henry Holt, blithe in his eighties as any youngster of sixty, has correctly solved the riddle of existence, then he and they, who have preceded us across the Great Divide, may still gather in convivial friendship around our board and silently join our fortnightly trysts.

Mark Twain seemed to come back a few nights ago, when an old story about him was told in a new way. He had always been interested in the Baconian controversy. "When I get to Heaven" he said, "I am going straight to Bacon and ask him if he really wrote all those plays of Shakespere."

"But suppose he's not there," suggested one of his listeners.

"Then you can ask him" was the ready retort.

And Hopkinson Smith reappeared the same night. "They say that New Yorkers are lacking in the courtesy we find so general in the South. It is a mistake," he said. "The other day I stood at the end of a long line of men who were waiting to buy their tickets at the Grand Central Railway Station, when a man, under a mild alcoholic stimulus, thrust himself forward, banged down half a dollar and demanded a ticket to Buffalo. 'You must take your turn in the line,' said the ticket agent. 'Anyway, you can't go to Buffalo for half a dollar.' 'Where can I go?' asked the inebriate. And," said Hopkinson Smith with deep solemnity, "every man in that line told him where he could go! Does not that prove the innate kindliness and courtesy of the average New Yorker?"

Speaking of the "Little Problems of Married Life" reminds me that a lady once protested that a bachelor was the least competent of authorities on marriage problems. "But Madam," replied Jordan, "do you think an oyster is the best judge of a pearl?"

"Nowhere," once remarked Henry Holt, "do I hear such good talk as at the Authors Club."

Have the minds that habitually responded so brilliantly to such small stimuli as these become as raindrops falling into the ocean? Are they no more than last year's earth-mold?

In the Fall of the year Nature's seeming wastefulness grows pathetically impressive. The leaves in countless

forests flutter down to mingle with the soil. Their delicate lacework of veins; their miraculous power to seize
an atom of carbon from vagrant air-currents and separate it from its accompanying atom of oxygen as no
human chemist can do; the magic of color and fragrance
of flowers, all seem wasted and lost. No less pathetically impressive is the apparent waste of human life. While
the mind is functioning in its perfection, something hap-
pens to the body containing it, and down flutters the
intellect, seemingly inert, with all its aims and ambitions
unattained, its poetry and brilliant imaginings unex-
pressed, its aspirations unsatisfied.

But in the Spring, other leaves come and other flowers spread their fragrance and their beauty to the sunshine, and are made richer by the autumnal death that
preceded them. Even so, other minds reach maturity,
and grow in greatness and breadth and beauty by im-
pulsions derived from predecessors. The unspoken
thoughts, the unwritten poems, the high aspirations of
the race, are passed on to a new generation, enriched
and fertilized by those who have gone before. Equally
with the flowers of the field and the leaves of the forest,
the human mind may enjoy an objective immortality in
what Henry Holt called the "Cosmic Consciousness,"
while yet they live in the memory of those they loved
and by whom they are beloved.

Nearly half a century ago Charlie de Kay, who, happily, is still with us, got his brother-in-law, Richard
Watson Gilder, to invite half a dozen of his literary
friends to his house at 103 East 15th Street, in order
to form a club, "for the promotion of social intercourse among authors." The house, as may be seen

HOUSE IN WHICH THE AUTHORS CLUB WAS ORGANIZED

NO. 103 EAST 15TH STREET

from the accompanying plate, was an ideal birthplace for such an enterprise. It was beautiful in its simplicity —a veritable poem in brick and graceful lattice-work. The date was October 21st, 1882. There were present, besides the host, Noah Brooks, Edward Eggleston ("the Hoosier Schoolmaster"), Laurence Hutton, Brander Matthews, Edmund Clarence Stedman and Charles de Kay. No doubt they smoked their pipes as they sat about the open fire, seasoned their sober discussion with Attic salt, brightened it with quip and quirk and quaint fancy, as was their wont when together, and, so well did their minds meet, that the Authors Club was organized forthwith. Three weeks later another meeting was held, when the club was formally "founded."

Of the twenty-five "Founders," Charles de Kay is the only one left; but the others survive in the memory of the fast-thinning ranks of those who knew and loved them. Some stayed with us long enough to enshrine their memories in a beautiful book which the Authors Club published in 1893—*Liber Scriptorum*, a monumental work containing stories, essays, poems, reminiscences, exclusively by members, who all signed with pen and ink, their contributions in each one of the limited edition of 251 copies. Of the 109 men who made this remarkable book, fourteen were "Founders" of the Club. Henry Mills Alden, author of "God in His World: an Interpretation," contributed an exquisite "fireside study" under the title "Flammantia Mœnia Mundi"; Hjalmar Hjorth Boyesen, a poem, "The King's Bastard"; Noah Brooks, a review of his early reading under the title "Books of an Old Boy"; Edward Eggleston, a ghost story entitled "In Defence of the

225

MILLIONAIRES AND GRUB STREET

New York, November 1, 1882.

DEAR SIR:

It has been determined to form, on a simple and economical plan, an association of gentlemen connected with literature in its various branches.

You are respectfully asked to meet the undersigned on Thursday ·evening, November the 9th, at eight o'clock, in the house of Mr. Laurence Hutton, West Thirty-Fourth Street, No. 229, for the purpose of organizing a New York Author's Club.

NOAH BROOKS	BRONSON HOWARD
JOHN BURROUGHS	LAURENCE HUTTON
S. S. CONANT	CHARLES DE KAY
GEORGE WM. CURTIS	HAMILTON W. MABIE
EDWARD EGGLESTON	J. BRANDER MATTHEWS
SIDNEY HOWARD GAY	EDMUND CLARENCE STEDMAN
RICHARD W. GILDER	RICHARD HENRY STODDARD
EDWARD L. GODKIN	RICHARD GRANT WHITE
J. H. G. HASSARD	WILLIAM WINTER

To Brander Matthews, Esq
East Seventeenth Street, No. 350
New York.

Dead"; his brother George Cary Eggleston a witty article on "The Literary Disadvantages of Living Too Late"—under which so many present-day writers are laboring; Parke Godwin, a scholarly study of the influence of "The Germans in America"; Bronson Howard, an analysis of his "Shenandoah" under the title "History In A Play"; Laurence Hutton, an account of "The Book of My Babyhood"—namely *David Cop-*

perfield; Hamilton W. Mabie, a lovely prose-poem,
"My Search for the Goddess," which he character-
istically finds in the heart of the woods and in the song
of birds; Brander Matthews, a humorous sketch "On
the Transfusion of Indigestion"—(Emerson ate the
pie and Carlyle suffered from it sympathetically!);
William Starbuck Mayo, a poetical reminiscence of
Dante entitled "Buondelmonte"; Edmund Clarence
Stedman, a delightful poem "Fin de Siècle"; Charles
de Kay, a swelling, tumultuous "Ode to Phoenix the
Sun."

Other contributors whose memory is embalmed in
this unique volume—now greatly sought by collectors
—are Will Carleton, Andrew Carnegie, Julius Cham-
bers, John Denison Champlin, John Vance Cheney,
Mark Twain, Titus Munson Coan, Alban Jasper Conant, Moncure D. Conway, Maurice Francis Egan,
Harold Frederic, Daniel Coit Gilman, Arthur Sher-
burne Hardy, Henry Harland, John Hay, William D.
Howells, Henry E. Krehbiel, George Parsons Lathrop,
"Bill" Nye, Charles Henry Phelps, Horace Porter,
Theodore Roosevelt, Josiah Royce, Oscar S. Straus,
William Hayes Ward, Charles Dudley Warner, and
many others who have since joined the silent majority.
Of the 109 members who wrote for this book in 1892,
less than a score remain.

In 1921 a "Second Book of the Authors Club" was
published, bearing the same title, *Liber Scriptorum,*
as before, and uniform with it in format.

This was happily described by a reviewer as "a pleasant sentiment, not lacking a tinge of romance. For its
purpose is to leave a substantial record of the Club
itself as a whole and of its component personalities,

like mileposts along the path of its history, or, like a portrait to be hung in a gallery of ancestors, for the interest and edification of the generations of Authors Club members yet to come."

Unlike its predecessor, it is especially rich in records of personal experiences, some of great historic value. Frederick S. Dellenbaugh, who made the romantic boat trip through the Grand Canyon of the Colorado in 1871 with Major Powell, tells of their navigation of a particularly dangerous fall and rapids between the mile-high walls of the canyon. He calls it "Running the Sockdolager." Judge Charles Fraser Maclean was present at Sedan, when Napoleon III surrendered himself and his army to the Prussian monarch, and his story is full of interesting detail. Frederic Courtland Penfield, who was American Ambassador to Austria-Hungary at the outbreak of the World War, relates his experiences in "Searching Darkest Russia for a Mislaid Savant." Dr. Louis Livington Seaman was in Antwerp when the first bombs were dropped on that city from a Zeppelin, and his story is full of horror—and interest. So are the telegrams which he sent to the State Department in Washington concerning this breach of international law and civilized usage. Marcus Benjamin, of the staff of the United States National Museum at Washington, contributes a series of Pepys-like recollections of his contacts with important visitors to the museum. Dr. George F. Kunz tells of an interesting experience he had in Russia "When Nicholas II was Czarevitch." Don C. Seitz versifies the "Yoshiwara" in Tokio. John Uri Lloyd describes "A Storm in the Desert" which he experienced in Africa. And so on,—nearly six hundred pages of stories, essays, sketches, critical

AUTOGRAPHED MENU OF AN AUTHORS CLUB DINNER

and scientific articles, poems, personal adventures or experiences, all done with the skill of practised writers.

The names of four ambassadors as members of the Authors Club will not be unnoticed in these lists. Besides those named—though mention should be made of President Roosevelt and Secretaries of State John Hay and Elihu Root—were their Excellencies Andrew D. White (Germany), Lloyd Brice (The Netherlands), James W. Gerard (Germany), David Jayne Hill, (Germany), Walter Hines Page (England), Thomas Nelson Page (Italy), General Horace Porter

229

(France), Dr. Henry Van Dyke (The Netherlands), Oscar Straus (Turkey), Robert Underwood Johnson (Italy), and representing France here, Ambassador Jusserand. It seemed at one time as if the Administration in Washington could not find anyone fitly to represent the nation in a diplomatic way unless it applied to the Council of the Authors Club for a recommendation!

Another famous book was published by the Authors Club. Like the others, it was written exclusively by members—*Feodor Vladimir Larrovitch: An Appreciation of his Life and Works*: edited by William George Jordan and Richardson Wright. This was the book I offered to Henry Clay Frick, who did not understand it. It was the outgrowth of an evening of delicious fun when, on April 26th, 1917, was held a centenary celebration of the birth of this mythical personage. The program, announcing the auspicious event, carried the following quotations, which, of course, are just as illusory as Larrovitch himself is unsubstantial.

The forthcoming definitive edition of the works of Larrovitch, to be published as a centenary tribute, will be hailed with joy by all lovers of Russia's novelist, patriot and philosopher. Surely, it is a sign of the re-awakening of Russia that the voice of this great author should speak again in this hour of the nation's fight for world liberty. Russkoe Slovo, December 12, 1916

From out the land of sunrise, dispelling the murk of evil report, rises the figure of Larrovitch ... to whom the world will some day pay just tribute. James Trotter in The London Times

Plusieurs, sans doute, ont défini l'âme Russe, mais il n'est aucun qui l'ait analysée aussi clairement dans tous ses attributs que Téodor Vladimir Larrovitch. Marcel Lanatiére

We hear much of Dr. Samuel Johnson's Literary Club, when Goldsmith, Garrick, Reynolds, Burke, Boswell, Gibbon and others used to meet and talk as men never talked before. I doubt whether they reached higher flights of fancy than did the Authors on this Saturnian night. The rooms were crowded with members and invited guests. My own guest was one of the Belgian Commissioners, who was associated with the State Department in the prosecution of the war. His mystification, as he listened to the homely details of Larrovitch's boyhood was almost pathetic. Finally he exclaimed: "But I do not understand! You say he never existed, and yet I am hearing eloquent extracts from his works, his beautiful poems, and we are told how the elders of his village patted his curly head and called him endearing names."

"Those names, if translated, might not sound so endearing," I answered; for, expecting to have Paderewski as our guest, Richardson Wright, in his clever essay, had used the Russian equivalent for the expletive in common use in the West which begins with "You son of—etc." We had looked for an appreciative laugh from the great statesman-pianist, but he did not arrive in time.

"You have a word in French," I explained to my guest, "which covers the case. That word is *'blague.'*"

"Ah, vous autres Américains, que vous êtes des blagueurs!" exclaimed my guest. "Je ne vous comprendrai jamais!" He was nevertheless relieved: he had feared his failure to "connect" was in some way due to his imperfect understanding of our language!

The essays were so clever, the recollections of Larrovitch so impressive, the list of his works so convincing, the authorities quoted so serious, it would have been a waste of excellent literature to let them die. So they were published in a book, and sent to reviewers without explanation. It was cruel, for some of them "fell for it"; amongst others the sapient *Boston Transcript*. Here is an editorial comment on the personality of Larrovitch and the *Transcript's* reaction to the book:

LARROVITCH

Some day no doubt we shall have to take a positive stand in the matter of Larrovitch. We may have to take him up in a serious way, if you get what we mean. But it is a puzzling problem. Of course, in the face of Mr. Jordan's argument and the weighty considerations put forward by the Boston *Transcript's* literary expert, it is absurd to accept the crude brutality of those who label him as a sort of 'Mrs. 'Arris,' and claim there 'never was no sich a person.' Have we not the ponderous critique elegantly put forth by the Authors Club as visible evidence of his solidity? . . . It is a work of erudition—and several other things.

Now the learned critic of the Boston *Transcript* tells us that "in the study of the life and work of Larrovitch many illuminative points of view are opened." That seems profoundly and beautifully true. "He himself" says the *Transcript*, "epitomized that curious blending of the East and West which perhaps accounts to-day . . . for that baffling combination of *laissez-aller* and revolutionary initiative" which is Russia. In the face of this, shall we not hail Larrovitch as a "find?"

Larrovitch is truly a "find," and the day is not distant when collectors will realize it, and will compete in auction rooms for a copy of this record of his life and works.

I am tempted to quote Clinton Scollard's beautiful tribute to this great personage who, created out of the

ambiant air of the Authors rooms—itself still pregnant with many unborn masterpieces of literature—has
become an actual and leading entity in the republic of
letters.

What I shall say of Larrovitch shall be
    As though one spoke of twilight in the spring
    Of vernal beauty come to blossoming
Too soon, to fade and be but memory—
The memory of a something to which we
    In our exalted moments fain would cling,
    Frail and ephemeral as the white moth's wing,
Or as the prismy spindrift of the sea.

Let us forget the chill Siberian snows,
    The stark Caucasian heights let us forget;
These girdled and oppressed him, and his woes
    Wake in our hearts a passionate regret;
So be there strewn above his long repose
    Sweet sprays of the Crimean violet!

Richard Henry Stoddard, the well-beloved poet,
warmly reciprocated the affection in which he was held
by his fellow members, and testified it by bequeathing
to them his priceless collection of first editions, rare
manuscripts, and scores of letters, incunabula and the
like, worth a fortune at auction prices. Many of these,
suitably framed, now hang on the walls of the Club
and add materially to its charm.

At a complimentary banquet which the Club honored
itself by honoring this distinguished poet, Judge Henry
E. Howland, told a fanciful story of a recent call
he had made on Mr. Stoddard. The poet was busy

JOHN DENISON CHAMPLIN II

in an outhouse at the rear of his home, and Mrs. Stoddard entertained the judge until her husband had finished the work upon which he was engaged. Whatever this was, it was accompanied by sounds of vigorous hammering, and the employment of many ejaculations which penetrated the house. Presently, after an outburst of strong expletives and a specially loud crash of a hammer, Mrs. Stoddard went to the back door, and in her gentle voice, inquired,

"Richard, whatever are you doing?"

"Opening a can of oysters," was the unexpected answer.

"What are you opening it with?"

"With an ax of course. What do you suppose I am opening it with?"

"From your language we thought you were opening it with prayer."

The banquet hall shrilled with mirth; for Stoddard was noted for his soft and gentle manner, and nothing could be more incongruous than the image pictured by Judge Howland and the known habits of the poet.

A similar complimentary dinner was given to Andrew Carnegie, who in his speech of acceptance, modestly proclaimed himself a "poor author." And sympathizing with other poor authors, he gave the Club a quarter of a million dollars to relieve the distress and destitution which not infrequently overtake those who depend solely on their pens for a livelihood. Less than ten percent of the annual proceeds of this fund has been used for the benefit of members of the Club, the rest going to the alleviation of suffering among other writers and their families. The fund is secretly administered by trustees, who are the only ones to know the names

235

of recipients of the Carnegie bounty. The authors naturally regard this as the wisest and most useful of Mr. Carnegie's many benefactions!

In 1916 the Authors Club in New York and the Bohemian Club in San Francisco joined to celebrate one of the miracles of modern science by dining to-gether—on opposite ends of the continent! Each of the six hundred sitters at the table in San Francisco, and each of the two hundred members of the Authors in New York, had a receiving-telephone attached to his ears, so that he could hear the speeches, songs and wit-ticisms sent back and forth across three thousand miles of space. Before the days of the greater marvel of radio, this was an epoch-marking experience; especially when the waves of the Pacific ocean were heard break-ing against the rocks of the Cliff House, and a moving picture of them—or others like them—was simul-taneously thrown upon a screen in New York!

Some fifteen years before, I had published in the *Overland Monthly* a set of verses by Rossiter John-son. This became the official anthem of the Authors Club. The first verse of it was now sung in New York, and the second verse sung in San Francisco—across the mountains, prairies, and rivers of the continent into our cozy quarters, where it had sounded every Watch Night for a dozen years or more. This is the song:

The Rolling World.

Opening Song, Watch-nights, at the Authors Club

Words and Music by . . . . ROSSITER JOHNSON

Oh, the rolling world it rolls alway—
Rolls and rhymes—rolls and rhymes!
And for the song there's a bill to pay—
Dollars and dimes—dollars and dimes!
Oh, what a rolling world!
Here's a dime for me and a dollar for you,
And more on the bush where the last ones grew—
Oh, what a rolling world!
R-o-o-s-t high! s-i-n-g low!
Never mind the rolling world!

Oh, the rolling world it rolls alway—
Rolls and whirls—rolls and whirls—
Rolling up lumps of moistened clay
Into boys and girls—boys and girls!
Oh, what a rolling world!
Here's a girl for me and a boy for you—
And we'll change them around, if that won't do!
Oh, what a rolling world!
R-o-o-s-t high! s-i-n-g low!
Never mind the rolling world!

Oh, the rolling world it rolls alway—
Rolls and sings—rolls and sings!
And as it rolls it seems to say:
"Get up, little poets, and try your wings!"
Oh, what a rolling world!
Here's a rhyme for me and a verse for you,
And the capital letter that marks them true
All over the rolling world!
R-o-o-s-t high! s-i-n-g low!
Never mind the rolling world!

Oh, the rolling world it rolls alway—
Steady and true—steady and true!
And the reason is, the wise men say,
It has nothing else to do—nothing else to do!
Oh, what a rolling world!
Here's a hint for me and a moral for you—
How steady we shall be when we've nothing else to do
But roll with the rolling world!
R-o-o-s-t high! s-i-n-g low!
And hurrah for the rolling world!

237

MILLIONAIRES AND GRUB STREET

An interesting discovery has been made while these recollections are being written. It is that an Authors Club was formed in New York as early as 1837. Here are the documents relating to this Club which have just reached me, through the kindness of my friend, Mr. Samuel H. Wandell, former secretary of the Authors Club, whose painstaking researches and publications have removed from the memory of Aaron Burr much of the discredit attached to it by ignorance and prejudice.

> Upper Longfield,
> Bristol, Rhode Island.
> [December — 1929]

Dear Mr. Wandell:

I wonder if there is anything in the Club archives to throw light on a document I found in a Providence bookshop, not long since? I enclose a copy of it, which may be of interest to some of the Authors Club members. The present Club, I believe, only goes back to the 'eighties or thereabouts. This Authors Club of 1837 was evidently a new thing, and I am curious to know how long it lasted and what became of it.

I am especially interested in the presence of Cooper's name on the lists. He was evidently elected a member and "appointed" 2nd vice-president at the same time. Just then Cooper was utterly at odds with everything American, including her writers, and it was in 1837 that he took occasion (In "Home As Found") to belabor the New York *literati* with extraordinary bitterness. I should guess that he never accepted his election to the Authors Club, especially as it offered him the post of third fiddle in the band.

> Sincerely yours,
>
> H. W. BOYNTON.

(Enclosure)

238

The Authors Club

New York, May 17th, 1837.
571 Broadway Opposite Niblo's

Dear Sir—

At a meeting of the Author's Club held pursuant to special notice at the Library of the Museum of Natural History on the 9th Inst.—

Washington Irving was appointed President,
Fitz Greene Halleck, First Vice-President,
James Fennimore Cooper, Second Vice-President,
Caleb Tickner, M.D., Treasurer,
Rev. J. F. Schroeck(?), D.D., Editor,
Solyman Brown, Secretary.

Greenville Mellen		
Rufus Dawes	Publishing	Executive
Rev. Calvin Colton	Committee	Committee

The following new members were also elected in addition to the first fifteen a list of whom were transmitted to you on a former occasion:

Richard Henry Dana	Jared Sparks
Rev. John Pierpont	Samuel Jackson, M.D.
Jas. G. Whittier	George W. Holly
Wm. G. Simms	James E. De Kay
Caleb Cushing	Wm. P. Palmer
Chas. H. Hoffman	Washington Alston
Theo. S. Fay	John Inman
J. F. Cooper	Rev. Timothy Flint
Chas. A. Lee, M.D.	James Hall
Thomas Cole	Thomas Sully
Robt. Walsh, Junr.	James Brooks
His Ex. Edw. Everett	Rev. C. S. Henry

Rev. M. Eastburn

Will you have the kindness to allow me to present for your signature the following simple Article of Association to be published on the cover of our periodical?

(Here a short document was evidently attached by wafer.)

A prospectus of the proposed work together with a copy of

the Constitution of the Club will be forwarded to members as soon as printed.

I am most respectfully,

SOLYMAN BROWN,

Secretary.

Fitz Greene Halleck, Esq.

Mr. Wandell writes: You will observe that this letter is signed by "Solyman Brown, Secretary." Brown was the author of several political pamphlets, was an Anti-Federalist. He seems to have been a literary dentist. In the work *John Jacob Astor, Landlord of New York,* by Arthur D. Howden Smith, New York, 1929, we find references to Solyman Brown as the partner of a young dentist who was engaged to marry Astor's daughter.

Charles de Kay, to whom I referred for enlightenment concerning this early Authors Club, writes from East Hampton, L. I., under date May 17th, 1930:

It seems to me that I have heard of an early Authors Club but I think it must have gone out of existence when Washington Irving went to Europe for so long a time. I can just recall Washington Irving as shown me in the street, although I must have met him elsewhere. My recollection is much clearer of Fitz-Greene Halleck.

Dr. James E. de Kay was the only brother of my father. He is the author of the five folio volumes on the fauna of the State of New York. A small brown snake and a small shrew-mouse as well as other "critters" were named after him. There is a niche in the entrance hall to the Natural History Museum which is reserved for my uncle's statue, but neither I nor his grandson of the same name, living at Babylon, Long Island, are well enough off to fill this niche. Perhaps in time the Museum itself will fill the void.

I have no idea when the first Authors Club came to an end.

Neither have I. Nobody seems to know anything about this early Authors Club. That is why I have reproduced the only known documents relating to it.

During the forty-eight years since the little group of writers met in the Gilder home in East 15th Street, to organize a club "for the promotion of social intercourse among authors" only one woman was admitted to membership. This was Julia Ward Howe. She was made an honorary member and probably never attended a meeting. At infrequent intervals, however, ladies were invited and admitted to the Club, and even attended dinners within its sacred precincts. But there was a strong feeling among the younger members that since women writers were no longer "authoresses" but "authors," it was an anachronism to exclude from membership, solely because of their sex, authors who were contributing so largely and so efficiently to the literary output of the day. The older and more conservative members, however, held that the character of the Club would be so changed by the admission of women that it would cease to conform to the ideals of its founders, and its meetings would lose their delightful informality. The subject was debated over a period of several years, and came up for a vote at every annual meeting. Until 1930 the regular motion for the admission of women writers to full membership was outvoted; but last year the advocates of feminism won, and, with a holy joy, nominated—and at the next meeting elected—Ida Tarbell, Edith Wharton, Willa Cather, Fannie Hurst, Leonora Speyer, Alice Duer Miller, Sara Teasdale, Margaret Widdemer, and, a fortnight later, Agnes Repplier and Ellen Glasgow.

241

The revolution—or evolution as some prefer to re-gard it—is too recent for us to judge as to its ultimate effects. That it is a progressive one and in keeping with the spirit of the times cannot be gainsaid. Now that ladies have themselves become votaries of Nicotina, there may be no diminution of our physical ease, while there may be some enlargement of our moral and spiritual natures—"a consummation" if not devoutly to be wished or entirely necessary, is yet one not to be deplored.

CANADIAN INTERLUDES

CORNELIA TRENCHARD

O F course that is not her real name, any more than
Digby, Nova Scotia, is her present home. But she had
lived at Digby, and when, at the age of six years, she
was taken thence to St. John, she really and truly originated the little prayer that has since been credited to
a host of youngsters: "Good-bye, God; I'm going to
New Brunswick to-morrow!" And she did; but not
seeing anybody who looked like God on the boat across
the Bay of Fundy, she long refused to believe that He
was on the mainland.

A few years later she said another thing that betokened originality. Her mother noticed that she was
sucking a sour-ball—that delectable mass which con-
fectioners impale on a skewer, to be twisted and rolled
over the infantile tongue in sticky delight. "Where did
you get that?" asked the mother. "Well," slowly answered the angel-faced babe, "Angus Cairns lost a
penny, and while he was looking for it I spent it!"

She was just sixteen when I first saw her. It was on
the steps of the church; and the khaki-clad regiment
was just swinging round the corner of the street, with
the band playing "Onward, Christian Soldiers!" She
had the face of Raphael's Madonna. Spiritual exhalta-
tion shone in her eyes—or so it seemed to me. And the
occasion warranted it. Tall, sun-burnt and ruddy, a

thousand young Canadians, called from logging-camp and farm, were marching in rhythmic step to the stirring notes of Sullivan's immortal hymn. It was their last church-parade before leaving for France. The congregation of women and elderly men had gathered about the church door to greet the soldier lads, and then to join them in their farewell service. Cornelia's two brothers were already "somewhere in France." Her father, too old to serve at the front, was doing "his bit" in other ways. He smiled a greeting to me as the soldiers clattered up the steps, and I joined his little party.

In church I shared Cornelia's hymn-book, and her sweet girlish voice trembled with patriotic fervor as the martial strains from brass instruments intoned the beautiful service—for the usual organ was silent on this day of days. The jingle of spurs and the rattle of scabbards in the officers' pew across the aisle formed a staccato accompaniment to the diapason of deep masculine voices chanting the Te Deum; and above all rose the silvery notes of Cornelia's girlish voice in ecstatic earnestness. The sunlight filtered through the colored glass of a memorial window above her head, and made for it a flickering halo of blended colors. Here were all the elemental forces that make for love and patriotism. And love there was! Who could look on Cornelia and doubt it?

Somewhere in the middle west, in Saskatchewan or Alberta, a plain English couple had pre-empted a government farm, and their son, barely turned eighteen, had been among the first to respond to Canada's call for recruits. He was now in the church, a few pews from me, a kettle-drum by his side. With all the amazing flourishes of sticks which characterize British drummers, he had marked time for his regiment as it marched through the town. With less noise and display he had beaten a tattoo on little Cornelia's heart; though this I did not find out until later, when Cornelia led me to the camp and gave me her childish confidence.

The boy himself was a sturdy youngster with a sunny smile, the bluest eyes and a ripe-apple complexion that many a girl might envy;—otherwise not remarkable except for the glory that was his in his glowing youth and in the distinction which Cornelia had conferred upon him. These I might have envied, even on the eve of his departure for the blood-sodden fields of France, had my sympathy been less altruistic. But to me it was so idyllic—this beautiful combination of youth, patriotism and love—that I savored it as I would an exquisite poem or a lovely landscape. It was ethereal, heavenly, made so by the spiritual beauty of the maid, whose mobile features were as a delicate instrument upon which her emotions played the softest music.

It was early night when the regiment marched through the town to take the train for Halifax, the band playing "We'll never let the old flag fall!"—the most soul-stirring musical product of the war. Rockets and flares were lighted on balconies and sidewalks by the townsfolk, who thus tried to give the occasion a festive look. It was a sorrowful failure. Tears struggled with smiles, and won in the contest.

I was again with Cornelia and her sadly reduced family. The drummer-boy could not leave the ranks

245

until after the band had reached the station, and then only for an instant. Cornelia was at my side one moment; in the next I missed her, and turned just in time to see, in the half-light of a standing automobile, a khaki-clad figure with a drum on its back, and two arms clasped about its neck. Cornelia was wearing a silver-gray dress, and this was the color of the sleeves I saw. The light was suddenly turned aside, and friendly darkness enveloped the lovers. A moment later Cornelia's hand slipped into mine, and we turned away home. If I did not see the beautiful eyes shining with tears it was because there was no light to reveal them; but the little hand quivered in mine in unspoken misery.

Throughout the broad Canadian dominion, in every town and hamlet, Cornelia's sisters in their thousands twined their arms around departing loved-ones and turned away into the dark with courageous silence. And from far-away France came to them, as it did to Cornelia, a single telegraphic sentence, witheringly brief, that will tinge with grey the lustre of the longest life. It was at Vimy Ridge that the drummer-boy beat his last tattoo; and his sunny smile, his baby blue eyes and apple complexion are all that remain as a memory to me. What was in Cornelia's heart I dared not look to see.

According to official figures, Canadian casualties, up to eleven days before the signing of the armistice, totalled 34,877 killed in action; 15,457 dead of wounds or disease; 152,779 wounded, and 8245 presumed dead, missing in action and prisoners of war— a total of 211,358!

CANADIAN INTERLUDES

PROFESSOR CHARLES TOWNSEND COPELAND

My love of contrasts was gratified in an unexpected
way. In this delightful little resort on Passamaquoddy
Bay, I was able to join to a beautiful love idyl a succession of intellectual exercises of the highest rank. I
count it as a signal honor that I found myself seated
at the same hotel table as Professor Charles Townsend
Copeland, the beloved "Copey" of countless Harvard
graduates.

At first I did not realize the distinction which had
accidently come to me. Half a dozen people were at
the table when I was first shown to my seat. There was
an empty chair at the head of the table. Presently a
gentleman of slight figure, scholarly look and wearing
thick glasses, appeared and took the vacant seat. After
a friendly glance at the company, he took a little book
from his pocket and became so absorbed in it that he
paid little heed to the food placed before him, and
none at all to the rest of us. In a whispered aside to
my nearest neighbor I inquired who the unsociable
vis-a-vis was; but his name meant nothing to me then.
I did not expect to find myself opposite to the most
popular member of the Harvard faculty, and felt a
little piqued that so far from joining in our innocent
chatter he seemed bored by it. Thinking that perhaps
the talk was on too lowly a plain for his professorship,
I mischievously essayed to raise it by a reference to the
law of equivalents. Speaking of the equations of motion in generalized co-ordinates, I brought the subject
down to what I thought might be the general level of
understanding by adding "and, as you know, action and
reaction are equal." This producing no effect other

247

Copyright Piric MacDonald

CHARLES TOWNSEND COPELAND

than to mystify two elderly spinsters, I went on with a serio-comic demonstration of the application to sociology of the mechanicistic formula that all motion takes place along the line of least resistance. Again the remark overshot its target: "Copey" did not flinch! Defeated, I became as silent as the pedagog himself.

The talk then became general—except for the professor and myself. But *Alice for Short* being mentioned, I could not resist the temptation.

"I once wrote an interesting letter to William De Morgan, the author of that book," I said.

"What was it about?" queried my neighbor.

248

"It was dictated to me by Herbert Spencer, and contained his famous definition of life." I noticed that my silent vis-a-vis showed signs of interest. "Would you like to hear it?" I asked of my neighbor.

"I believe I've heard it, but I'd like to hear it again."

"Life is the definite combination of heterogeneous changes, both simultaneous and successive, in correspondence with external co-existence and sequences," I quoted.

The professor looked up. "Did I understand you to say that you were acquainted with Herbert Spencer?" he asked.

I assured him that I had known Spencer well.

"Then perhaps you can tell me if it is true that he used to apply a pair of ear-pads to shut out inconsequent chatter."

I gravely answered that he had been rightly informed. The merry twinkle in his eye ought to have warned me!

"Happy expedient!" was his comment, as he returned to his book.

A shout of laughter from the rest of us, and a quizzical glance from the professor, who simulated surprise at our mirth, broke the conversational ice and made the meal a merry one. When I got to know him better I realized that it was part of "Copey's" humor to fire a devastating shot like that and look unconcerned.

"All *Gaul* is divided into three parts," he is said to have quoted as three undergraduates stamped noisily into a room where he was speaking; but this Parthian shaft he disclaims, and credits it to Professor Kittredge. *Si non e vero e ben trovato.* It bears the true Copian stamp!

249

After a meal or two, during which I made several discrete probings, I discovered a chink in dear old "Copey's" armor: he hated the mechanical age in which we live and abhorred new inventions. He had no use for the electric light, and the telephone, with its jangling imperiousness, was anathema to him. Less academic in my training, I had found poetry in a Bessemer converter, and romance in a slabbing mill, and said so.

"Mere sentimentality!" he had incautiously exclaimed.

"Mere sentimentality!" I echoed. "That is how Darwin's beautiful monograph on the useful functions of earthworms would appear to the earthworms themselves."

He flushed, then smiled and said "Continue!" as if I had been at recitation in his class. So I continued.

"Even Ruskin, who went into volumes of rhapsody over the imaginings of painters and architects, was blind to the beauty of that form of imagination which takes the crude ore of the earth and endows it, as a machine, with human ingenuity and superhuman precision and patience. The dreams of the inventor, the conceptions of the merchant, the imaginings of the great industrial organizer, are none the less poetical because they emerge from the realm of fantasy into that of fact. An ideal that becomes an actuality, as a wonderful piece of mechanism or an elaborate commercial organization, is as truly a poem as if it had merely been thrown into dreary hexameters and left there."

"So you find poetry in machinery," he commented.

"I prefer the spirit that found 'sermons in stones, books in running brooks' "—

" 'And good in everything!' " I could not stop the interruption: it slipped out! "Do you realize," I ventured, "that the poetry of America most often finds its expression in a machine rather than in an ode? The imagination that inspired Tennyson is, in essence, no different from that which excited Robert Hoe when he built his double-sextuple press to print two hundred thousand eight-page *Heralds* an hour."

"When Carlyle was told that the American people doubled their numbers in twenty-five years, he questioned the benefit to civilization of 'sixty million dollar-hunters over thirty million.' One may not improperly ask why two hundred thousands *Heralds* an hour." It was in some such way that "Copey" met my argument. I declined to agree with him!

After that we got on famously. My dissidence stimulated him, and in the quiet of his room, where I soon became a welcome guest, or along the country lanes where we walked, he talked as I fancy Oliver Wendell Holmes must have talked. It was like hearing a new autocrat speak—not like a book, but one alive with "thoughts that breathe and words that burn." Then his voice was as beautiful as the thoughts he spoke; and when he read aloud it was music. I recall one heavenly night as we walked through the soft Canadian air, and the stars seemed to have come down close to earth to inspire him to speak of things celestial. It was a benediction—a prose poem, and, with his beautiful voice, a song of thanksgiving. All too soon we arrived at his cousin's house, where he was persuaded to read to us—a small sympathetic group. Whether it was because of our solemn talk on the way, or whether the company was exceptionally harmonious, he read, first a chapter from Dickens, and then from one of the gospels, in a way that made each sentence sound like a passage from an oratorio. I recalled a rehearsal when Sir Joseph Barnby, who had the most beautiful voice I ever heard, showed the choir he was conducting how to render the dramatic passages from Mendelssohn's "Elijah":— "The deeps afford no water, and the rivers are exhausted. The suckling's tongue now cleaveth for thirst to his mouth; the infant children ask for bread," and so to the end of the page, as the phrases are passed from voice to voice in exquisite succession. That is how Copeland read on this night of nights.

Lest my enthusiasm be deemed overwrought, I hasten to remind those who know, and to inform those who do not, that Professor Copeland, for a quarter of a century has made an annual trip to the Harvard Club in New York, simply to read to an audience of his old students, who come from the ends of the earth to hear him and to greet him. He is the only member of any faculty who has his own personal alumni association, numbering some hundreds of devoted graduates; and on these occasions they flock to meet him from everywhere.

Of all this hero worship I was happily unaware; else had our friendship developed along more formal lines. For I loved to tease him in a way that would have shocked his worshippers. One day he spoke of himself as an old man. He was not yet sixty. I remonstrated. My belief is that to give expression to an unpleasant thought often makes it a fact. Not that old age is itself unpleasant; but in a world wherein is so much of beauty and interest, it is not well to encourage the thought of leaving it. As I rose from the table I said: "If any one should ask me, I should say you were a dapper young man, with an unconvincing pretence of senile decrepitude!"

"And if anyone should ask me," he countered, "I should describe you as a cosmopolitan Englishman, with a trenchant turn for satire!"

His mental processes were so rapid that it would have been surprising if he had not had a trenchant turn for satire himself. On one of our walks that I recall we indulged in a game of dialectical fooling around the speculation: "Why do the lives of elderly spinsters so often display an intellectual barrenness rarely found in elderly bachelors?" The discussion came to a sudden end as I led it into forbidden reaches. Thus:

"Has the uni-lateral standard of sexual morality anything to do with it?" I asked.

Receiving no answer from the celebate at my side I joined another query:

"If it has, is not the remedy self-evident?"

"If the remedy be self-evident, then it is not debatable."

A playful conceit, punctured by a keen satirical touch!

Some years afterwards I called upon him in his chambers in Hollis Hall, Cambridge, taking with me one of Boston's most prominent business men—one whose imagination had expressed itself in the building, equipping and managing of a dozen or more spinning and weaving factories.

"A graduate of Harvard, of course," said Copeland, on learning that my friend was a Bostonian.

253

Nothing else was conceivable in one whose life centered in Cambridge.

"No, Brown University," was the unexpected reply.

"Ah! too bad, too bad—for Harvard!"

And yet my friend was not without academic distinction. He was president of the board of trustees of Wellesley College and a trustee of his own alma mater.

Again I found the genial "Copey," as I had come to regard him, saddened by death. Many of his young student-friends had gone to France, and had had their high hopes quenched in the welter that made the world safe for—politicians. It was all so far from the gentle life of Cambridge, and so different from the high hopes their dear "Copey' had instilled in them! But he himself is still active in well doing. On Wednesday evenings a lamp in his window in Hollis Hall is notice that Charles Townsend Copeland is at home, and that all properly-accredited and well-behaved visitors will be welcome to share in an intellectual treat such as is rarely offered these days. For myself, I like better to think of him as I knew him, amid the scenes on Passamaquoddy Bay that Cornelia Trenchard had hallowed.

GENERAL THE HON. SIR SAM HUGHES, K. C. B.

Returning from England in 1901, I was asked by the purser of the Cunarder to take charge of the usual entertainment on board in aid of the seamen's charities, and I got Mr. Chauncey M. Depew to act as chairman of the concert. He presided with his usual aplom and told a number of stories. One of these, at which he himself laughed most heartily, was an old one that had been told to me years before by John Fiske, and I had quoted it in *Uncle Sam at Home*, which I wrote in 1885 and published in 1888. It had to do with an "improvement" of the usual patriotic toast, running:

"The United States, bounded on the North by Canada, on the South by the Gulf of Mexico, on the East by the great Atlantic and on the West by the broad Pacific."

The "improvement" was as follows:

"The United States, bounded on the North by the North Pole, on the South by the Antarctic Ocean, on the East by the Gulf Stream and on the West by the illimitable ocean."

"But," said Mr. Depew, "not satisfied with this, a gentleman from Duluth got up and said:

" 'I propose as toast, the United States, bounded on the North by the Aurora Borealis, on the South by Infinite Space, on the East by the Precession of the Equinoxes and on the West by the Day of Judgment!' "

The story was received with shouts of laughter. Even had Mr. Depew's enjoyment of it been less hearty, I should have hesitated to tell him of its ancestry.

MILLIONAIRES AND GRUB STREET

Canadian Official Copyright

GENERAL THE HON. SIR SAM HUGHES, K. C. B.

Moreover, I still held Carnegie's whimsical theory that, by all the rules of equity, every joke was entitled to the recompense of a laugh, and an old story, well told, to an adequate reward. So I laughed almost as loudly as did Mr. Depew, and silently paid tribute to John Fiske, who originated the yarn and gave it its deserved immortality.

Some years later I was again asked to get up the usual entertainment on a transatlantic liner. No Depew was on board; so there was no denial of the equal rights of the Dominion of Canada to a share in the glories of the amended toast. I accordingly picked as my chairman the handsomest and most distinguished man present, Colonel Sam Hughes, senior member of the Canadian House of Commons. This was ten years before the Great War, and before he was knighted for his incomparable services, as Minister of Militia, in forming, training, equipping and sending to sea an army of thirty thousand lusty Canadians within a few weeks of the outbreak of hostilities.

During these ten years I was privileged to be with Colonel Hughes in many places and under various conditions. I was his guest at the opening of parliament in Ottawa and at many sessions of it. I was with him during a parliamentary election in Ontario, and witnessed his unfailing good nature and ready wit in presence of antagonistic hecklers. I was his companion on a trip to Montreal, and on the train saw that he was acquainted with almost every man on board. Once I turned to see him in vigorous converse with a deaf man, using the finger alphabet as readily as he did his tongue—which, at times, was as keen as the sword he wore on state occasions. In Alberta, Saskatchewan, even in British Columbia, I have run across his friends who instantly became mine as soon as I mentioned his name. He had a genius for friendship, and his confidence once given, was never shaken. Which was not always the best for himself!

In the *Daily Star* of Montreal I once saw a cartoon of Sir Sam Hughes, in a "tin-hat" marked "integrity," with bombs exploding above it and, falling harmlessly from it, missiles marked "jealousy, personal spite, cowardly innuendo, mean untruths" and such like products of political antagonisms. Under it all was the legend *"Can't even dent it!"* But they could, and did!

Sir Wilfred Laurier, his political opponent for years, being asked the reason for the honor of knighthood which had been conferred on General Hughes—ignoring the splendid work he had done in calling from the furthermost parts of the Dominion the first of half a million men that formed the great army Canada sent overseas—is said to have replied with a Gallic shrug: *"Le roi s'amuse!"* A clever pun, but in execrable taste, if true!

To the *Canadian Magazine* Britton B. Cooke contributed an article from which I am tempted to take a paragraph or two, in which, almost in epic form, a scene is put before us of Sir Sam Hughes's first great achievement after the declaration of war—an achievement such as no one had ever dreamed of as within the bounds of possibility. This scene occurred in September, 1914, one short month after the war began, in August!

Says Mr. Cooke:

Homer Watson, the Canadian artist, is painting, in his studio in the hamlet of Doon, a tremendous canvas, one of three ordered by the Government in commemoration of the mobilization of the First Canadian Overseas Contingent at Valcartier last year. This canvas shows, against a background of Laurentian Mountains crowned with September sunlight, the great Valcartier plain covered with our soldiers "marching past" the Duke of Connaught and the Minister of Militia, and a blot of spectators in the foreground just behind the Royal Standard. Between this fluttering piece of colour and the mountain background are thirty thousand sons of Canada, organized, uniformed, and armed for war—thirty thousand stalwart men

258

swinging across the plain under the clear hot sky, thirty thousand bayonets glancing in the brilliant light and forming where the long lines back in the middle distance swing round the turn into the stretch leading past the Governor-General and the Minister, a figure like a fan of burnished gold flung against the gray-greens of the hills behind.

It is a stirring picture. It was a stirring scene.

Here was not a mere assembly of uniformed and orderly men, but a unit, a force—the thunderbolt forged by a young nation, a terrible instrument, keen, hard as adamant, true as steel, now ready to be launched—as it has already been launched—in the defence of Christendom. This was the force of which General Drain of the United States Army, looking on, said: "I would rather command this army than any army on the battlefields of Europe, or in the reserves of Europe. It is not a body of soldiers. It is an army of non-commissioned officers!" This was the force that stopped the breach at Langemarck. It had been gathered from the far ends of the nation, from the coal mines of Nanaimo to the docks of Halifax, from the rock streets of Prince Rupert to the cobbled pavements of the city of Quebec, from tall office buildings in Winnipeg, and lonely farm huts on the prairie, from old families in old Ontario counties to sombre interiors of banking-houses. They had been plucked from the decks of lake ships and the tops of swaying railway cars, from schools, and from factories by the call of war. Here, now, they moved like the fingers of a hand or the unerring parts of a great machine. It was as though a Saskatchewan wheat-field, as wide as the horizon, had turned its stalks into armed men, its wild flowers into banners, and the prairie wind into the music of war. The crowd, the staff officers, the blasé newspaper-writers, were touched as men are not often touched.

When the last officer's sword had flashed in salute, one newspaperman touching another's arm, pointed to General Hughes, grim of face, his white close-cropped hair gleaming under the edge of his service hat, riding soberly from the field.

"Look at Hughes!" whispered the reporter. "What must a

man feel like who has risen from a farm boy in a dull Ontario county to a position where it lies in his hands to give form to this first big unit sent by this country to the war?"

"What must it feel like," retorted the other, "to have accepted the responsibility and to have *achieved*—what we have just seen?"

Within two weeks the fleet of transports sailed to England. The first section of a gigantic piece of organization was thus completed under the hands of this one-time Canadian country boy, private in the militia, school teacher, political worker. In unhappy Germany the task would have been accomplished with even greater speed. In England, rich in military traditions, and with at least a nucleus of war organization, it might have been done—though it was *not* done—without any mistakes whatsoever. The fact that Canada, a non-military nation, without real previous experience, without preparation before the declaration of war except the ordinary preparation for militia manœuvres, collected, equipped, mobilized, and trained thirty thousand men without one serious mishap, is due to the genius —for it required genius—of General Sam Hughes. Criticisms have been raised and have died. Errors have been found in departments. Dishonest members of Parliament and dealers in supplies have attempted to take advantage of the nation's necessities. But no loss of time, no slip of memory, no blame, worthy under the circumstances to be considered, attached to the Canadian Department of Militia and Defence. On the contrary, with General Sam Hughes at its head, the department executed its task in a way that brought praise from the military chiefs of Great Britain, whose praise is never given without cause.

This is only one chapter in the life of my friend— a chapter, however, that marks the initial momentum that carried the Canadian nation into the war with more than six hundred thousand enlistments, one in thirteen of the entire population of the Dominion! If I were writing his biography I would tell of his having

constructed—even while raising the army just described—the equivalent of a town accommodating
thousands of inhabitants, with its miles of streets,
water-supply, drainage, telegraph and telephone systems, churches, a theatre, post-offices, and all the other
things needed to make life safe and comfortable; and
all within a few weeks in what had been a wild waste.
This was Valcartier Camp, which I visited as the guest
of the commandant, Sir Sam's brother. I would relate
some of his adventures when commanding a troop of
Canadian horse during the Boer War in South Africa,
where his impetuous gallantry was mentioned several
times in despatches. I would tell of his work under Sir
Garnet Wolsey in the Riel rebellion; and I might be
tempted to mention his service in defence of the Dominion during the silly Fenian invasions across Niagara River, when Hughes was still in his teens. But I
should hesitate to tell of his rushing off to Montreal
with a dozen other wild Orangemen, to break up a St.
Patrick's day parade! Hughes was an Irishman and
dearly loved a fight!

Bearing on his services in South Africa, with which
Canadians were imperfectly informed, I may mention
an incident that happened while I was in Lindsay. Lord
Milner, who was High Commissioner of South Africa
during the Boer War, finding himself in Toronto, had
his private car attached to the Lindsay train and, with
complete absence of ceremony, had himself taken to
call on Colonel Hughes at his home. This was no
slight distinction, as Lord Milner was the guest of
Canada, and, to pay honor to his friend, he had to
forego some official function that had seemed to his

hosts of greater importance than an informal call upon Colonel Hughes.

But Colonel Hughes himself would have done just such a thing to mark his friendship. Reading that my daughter was to sail from Montreal one midnight, he hastened from Ottawa and met her at the dock with a steamer basket, and waited until the ship sailed.

Unknown to him, the water commissioners of Lindsay had invited me to come from Philadelphia to look into their water supply. I naturally sent him a note telling of the time of my expected arrival at his home town. The commissioners were at the station to meet me, and a more or less formal luncheon had been ordered at the local hotel for us all. But Colonel Hughes was also there, and he, too, had counted on my lunching with him and his family. The water commissioners gracefully gave way, though in a manner that amused while it embarrassed me; and while I was sitting at meat with the charming wife and daughters of my friend, the commissioners ate their lunch in their own company. My session with them came later—at the water works, when, despite their natural disapproval of my desertion of them, they gave me a contract to put in a filtration and ozonizing plant to treat the entire water supply of the town!

AN ADVENTURE IN SANITATION

WILLIAM W. GIBBS used to be regarded as the
J. P. Morgan of Philadelphia, which was not exactly
fair to Mr. Morgan. He was nevertheless an important
figure in the financial streets of the Quaker City. He
founded the United Gas Improvement Co., The Stor-
age Battery Co., The Alkali Co., the Marsden Co., developed the Welsbach gas mantle into commercial use,
controlled at one time, by stock ownership, the Philadelphia and Reading Railroad, and did many other
things more or less financially sensational.

The Marsden Co. was not an unqualified success, so
far as the investing public was concerned; but it was
generally believed that Mr. Gibbs had profited largely
by the promotion of the company, in which he had displayed a master hand. One of Gibbs's sons was showing a friend through the handsome mansion in Ritten-
house Square in which he lived, and remarked in a
charming little room, "this is Pa's den." "I suppose the
whole house is Ma's den!" was the unexpected punning
rejoinder.

At the time of my first meeting with Mr. Gibbs in
1904 he had just formed the United Water Improvement Co., designed to eclipse the United Gas Improvement Co. which had grown to be one of his great financial successes. Because of certain experiments in electricity I had made in Boston that winter, Gibbs invited
me to join him in his new enterprise. He had bought

the Vosmaer system of purifying water by electrically-produced ozone, a Dutch invention brought to America by my friend George J. Cory, who had been U. S. Consul at The Hague. Gibbs's offer was a liberal one and I accepted it. I was to be vice-president and treasurer of the company, and J. Hampton Moore, afterwards mayor of Philadelphia, was to resign these offices in my favor.

I was no sooner committed to this enterprise than I received word from Mr. Frick that President Roosevelt and Attorney General Knox wished me to go to Panama to write a book about the work being done on the canal by Chief Engineer John F. Wallace, which had been adversely reported on by Poultney Bigelow. I was not favorably impressed with the proposition. Panama was not the health resort it has since become. Indeed, that very year there was an outbreak of yellow fever, and a general exodus of the workers, including the chief of the staff! Moreover I felt committed to Gibbs. "But Gibbs is a speculator," objected Frick, who had himself just refused Roosevelt's appointment to the Board of Panama Commissioners. So I held to my own plan and went to Philadelphia to live, occasionally breakfasting with Frick at Sherry's on my visits to New York.

A plant to demonstrate the Vosmaer system was being built on the banks of the Schuylkill, under the direction of a man from Holland. It was ostensibly designed to treat a million gallons a day of the repulsive waters of the river, just below a large sewer and the outfall of the slaughter-houses of the city—the vilest compound they could find; such was Gibbs's faith in the efficiency of ozone purification. But the Dutch engineer did not share his optimism; and secretly installed a system of pipes that enabled him to pass the city water through the apparatus. This he did whenever a demonstration of the process was held. Visiting engineers, scientists, sanitarians, equally with Gibbs and myself, thought he was purifying the vile water that ran past the plant, with its billions of bacteria, its slaughter-house filth and sewage, while, as a matter of fact, he was simply taking the city water through concealed pipes and bringing it out of the apparatus bright and sparkling, and so free from pathogenic bacteria that visitors were amazed and Gibbs thought he had the world of sanitation by the tail! All of this was discovered only after the Dutchman had gone back home and repair work had uncovered his buried pipes. Some workman, however, sold the information to a newspaper man, and a New York paper came out with a sensational article charging Gibbs and his company with purposeful deceit. In our happy ignorance we treated the revelation with disdain, and offered to purify the entire water supply of Philadelphia—some three hundred million gallons a day—at a fraction of the cost of slow sand filtration. The mayor of the city, duly impressed, visited the plant and drank the treated water with gusto, thinking it was Schuylkill water, which he remarked had always been better tasting than that taken from the Delaware!

Vosmaer himself, in Holland, had no knowledge of what his subordinate had done in this foolish substitution of the city's partially filtered water for the unmodified sewage of the river. He had never claimed that his system—or any other—could deal satisfactorily with sewage; and, on his arrival in Philadelphia, he said it was a futile gesture on the part of Gibbs to put the plant in such a location and subject it to such a ridiculous test. There was abundant evidence in Paris, Nice, Wiesbaden, Paderborn and other places in Europe to show that ozone will kill bacteria in water, removing, as well, objectionable tastes, smells and colors, and that the process was economical and efficient to a degree reached by no other means of purifying municipal water supplies. It was a silly thing this Dutchman had done. That the patents had not been wholly paid for is the only reason I can think of for his moronic act. And this adjective fits his mentality also!

Before this discovery an offer had been made to the city of London to establish there a demonstration plant to treat a million gallons a day, and show how superior ozone is to sand filtration. The offer was accepted, and I went to England to superintend the installation. While waiting there for working plans from Philadelphia— delayed, as I later discovered, because Gibbs had run out of funds—I ran over to Paris to look into a somewhat similar system of treating municipal waters by ozone. This was also a Dutch invention, then being demonstrated at Joinville-sur Pont, where the city of Paris takes part of its water from the Marne. Here they used a very high voltage—some 30,000 as against our 12,000. The Dutch engineer took me over the plant, but his French was defective, and I misunderstood his description of the electrodes he was using. I thought they were hollow. They were solid. Like a flash the idea of a hollow electrode came to me, with its obvious advantage of having air pass through it, and directly into the core of the brush discharge. All the methods of producing ozone up to that time had passed

266

the air *across* the discharge. My idea was to force it into the cone of the discharge itself, and so through the flaming walls of the cone, thus bringing every molecule into actual contact with the discharge. The conception was revolutionary, as I found on testing it in a small apparatus I built on my return to London. I made so much ozone with my little apparatus that people living in the same street complained to the authorities of the smell!

Without awaiting further word from Philadelphia I got on the steamer with my little ozonizer, and returned to Philadelphia, greatly to the astonishment of the president of the company. Nor was he altogether pleased. My simple apparatus had cost $500. A Vosmaer machine of no greater capacity had cost $15,000. The plant on the banks of the Schuylkill represented an outlay of $200,000—contributed by Gibbs's friends; and here was a simpler demonstration that he thought would discredit him. So he would have none of it!

As I had not occupied a technical position in the company, I was free to patent my invention and use it as I pleased. Having advanced to Gibbs considerable money during the development of his enterprise, I now offered to make over to him all my rights in the new invention if he would reimburse me. This he was unable to do; and, in default, we made a friendly agreement that I should be free to exploit my invention in my own way, but giving him the first opportunity to buy it for his company if its superiority over that of Vosmaer was demonstrated in practice.

The town of Lindsay, Ontario, had made some inquiries about ozone purification while Gibbs and I were discussing our affairs, and it was agreed between us that I should be free to make an arrangement with the authorities of Lindsay to demonstrate my system there. I therefore left for Canada the next week, and was met at the train, as I have elsewhere related, both by my friend Colonel Hughes and the water commissioners of the town. I offered to install an ozone plant that would give to the entire supply of the town a water free from color, taste or smell, sterile of pathogenic bacteria, and holding an increased amount of dissolved oxygen; that the cost of operation should not exceed one dollar a million for electricity. If I failed, the town would owe me nothing; but if I succeeded I was to receive the sum of $7250, this being less than one-third the estimate the town had considered paying for a filter, similar to one that I agreed to build as a part of my system. Of course, the commissioners, having nothing to lose, promptly accepted my offer, and thereupon I became a member, for the time being, of this charming community on the Kewatha lakes, and had one of the most delightful experiences of my life. The hospitality of Canadians is proverbial.

Details of the building of this purification plant might be interesting, but not to the general reader. *The Canadian Engineer* sent an expert to report on it, and on Nov. 6, 1908, published an account of his visit. This was quoted by daily papers throughout Canada and the United States, and caused some sensation among sanitarians. Here are a few extracts:

First municipal ozonizing plant to treat the entire water supply of a town on the American continent.

Constructed under contract with the town of Lindsay by J. Howard Bridge, the inventor and patentee.

Daily capacity, 1,500,000 gallons.

An Adventure in Sanitation

Cost, including pre-filter, $7,250.

Cost of operation 8 H. P., for which the town pays $35 a H. P. year. This equals $280 for the treatment of 547 million gallons yearly, or 51c per million.

There are no other costs, the plant being operated by the regular employees of the pumping station.

Besides breaking all water-works records for cost of installation and economical operation, Mr. Bridge broke all records for rapidity of construction, which in the purification of a public water supply is of almost equal importance. Mayor Begg, of Lindsay, turned the first sod on August 24th. The plant, including a pre-filter of reinforced concrete, was completed and in operation on October 23d—a little over eight weeks. * * * The raw water is strongly charged with vegetable matter derived from the lake and surrounding swamps, and this, besides affording a rich pabulum for bacteria, imparts an unpleasant odor and taste to the water. As a result the citizens have had recourse to well water, which in itself has not always been above suspicion, and typhoid fever has been quite prevalent in the town. (Fifteen cases in the hospital. Later, none.)

The new system includes a modern rapid filter of reinforced concrete, a sterilization well forty feet deep and about six feet square, and a purified water basin from which it is pumped directly into the mains of the town. The system is so contrived that the water passes entirely by gravity from the river through the filter and sterilizing well to the suction pipes of the pumps; while in the electrical part of the plant there is a similar absence of mechanical means, so that with the exception of an electric blower of ⅛ H. P., there is not a wheel turning anywhere. By an ingenious automatic device, the graded opening of a single valve admits varying quantities of water to the apparatus as required by the needs of the town. At ordinary times the pumpage is five hundred gallons a minute. During fires this may be doubled; in either case the rate of filtration and ozone sterilization is simply regulated by the operation of a raw-water valve, and no other attention is required. So, too,

269

when the pumps are completely stopped, provision is made by which the ozone produced is automatically drawn from the ozonizers, so that these may safely run continuously should the attendant neglect to turn off the electric current supplying them. * * * The Howard-Bridge system has demonstrated its superiority to that tested by the officials of New York City, who showed that the cost of ozone in water purification is only twenty-five per cent of the whole, the remaining seventy-five per cent being used up by the air-pump and refrigerating machine. In regard to the efficiency of the Lindsay plant, there can be no question as to its having already met the chief conditions called for in the contract made with the town. * * * The effluent of the plant is clear, bright and palatable, and it is free from objectionable color, taste and smell.

When the bill was rendered to the town for electric power supplied to the ozonizer, it was found that the current consumed cost only forty-four cents per million gallons for the plant's capacity!

The little town of Lindsay, on the amber-colored Scugog, at once became the Mecca of engineers, filtration experts, chemists, bacteriologists and sanitarians. Delegations came from cities in the United States and distant parts of Canada to see the working of the plant; and I received scores of letters of inquiry, and invitations to visit cities as remote as St. Petersburg, Barcelona, and even Bangkok, Siam.

Pembroke on the borders of the province of Quebec, had an outbreak of typhoid fever, and the mayor urged me by telegraph to rush over there at once. I did so, and found the town hall so crowded that I had to be helped up to the platform across the footlights. They had had, as I remember, forty deaths from typhoid, which meant ten times as many cases. I had not known that I was to address a crowded house of townsfolk, all excited because of the unsanitary conditions that prevailed, and many of them were in mourning. The professor of hygiene from McGill University was speaking when I was hoisted across the footlights, and to my dismay he promptly stopped and the mayor at once turned the meeting over to me. I had written quite extensively on subjects about which I was expected to speak, and I was able to interest the meeting despite one vociferous heckler, who fortunately for him had not confined his drinking to town water.

Next morning the mayor drove me along the Ottawa River in a sleigh. It was many degrees below zero, and the ice was inches thick. There was nothing to do at that season except to boil all water for domestic use! But I suggested that when the ice went out, a number of floats be put into the river down stream near the sewer outfall to mark the direction of currents. For I had noticed a little headland projecting into the river just above the water intake, of just the form to create an eddy. This proved to be the case, and the cause of the typhoid outbreak: the floats were carried up the river to the intake supplying the town's water, showing that the people had been drinking their own sewage!

An allied condition was found at Ottawa, the capital of the Dominion. The authorities there asked me to meet the water commissioners, and we had several sessions together. When I mentioned "sewage," they became very indignant. I called for the bacterial reports of the Medical Health Officer, which I had previously studied, and pointed to a plus sign under the heading "B.Coli." "What does that mean?" they asked. "It indicates the almost constant presence of the Colon Bacillus in your water, and that shows that sewage from

271

Aylmer, and possibly other towns up-stream, is mixed with your drinking water." Next morning, the Ottawa papers came out with scare heads, one of them with a whole page report of the meeting.

Far more shocking conditions prevailed in Western Pennsylvania. I went a hundred miles up the Monongahela valley, and found that every one of the score of towns along its banks took its water untreated from the river and discharged its sewage into it! These towns were often only a few miles apart; and typhoid fever was endemic among them. Pittsburgh took a part of its water from this badly-polluted stream, and had a typhoid rate in 1907 well above a hundred per 100,-000 of the population, as against fewer than seven in England. At Niagara Falls the published rate was just as high, owing to the admixture of the sewage of Buffalo with the water supply of the town; and this did not tell the whole story, because thousands of visitors became infected, and took the disease to their home towns, to further spread sickness and death.

The city of Lynn, Massachusetts, sent a delegation to Lindsay, and inspired by what they saw there bade defiance to the State Board of Health, which was insisting on their adopting a costly system of slow sand filters. Pressed by the board, Lynn appealed to the legislature. A committee of the Senate was appointed to investigate the matter and take testimony. I appeared before this committee and spoke and was cross-examined for an hour or more, receiving the usual fee given to experts in hydraulic engineering—a far cry from Herbert Spencer and the other things I had been doing since he wrote Professor Youmans that he had tried in vain to dissuade me from engaging in the strenuous life of America!

The success of the Lindsay plant resulted in contracts with Baltimore and Ann Arbor for similar installations, but much larger and with unconditional advance payments. These plants were to have a purifying capacity of three to ten million gallons a day; and on the strength of this evidence of marked success, Gibbs called me back to Philadelphia to join in the formation of a new company, bearing the old name, this time with a capital of ten million dollars in shares and $110,000 in debenture bonds. The bonds were given to me, with one-quarter of the total shares, in return for my patents and the contracts I had made with Baltimore and Ann Arbor.

Two and a half millions in stock and $110,000 in bonds looks like a high price to pay for my little $500 ozonizer with all its possibilities. Vosmaer's patents, priced at $100,000 cash, had cost Gibbs $200,000 to demonstrate their impracticability.

A comparison of values was made by Edwin F. Dwelley, city engineer of Lynn in his report to the City Council. He says:

While the Vosmaer system was in many respects superior to anything that had preceded it, it involved three distinct steps each with its attendant expense. They consisted of first drying the air, then producing the ozone from the dried air, and last the forcing of the ozonized air through the water.

About this time, Bridge perfected his apparatus which, in simplicity and effectiveness, seems without doubt to place the purification of water by ozone on a basis such that it will be an indispensable part of any complete water works.

The Bridge system has been installed side by side with the Vosmaer system for comparison and the result seems to be a complete confirmation of the claims made for the Bridge sys·

273

tem. I have personally examined the operation of these two systems at Philadelphia.

Before taking up the discussion of any special system with
regard to its practicability and desirability as a part of the Lynn
Water Works, it will be well to state that there is absolutely
no doubt as to what the ozone treatment will accomplish with
a water in the way of removing taste, odor, organisms and
bacteria. It will go further in these directions than any known
treatment. By the use of ozone it would, unquestionably, be
possible to produce an absolutely sterile water, should that seem
desirable and a water could be made absolutely safe, with
ozone, against any and all suspicions as to the presence of
pathogenic bacteria in the ozonized water. * * *

The Howard-Bridge system differs from all others in its simplicity. Until Bridge designed his apparatus, the production of
ozone and its application to the water to be treated involved
three distinct power consuming mechanical steps. First, the air
had to be dried. This was usually accomplished by refrigera-
tion and was an expensive process, because of the amount of
power consumed, and the liability of the refrigerating machine
to get out of order. Second, the air was passed through the
ozonizer, where it became charged with ozone. Third, the
ozonized air was then forced through the water by an air pump
against a head of from 25 to 40 feet.

The drying of the air was necessary on account of the copper
usually used in the construction of the ozonizer as the ozonized
air, if not dry, attacked the copper, and rapidly cut down the
efficiency of the machine. In using aluminum electrodes in his
ozonizer and avoiding the use of all copper, Bridge rendered the
use of the refrigerating and drying machinery unnecessary, thus
cutting out fully one-third of the expense, and one of the most
potent sources of trouble.

In the Vosmaer system, as has been stated, the use of any
dielectric other than the air was dispensed with, but the neces-
sity for the delicate adjustment of the electrodes, where air
was depended upon as a dielectric, greatly increased the cost of

installation and operation. Bridge designed an ozonizer using a dielectric of micanite which has been shown to be very little liable to fracture, and which has worked perfectly using very high voltages in the ozonizer. Further, the Bridge ozonizer is so constructed in small units that should one unit get out of order, something that might, of course, happen, it can be instantly replaced almost as easily as one book could be taken off a shelf and another substituted for it.

In all the processes for producing ozone by electricity, previous to the Bridge process, the air was drawn through a more or less confined space in which a brush electric discharge was taking place, so that only a portion of the air passing came in contact with the brush and was ozonized. In the Bridge apparatus every particle of air has literally to break through the discharging brush several times, thus practically all the air comes in contact with the brush and a very much higher concentration of ozone results.

Another source of expense in the earlier systems was the method forcing the ozonized air through the water being treated. This required an air pump and special apparatus. The Bridge system takes advantage of a well-known physical law, which is as simple and universal as the law of gravitation and makes the water itself do the work formerly done by the air pump. * * *

I have spent much time in studying the Bridge system and apparatus, and I am fully convinced that it is an indispensable part of a perfectly equipped water works, where the desire is to produce a domestic water that shall be beyond criticism.

If it were of any present day interest I could tell of contacts with politicians who controlled, to their own advantage and that of their friends, situations involving the health and even the lives of the communities in which they lived—purposely delaying the improvement of a city's water supply until favored contractors were ready to bid for the work. Philadelphia had a typhoid

275

rate that would have justified the hanging from Market
Street lamposts of half a dozen of its bosses. At Roch-
ester I was not allowed to see even the plans of a costly
addition to the water works until I appealed to the local
boss, George W. Aldrich, who asked me to come to his
home after dark. The next day I was received at the
City Hall with almost regal honors, and driven to the
water works in a carriage!

Happily these days are passed; and the reason is one
that gave safety to municipal waters all over the world
and incidentally put ozonization into the discard.

At Lindsay I had used chlorine to sterilize the plant
before starting it, and again before bacterial counts
were made. For this I was roundly condemned by some
of my antagonists—of whom I had many! A rising
bubble of ozone has no action on a bacterium that is
safely lodged in the interstitial walls of a concrete well;
so I allowed a chlorine solution to stand in the apparatus, and ran it off into the river before passing the
ozonized water into the mains.

Someone else discovered that chlorine, as an active
germicide, could be safely used in drinking water. And
the process was easy to install and cheap in operation:
it called only for a tank and a few pounds of a chemical that had been almost a waste product. Hence chlor-
ination has been adopted by municipal authorities all
over the world, sometimes as an adjunct to filtration,
which had never been completely efficient, more often
as the only means of giving safety to public water supplies. Typhoid fever has disappeared from the mor-
tality returns of hundreds of cities and towns, and
ozonization, in the most promising period of its development, has fallen into "innocuous desuitude."

Gibbs never recovered financially from the disaster. He died a comparatively poor man not long after his disappointment. To me the experience brought many friends in Canada, Baltimore and at the University of Michigan. The paper I read in 1907 before the Franklin Institute of Philadelphia on Ozone : its Nature, Production and Uses, is still regarded as authoritative. Advertisements in magazines show that electrically-produced ozone is again attracting the attention of sanitarians. No progressive effort is ever entirely lost, however disappointing it may be to the individual who makes it.

CHARLES RANLETT FLINT

THE FATHER OF TRUSTS—AND THE LOG OF THE "ARROW."

IT would be hard to find a man of greater versatility than Charles Ranlett Flint. At this writing he is in his eighty-first year and has recently gone back into business. Three years ago he took unto himself a wife and retired from work. This was no "triumph of hope over experience," as second marriages often are; for the first Mrs. Flint was one of the finest women it has been my privilege to know. She was "the perfect partner," as stated in the dedication of Mr. Flint's fascinating book *Memories of an Active Life: Men and Ships and Sealing Wax,* published by the Putnams.

It has been wisely held that when a man has been happily married to a woman for nearly half a century, it is a compliment to her and a testimonial to her worth if he elects a successor. I have known Mr. Flint a good many years and seen him in positions of difficulty; and he has always excited my admiration by his wisdom and excellent judgment.

He is spoken of as "the Father of Trusts"—nearly a score of them. But he is their mother also. As a father he only begot them; but, as mother, he conceived them, gave them birth and nursed them through their infancy. I have said he is a man of great versatility!

When Don C. Seitz was asked by an inquisitive Sen-

278

atorial Committee "What is your position?" he truthfully answered "I am general manager of the World."
"Some Job!" exclaimed his astonished questioner.
When one finds among the score of corporations that
Charles R. Flint fathered, mothered and nursed to maturity, industrial giants of such amazing diversity as
the U. S. Rubber Co., the American Chicle Co., The
Schloss-Sheffield Steel and Iron Co., The U. S. Bobbin
and Shuttle Co., the American Caramel Co., the American Sewer Pipe Co., The International Emery and
Carborundum Co., the National Starch Co., the American-Hawaiian Steamship Co., the American Woolen
Co., the International Business Machines Co., The
American Trading Co., and some others, one is forced
to echo the senatorial exclamation: "Some Job!"

But that is only half the story of Flint's achievements.
From chewing gum to battleships seems an impossible
jump; but Flint made it. He fitted out a fleet of war
vessels for the Brazilian Republic, in 1893, including
the famous dynamite ship the "Nictheroy"; and a couple of years later purchased the cruiser "Esmerelda"
from Chile and delivered her to Japan during her war
with China—the first time in the history of the world
that a war ship had been sold to a belligerent. He sold
twenty sub-marines and torpedo boats to Russia when
she was on the verge of war with Turkey. He arranged
with President Cleveland to infest the seas with American Privateers when the Venezuela tangle threatened
war with England—that is threatened it in the minds
of fire-eating congressmen and yellow journalists, all
"unbeknownst" to England! For at that time America
had not signed away the right—or the wrong—to
license private citizens to make war on a public enemy.

MILLIONAIRES AND GRUB STREET

Flint was the first to finance the Wright brothers in their epoch-making invention of the flying machine. His partner, Ulysses D. Eddy, used to stop at my apartment in the Dakota on Sunday afternoons and take me for a walk in the park. Sometime early in the century he came in for our usual walk. In the park he said: "The world is soon to be thrilled as never before. I have seen a man fly—not a few feet, but round and round a race-track, like a bird!"

He had just come back from Dayton, where he had gone in the interest of Flint, Eddy and Co., to investigate the Wright Brothers' claims. Mr. Eddy was one of those quiet, forceful characters who impress one as much by their restraint as by their mental power. His appearance suggested Michael Angelo's "Moses." In his way, which was different from his partner's, he was as great a personality as Flint. On this occasion he was as solemn as when describing a battle in which he had taken part during the Civil War. It was a victory— the conquest of the air, for which men had been contending for two thousand years! And American officialdom, committed to the inconclusive experiments of Langley—as were the salaried officers of the Smithsonian Institute only a year or two ago—treated the Wrights "snippily" and allowed the invention to go to Germany.

John Brisbin Walker asked me to write an article about Flint for the series "Captains of Industry" which he was publishing in the *Cosmopolitan Magazine* in 1902. In this, to mark Flint's amazing activity, I pictured him as attending three meetings of directors at once, one in person and two others by a telephone glued to each ear. I also described him as dictating to a sec-

retary an essay on industrial consolidations while steering his primitive "horseless carriage" in and out of the
traffic of Broadway. I gave it to one of Flint's secretaries to correct any statement of fact that I might have
got wrong. This young man's sense of humor, like himself, had not reached adolescence : the article came back
with these facetious descriptions deleted. Then I told
him a story:

When Andrew Carnegie wrote a motto for his
brother's fireplace, the builder came to him and asked
him to shorten it: it was too long for the fireplace!
"You mean the fireplace is too short for the motto.
Make it longer; and if the room is too small for the
fireplace, make the room bigger; and if the house is too
small for the room, pull it down and build a bigger one.
But at your peril, don't cut a letter out of that motto:
'Our Hearth our Altar; its Flame our Sacred Fire.' "

Needless to say, the deleted parts of my article were
restored; and Flint, whose sense of humor had achieved
its full growth and was always in working order,
laughed heartily at the story.

This sense of humor, by the way, occasionally took a
strange turn. For instance, on his yacht "the Arrow,"
the swiftest thing afloat, he would invite his overnight
guests to jump overboard, as he did himself, and then
give the sailing-master orders to get under way. In the
middle of Long Island Sound, before breakfast, and in
the costume of Adam, I failed to appreciate the joke,
until I noticed that sailing-master Packard had gone
just far enough to give it point, and was gracefully
swinging back to us.

Flint was great for exercise—probably still is in an
octogenarian way. He took it for granted that I could

ride a bicycle, and started off at great speed along the rough country lane leading from the Sound, where we had just landed, to the Wyandank Club in the middle of Long Island. I had been somewhat expert on those high-wheel affairs of the early eighties, but had had no experience with the so-called "safeties." I was not displeased, therefore, when I saw him totter a few yards and then topple over into the ditch. As I wobbled past him, I thought he would laugh it off; but he took it, as he did the disappointments of his business, as a matter of course and not worth mentioning. It was in line with his business philosophy. When he lost several millions over night, by *almost* cornering the crude rubber of the world, he told me that he had not "exposed his pocket nerve." Nor any other, I imagine!

Once, when we were motoring on a rough detour near Jamaica, a stone threw the wheels to starboard, and we ran gently into a tree. He was busily discoursing on some more or less recondite subject, but he did not let the little contratemps interrupt his speech. He put the car in reverse gear, backed away and went on, both with his talk and his steering. I recall with amusement the surprise of a man on the sidewalk, who apparently thought the tree had saved him from being run down, and that some comment on the near-accident was called for.

It was usual for guests on "the Arrow" to write something in the log-book. On this famous yacht great corporations were planned, built, equipped and launched on the sea of industrialism, to be afterwards navigated around the shoals of the Sherman anti-trust law and brought into ports of prosperity. This trust-building involved the presence on the yacht of many men of

282

prominence—leaders in the world of finance, law, commerce, transportation, diplomacy, journalism; and these men generally contributed to the pages of the log-book a wise remark, witty comment or interesting anecdote. While some of them broke into mere verse and some into real poetry, nearly all the contributions were interesting and original. With Mr. Flint's approval I copied some of these, thinking to make a magazine article of them. I select a few from my Scrivener's Wallet.

As no attempt at order was possible in these scribblings, a selection of them may be made hap-hazard; leaving unquoted or unsigned, however, many bright comments on public men and affairs which the celebrities who wrote them might not care to see in print under their own names.

Of this character are certain comments on Theodore Roosevelt, scribbled across the translation of a letter from the Sultan of Morocco "to the great Loving and Exalted in his position of Splendor and Glory, First among the Great and Noble, the President of the Great American Nation, the Mirror of its Greatness, possessor of its Highest Position, Theodore Roosevelt."

Across this in colored ink a world-famed lawyer has written:

> He was a good man in his time
> Ere the pruning knife of time cut him down.

To this a leader in the financial world who is also a sportsman adds:

A fisherman caught an eel and cut his head off; the eel continued to wriggle; the fisherman said "The eel's dead but he doesn't know it."

And over it all in another hand comes the terse prophecy:

His epitaph: Resurgam.

Professor Jacob Gould Shurman wrote:

A man to be liberally educated must have a knowledge of the naturalistic sciences; a man to be liberally educated must have a knowledge of the humanistic sciences; and a man to be liberally educated must have a knowledge of the theological sciences; because in a knowledge of the naturalistic sciences we have a knowledge of nature; in a knowledge of the humanistic sciences we have a knowledge of man; and in a knowledge of the theological sciences we have a knowledge of that which is highest and best of all, a knowledge of God.

And here is an illuminating definition of art that calls, for wide publicity. It is by the well-known artist, F. R. Ruckstuhl.

My dear Mr. Flint:

You ask me for an original thought having a relation to Art. Permit me to add to your most interesting log my definition of a work of art:

Every human work made with a purpose of stirring human emotion is a work of Art; and a work of Art is great in ratio of its power of stirring the highest emotions of the largest number of cultured people for the longest period of time.

F. R. RUCKSTUHL.

Jules Huret, the well known French author and associate editor of the Paris *Figaro*, whom I took round the Carnegie works one freezing winter night in 1902, struck with admiration at the speed of the "Arrow," exclaims:

En cas de guerre, quelle chance de pouvoir fuir sur un bateau pareil!

284

This unheroic sentiment is approved by F. R. Cordley:

> He who fights and runs away
> Lives to fight another day.

But Ulysses D. Eddy added a little later:

> He who fights and runs away
> May yet learn to fight and stay.

And William M. Polk was prompted to this new version of an old saw:

> Thrice armed is he who hath his quarrel just;
> But four times he who "gits" his gun out "fust."

A lawyer, too well known to be named, writes:

For a client I will hammer the truth so thin that a gold leaf would appear thick; but I will not tell a lie.

Here is a string of anecdotes relating to various personages, the guests on this occasion including Governor Murphy of New Jersey, Wm. D. Guthrie, the great lawyer, Gustave H. Schwab, of the North German Lloyd Company, Captain Petrie and others.

Lord Aberdeen attended a dinner in New York while Governor-General of Canada. In honor of his Scotch entertainers he appeared in kilts. Aberdeen made a neat speech, and the applause had hardly ceased when Choate was introduced and proceeded to say some complimentary things of the last speaker, and to declare that if he had known that he was to be permitted to sit next to his distinguished friend the Governor-General of Canada, he too would have come "without his trousers." The kilted guest was soonest to catch the humor of the remark, and led the laughter it produced.

Someone inquired of Mr. Choate who he would like to be if he could not be himself. He paused a few seconds as if thinking over the list of the world's celebrities, and then his eye rested upon his wife. "If," he answered, "I could not be myself, I should like to be Mrs. Choate's second husband."

"A man who sings tenor always wants to sing bass," said J. G. Blaine when he heard that Andrew Carnegie was writing a book.

Ambassador Choate to American lady who inquired the name of a lady dressed very décolleté:
"That is Mrs. Chimeseoff, née Alloff."
> There was a young man of St. Louis
> Who married a beautiful Jewess.
> The stores she told—
> Not all of them old—
> He called her his Chauncey Depewess.

William M. Evarts, after dinner at home, a goose being the pièce de résistance, said:
"My children, a little while ago you saw a goose stuffed with sage. Now you see a sage stuffed with goose."

"No failure but low aim is crime."—W. W. Jacques.

"Good management of a corporation having several constituent companies largely depends on comparative accounting."—A. M. Ames.

Scotchman drunk, holding rail: "If I hold on to this rail I'll lose my train; if I let go I'll fa' doon!"

"Macdonald, how far to Glasgow?"

"Hoo did ye ken my name?"

"I guessed it."

"Then guess hoo farr 'tis to Glesgo!"

Woman: Does it make any difference which car I take for Greenwood?

A man: Not to me, madam.

"A pessimist is one who has been very intimate with an optimist."

"An optimist is one who when handed a lemon makes lemonade out of it."

I have recently heard a new definition: An optimist is one who sees a light which isn't there; a pessimist is one who tries to blow it out!

Lyman J. Gage in quotation marks inserts a verse, apparently borrowed from a revivalist:

No more, no more the earthly shore
Upbraids me with its wild uproar;
With dreadful eyes my spirit lies
Under the walls of Paradise.

The Grand Duke Boris of Russia went on the "Arrow" to West Point, and he and his suite wrote several pages of undecipherable Russian in the log-book. A marginal note reads thus:

The Grand Duke Boris was met on the West Point dock by Superintendent Mills and other officers. When being driven up the hill, he looked with manifest interest at the trees on the west side of the drive. We supposed that he was admiring these sturdy oaks until he remarked: "What fine limbs on which to hang the reporters of the American newspapers!"

Sir Philip Burne-Jones was taken on the "Arrow" to attend the dedication of the Stony Point Battlefield State Reservation, and his contribution to the log-book was a spirited sketch of himself shaking hands with the ghost of Anthony Wayne. In the book which he afterward wrote of his visit to the United States he naïvely mentions that up to this time he had never heard either of Anthony Wayne or the battle of Stony Point.

Charles D. Mosher, who built the "Arrow's" engines and was frequently Mr. Flint's guest, has written:

The efficiency of the turbine engine in economy of steam is fourteen and a half pounds of steam per horse power per hour, or about equal to a good triple expansion reciprocating engine with a consumption of one and one-half pounds of coal per horse power per hour. Whereas the best quadruple expansion reciprocating engines have produced a horse power for one hour on about nine pounds of steam and less than one pound of coal, which is over 50 per cent more economical than the best

1779 — 1902.

Modern representation of effete civilization to
Shade of Anthony Wayne

"Many happy returns of the day."

Stony Point.
N.y. July 16ᵗ 19·2·

turbine engine; besides which the turbine engine has only a
very small range at its economical point.

But the turbine, as might have been expected, has
greatly increased in efficiency since Mr. Mosher wrote.
Indeed, it has surpassed the reciprocating engine in
marine work.

Here is an unsigned complaint, apparently prompted by a recent loss:

> The rain it raineth every day
> Upon the Just and Unjust fellows;
> But chiefly upon the Just because
> The Unjust have the Justs' umbrellas.

The "Arrow" was a conspicuous attendant at the American cup races in 1903, and Sir Thomas Lipton came over to visit the steam yacht that held the world's record for speed. His autograph in the log-book is appended to a parody on Kipling's "Tommy Atkins" written by Clay M. Greene. This is appropriate in 1930, when Sir Thomas, in his eightieth year, has come again to try to "lift" the "America's" cup. It runs:

TOMMY LIPTON

There's a battle-battered trophy of the sea,
And its beauty's of the questionable kind;
But to yachtmen it's as priceless as can be.
We've defended it time almost out of mind.
Right gallant foes we've led across the line,
Who smiled upon the struggles fought in vain;
　But of all the men of fettle,
　Who have come to show their mettle;
　None so brave as he who's just come back again.
Oh!
Tommy, Tommy Lipton, we have welcomed you before,
And we hope again to welcome you a dozen times or more.
We have faith in our "Reliance,"
Whom we trust to rule the blue,
But losing, Tommy Lipton, we had rather lose to you.
We remember fair "Genesta" in our wake,
With the grim and lordly Sutton at the stick;
"Galatea's" hopeless turns about the stake,
With Captain Henn, that merry little brick.
We mind the fright the graceful "Thistle" gave

Until she met the fleeter "Volunteer";
  We forgive Dunraven's error
  When "Defender" proved a terror,
And the laugh on "Shamrock Third" we'd like to hear.
But!
        (Refrain as before.)

If you lift the cup, there's solace in the thought,
That you'll sweep the boards of yacht designers clean;
And teach them what they've never yet been taught,
That a yacht should never be a mere machine.
But, win or lose, this toast we give to you,
In glasses filled a dozen times or more:
  Here's good luck to our "Reliance"
  And your obstinate defiance,
And the Briton who's good fellow to the core.
So!
  Tommy, Tommy Lipton, etc., etc.

Gage E. Tarbell, under the exhilarating influence
of the yacht's speed, became prophetic:
  The past history of life insurance seems marvelous, but I do
not hesitate to predict that in twenty-five years from now
there will be a single company with assets equal to the present
combined assets of all New York State companies.

Admiral Brownson, at that time head of the Naval
Academy at Annapolis, insisted, during a discussion,
that the navy had contributed more largely to the success of the Revolution than was generally supposed, and
in support of his argument wrote as follows:
  In writing to Admiral De Grasse, who commanded a French
fleet in the West Indies, Washington, who was urging him to
bring his fleet to our coast, said: "Whatever the land forces
may do in this contest, it cannot be denied that the navy will
have the deciding vote."

Later Admiral Brownson sent the following letter to Mr. Flint, which was duly pasted in the log-book. It is fittingly quoted here for its historic interest:

Dear Mr. Flint:

The quotation of Washington's letter to De Grasse, which I wrote in your log, was substantially correct. It reads: "You will observe that whatever efforts are made by the land army, the navy must have the casting vote of the present contest." In writing to De Grasse *after* the surrender of Yorktown, he says: "The surrender of York . . . the *honor* of which *belongs* to your excellency." I wonder how many Americans know that— that the battle of Yorktown was practically won by De Grasse in his fleet action with Graves hundreds of miles from Yorktown. In July, 1780, Washington sent a message to Rochambeau by Lafayette to the effect that "In any operation and under all circumstances a decisive naval superiority is to be considered as a *fundamental* principle, and the *basis* upon which every *hope* of *success* must ultimately *depend*." But enough of the navy and its past glories! I find myself very busy, but am still cherishing the memory of the night at Coney Island and the beautiful summer's day spent on the "Erin" with Sir Thomas and yourself.

Very cordially,
WILLIARD H. BROWNSON.

Dr. Albert G. Male contributes two mathematical problems to the pages of the Log which some nautical reader may find pleasure in elucidating:

Supposing you start from the North Pole and steer a course due S. S. E. for thirty miles. What course would you steer to get back to the North Pole again?

Two steamers start off on a voyage of 3,000 miles at the same moment. On reaching their destination each turns back for the starting point at once. One goes out at the rate of 12 miles an hour and returns at 8 miles an hour. The other steamer goes at 10 miles an hour throughout. Which steamer arrives home first? (The distance is 6,000 miles in all, 3,000 out, 3,000 home.)

Frank A. Munsey, whose publications made his name a household word, has a half-page autograph inscription

TO A NEW ENGLAND BOY.

The New England boy is born with two great overshadowing purposes in life—purposes that are his whole life from the cradle to the grave—getting on in the world and getting into heaven.

"But the methods of the one closes the door of the other," Mr. Chauncey M. Depew comments on this.

Here is an interesting unsigned memorandum contributed by one of the visiting captains of industry:

Can you make a place for me in your office? I am a graduate of Harvard College; graduated last June.

Most certainly we cannot make a place for you in our office, knowing no more of you than we do. The mere fact that you are a graduate of Harvard College does not make much of a figure with us. *God* makes *men,* not colleges.

One's sympathy here is all with the college graduate. The rebuke is too severe for so mild an offense, if, indeed, such a naïve application can be deemed an offense. Moreover, the reply itself contains an argument in favor of at least a literary education; for it certainly was not the writer's meaning that God makes men and does not make colleges, which is what he says. The instinctive perception of case values which the graduate probably had is a rare possession among American business men, most of whom still say "between you and I," which to the college graduate would be the unpardonable sin.

T. H. Wheeler relates in the Log some recollections of the war. Amongst other things he says:

. If I were to enlist again, I would enlist under the name of Adam instead of Wheeler. I waited at Salisbury two months before they reached "W" on the exchange list. There were four thousand ahead of me.

At Utica I inquired at the depot for John Newton, "who was in prison with me."

The countryman's reply: "He is still in. You must have had a shorter sentence and you are lucky to be out."

John Hay follows his namesake into the flowery meads of verse:

> 'Tis well to be witty and wise,
> 'Tis ill to be grumpy and blue,
> 'Tis well to hang on to the old love
> Until you are sure of the new.

Sometimes the log-keeper jotted down brief notes of conversations. Here is such a page:

Beecher to committee who waited on him to call his attention to the fact that many in the congregation objected to his humorous illustrations. He replied: "If you knew how much I kept back, you would not say anything about what little escapes me."

Thiers was always serious in public, reserving his wit for his friends.

To Depew, Sunset Cox said that he felt his political influence had been seriously weakened because he had been witty in public.

Depew replied: "I once discussed this subject with Lincoln, who said there was no way that an idea could be so well impressed upon the people as by a humorous illustration. As to what a supercilious few might think of it, he didn't care."

Here is the Log's extract of a pleasant exchange of rapier thrusts of wit:

Walker: I do not drink or smoke.

Depew: Walker hasn't vices, but has *views!*

Walker: If Senator Depew had my views, what a great man he would be!

Barger: Success largely depends on luck.

Mills: It depends entirely on ability.

Barger: You went to California.

Mills: Judgment.
Barger: You were taken sick—didn't go to mines.
Mills: Judgment.
Barger: Speculation lucky.
Mills: Judgment.
Barger: How *lucky* you are to have such *judgment*.

John Hays Hammond writes:

There are mines and MINES. All mines are not holes in the ground owned by liars. The Chinese definition is good: "A place from which benefits are derived." (P. S.—Mr. Commissioner Wong "is dubious"—says no good authority for above etymology.)

Lewis Nixon is worth reading when he writes:

In the "Arrow" we see the perfection and maturity of the steam engine. In its blossoming there is seen the need by the world of further advance; its fruit will be the gas engine—no boiler, no steam, smokeless, noiseless, always ready.

"A Daniel come to judgment!" He foresaw the Diesel engine!

Truth in diplomacy has its place as it had in Jay Gould's policies. Here is what Gutowski writes:

Je crois qu'en diplomatie il vaut toujours mieux de dire la vérité: l'on ne pourra vous accuser de mauvaise foi et—l'on ne vous croira quand même pas.

John P. Holland, builder of submarines, writes:

Within sight of our course Bushnell, the father of submarine warfare, made his experiments, in the hope of developing a weapon with which to destroy his country's enemies. We already have good grounds for hoping that the complete development of his idea will more probably result in the ending of naval warfare than in the destruction of our enemies' ships.

Here is a tabloid symposium:

"Architecture is the mother of all the Arts."—S. B. P. Trowbridge.

"Finance is the father of architecture."—Frederick L. Eldridge.

"Finance vs. Architecture. The Coliseum: that, said the guide, is the greatest ruin in the world.

"I guess he never saw Pacific mail!"—L. J.

"If you leave money to a woman, it is either kicked or kissed out of her."—S. T. Tilden.

"The views of a crusty old bachelor—that is not my experience."—S. T. T. T.

The last time I was on "the Arrow" we had just been overboard for our matutinal dip. Flint was struggling with a refractory collar button.

"What was Herbert Spencer's religious belief?" he asked with characteristic irrelevance.

"He hadn't any. He was born without any spiritual sense—was color blind in this respect."

"What is your view?"

"I am hopeful, but don't know."

This is the last entry in the log-book of the "Arrow."

APPENDIX

A Playful Satire That Became a Prophecy

A denizen of Earth, Grizzle by name, finds himself unexpectedly on Jupiter. The giant planet is like the Earth in that every country, and even every one of its inhabitants, has a Jupiterian duplicate. Chicago is a city of sky-piercing towers built of glass. New York is filled with sky-scrapers that glitter in the sun with metallic sheen. Giant dirigible air-ships and other flying machines fill the air and flash across the oceans and continents of Jupiter as they are beginning to do on Earth. Talking-moving pictures are a commonplace there, and nearly fifty years ago, were known by the recently-coined name of "photophone." In the Jupiterian Chicago they had a Soviet system of communistic government. Here are a few extracts from *A Fortnight in Heaven*, which I wrote between 1880 and 1884, published in 1886 by Henry Holt & Co. in America and by Sampson Low Searle and Rivington in London:

PHOTOPHONE. The vague impression that remained was that the instrument was a moving photograph which reproduced every look and motion just as a phonograph reproduces every sound. To this was joined a phonograph, which, accurately adjusted to the gestures, and movements of the lips, repeated the words and all the inflections of tone in which they were spoken, so that they seemed to proceed from the lips of the image. The perspective was as perfect as in nature. A number of moving figures were represented in all the intricacies of cross-motion as accurately were the movements of an individual. . . . It is needless to describe how Grizzle enjoyed subsequent exhibitions of the powers of the photophone, as the instrument was inaccurately but conveniently called. . . . To describe what Grizzle did and saw, would be but to enumerate the possibilities of the photophone; and these the reader can imagine for himself. To illustrate the habitual discontent of man, however, it may be mentioned that before Grizzle had had long experience of the photophone, he was finding fault with it because it repeated only such events of the past as had been photophoned. . . . pp. 135-6.

This exhibition is described as taking place on an airship, the "Meteor" while on its way from New York to London, years before the invention of the toy-kinetoscope, which long preceded the first silent moving-pictures; and of course long before any "Zeppelin" had been thought of.

AERIAL-SHIPS. The golden spires of the Empire City mingled their radiance with the glory of the rising sun as the "Meteor" rose from her harbor and resumed her flight towards the Western Isles. Dotted here, there and about the blue heavens were other air-ships, flashing towards all parts of the globe; crossing mountains and seas, arid plains and unbridged rivers as indifferently as did the birds. Graceful and swift as the swallow's flight, more luxurious than the noblest of earthly palaces, these marvellous air-ships seemed to mark the acme of man's ingeniousness: art and science appeared to have reached in them their highest development. . . . As he flew over Long Island into the wide Atlantic, he joyfully hailed Far Rockaway and other places known to him. . . . He saw the Jersey highlands fade from view, and with them disappear from these pages the Western Republic, with its two hundred million people, its boundless fields and mammoth granaries, its vast mineral treasures, and the hundred other things which, by Grizzle's

297

time had raised it to the greatest civilization the world had ever seen. . . . pp. 129-30.

He discovered that every air-ship consisted of an upper and lower part, the former containing the buoyant force—the gas; and the other consisting of the heavier chambers, containing the batteries and the accommodation for passengers and crew. Whenever an accident rendered needful a descent on to the sea, the upper part was detached and allowed to float away, while the lower part, being a boat-like construction, rested upon the surface of the water. The electric force was then transferred from the aerial screw to the aquatic screw, and the passengers found themselves in a well-appointed, sea-worthy ship, provisioned for a long voyage, and independent of wind and tide. pp. 141-2.

Electricity from the air. Grizzle followed his guide to the engine rooms. Here he saw several immense batteries, by which the *Meteor* was propelled. Looking out of a window he was able to see the enormous screw, which revolving with fearful rapidity, drove on the ship with the speed of the wind. Grizzle watched it for a few moments in silence. "I little thought electricity had such power," he presently remarked. Then, with enthusiasm, "Nasty smelling engine-rooms and smoky funnels are here dispensed with; what a boon to the sensitively-organized!" But, reflecting, he presently abated his enthusiasm to ask if a steam-engine were not really required in the production of electricity, as he had observed on Earth. The question was hardly understood. Having explained that on Earth electricity is produced only by the aid of a steam-engine, with all its disagreeable accompaniments, he was told that the motor force of the *Meteor* was gathered from the surrounding atmosphere as the ship passed through it!

Writing nearly fifty years later, Mr. O. H. Caldwell, Editor of Electronics and former Federal Radio Commissioner, turns the ancient pleasantry into an impressive prediction. Thus:

APPENDIX

Within twice five years we may even be transmitting our energy over high-frequency radio beams in the ether, entirely without wires. Who can so no? Aeroplanes may be taking their power supply from such beams of radiated energy, which will also guide them. [This may sound the height of absurdity in January, 1931, and I would not seriously mention it here, were it not for the fact I have recently heard two of the sanest and most fruitful engineers in the country, each with world miracles to his credit, independently and confidentially propose the early possibility of this very thing.] *New York Tribune,* January 4, 1931.

From the New York Sun, September 21st, 1929
GLASS HOUSES. The use of glass as a major building material will be attempted on a large scale for the first time in America in the new Palais de France at Broadway, Central Park West, Sixty-second and Sixty-third streets, according to Irwin S. Chanin, head of the Chanin Construction Company.

Chicago, as Grizzle saw it fifty years ago:
. . . A crystal city, flashing in the bright sunlight, and throwing off prismatic hues with a splendor indescribable, and almost beyond the conceptions of mortals. There rose towers, minarets, and spires, apparently of solid crystal, but infinitely higher and more massive than any architecture he had seen before. Tier upon tier, street after street, all of solid glass; cornices, buttresses, columns of crystal moulded into exquisite shapes, sparkling and flashing. . . . pp. 14 and 16.

An American Soviet
When, thirty years ago, the Knights of Labor succeeded in uprooting the republican form of government and nationalizing all capital, a division of property was never contemplated by them. Since then the Internationalists, the Socialists, and the Communists have successively obtained control of the government, and in two decades there have been eight divisions of property—one ordered by the Socialists, three by the Interna-

299

tionalists, and four by the Communists. All this has tended to alienate the affection of many worthy people from our principle [*The State is the True God and Karl Marx is His Prophet*] and the spy system, necessary under a socialistic regime, has increased this tendency. As a result, many citizens have absconded, and defrauded the community of their labor! pp. 30-31.

INDEX

301

INDEX

INDEX

304

CPSIA information can be obtained
at www.ICGtesting.com
Printed in the USA
LVOW07s0620210817
545780LV00001B/104/P

9 781432 580087